Herring Fishermen
of Kintyre and Ayrshire

Herring Fishermen of Kintyre and Ayrshire

ANGUS MARTIN

Cover illustration: 'Below the Sleeping Giant' by Archie MacAlister

British Cataloguing in Publication Data
A catalogue record for this book is available
from the British Library

ISBN 1 899863 90 7

Typeset by XL Publishing Services, Tiverton.
Printed in Great Britain by Bell & Bain Ltd., Glasgow
for House of Lochar, Isle of Colonsay, Argyll PA61 7YR

Contents
·············

Illustrations

· · · · · · · · · · · · · · · · ·

Introduction

In 1974 I began researching a history of the ring-net. One of the main aims of the project was to tape-record those surviving fishermen, in Kintyre and Ayrshire, who had fished during the final years of sail and oar and manual hauling of nets, before the advent of motor-power transformed their lives. In 1981, the resultant book, *The Ring-Net Fishermen*, was published by John Donald Publishers Ltd.

The cassette-tapes and transcripts were then deposited in the School of Scottish Studies, Edinburgh, and that, I thought, was the project completed. I had no intention of listening to the tapes or looking at the transcripts ever again. In 1997, however, when I undertook to write an essay on the history of the Campbeltown fishing industry, I was forced to think again about the subject, and the more I thought about it, the more I began to wonder just how much material lay untranscribed in these tapes. *The Ring-Net Fishermen* was essentially a 'factual' work, and in the course of the transcription I disregarded many anecdotes and tales because they were too rambling – and therefore time-consuming – or lacked obvious relevance to the subjects I had decided to cover.

These 'lost' tales haunted me so much that I finally decided to retrieve the tapes and go through them once more, in order to compile the best of the material. Early in July, 1997, I went to Edinburgh, collected three boxes of tapes and brought them back to Campbeltown. I spent three months at transcription, working on the tapes at every opportunity, and, finally, at the end of September, the job was finished. The recordings were in remarkably good condition, considering the poor quality of the tapes and equipment I had used back in the 1970s. It occurred to me, though, that they weren't going to last forever, and I was glad that I'd gone through them again. But was there a book in them?

I began organising the stories and putting them into my computer, and by the end of October there was a book. This isn't it. That book – finally titled *Kintyre Fishermen In Their Own Words* – was accepted by a Scottish publisher and contracts duly signed. The stories in it had been transcribed faithfully in the form that I heard them, in other words in dialect.

I soon afterwards began work on another book, *The North Herring*

Fishing (published in 2001) which was to take the same form, i.e. stories in dialect, thematically arranged. I hadn't long started assembling the material when doubts began to plague me, chief of which was: *how many people will actually bother to read this stuff?* Much as I care about Scots, there suddenly didn't seem much point in assembling a book that probably wouldn't even sell as a remaindered title.

I wasn't long in changing my tack – I'd rewrite the material, rendering it easily accessible to all readers, but leaving a Scots flavour in the form of quotations. Having decided on that course for *The North*, I then began to fret about the earlier book, the proofs of which I still hadn't seen. Was it too late to cancel it and would the publisher agree to its cancellation? He didn't take much persuading, himself realising – I suspect – that he was sitting on a commercial dud. None the less I thank him for releasing me from the contract and freeing me not only to rewrite the stories in English, but also to incorporate fresh material from the Ayrshire side of the Firth as well as from Kintyre.

The bulk of the material is entirely fresh, but a small part of it appeared in *The Ring-Net Fishermen*, in edited form, and will be recognised by anyone familiar with that book. I have had to render a number of words phonemically, notably the element *eh*, as in *aweh* (away) and *deh* (day) which is pronounced as in *geld*, *weld*, etc. Place-names I have sometimes spelled as I heard them, when the pronunciation diverged significantly from that conveyed by Ordnance Survey spellings. At other times the spellings will be standard. There is no hard and fast rule. Most of the places mentioned in this book will be found in the Fishermen's Place-Names appendix in *The Ring-Net Fishermen*, which was reissued in 1996. Some others will be recorded on Ordnance Survey maps or Admiralty charts, but by no means all.

I have kept chapter notes to a minimum, preferring that the fishermen should, as far as possible, speak for themselves. Dates, however, have never been a strong point in oral tradition, and, where possible, a chronological outline is provided in the chapter notes. These notes derive almost entirely from *The Ring-Net Fishermen*. Additional information comes from the annual reports of the Fishery Board for Scotland, unless otherwise indicated.

I have used several stories from the late George Campbell Hay, poet and linguist, since these were heard by him from Tarbert fishermen during his boyhood in the village. Likewise, I have used a few stories from the late John Campbell of Dalintober (born 1904), though his practical experience of fishing was limited to about a year with Donald 'Moggans' McLellan in the *Victory*. He was of a fishing family, however, and his knowledge of the traditions was extensive. A few other stories came from non-fishermen – Harry McIver, Iver McKinven and Bob Miller – while Crawford Morans and Donald Blair of Tarbert were, like John Campbell, fishermen for a short time only. I have also drawn on the experiences of Tam Hughes – who fished for most of his life from Rothesay, on the island of Bute, though he was born in Pittenweem – and Jim Tarvit, his cousin from Cellardyke, who worked as a fisherman before becoming a fishery officer.

Of all the stories collected here, the one that most stirred my imagination was Hugh MacFarlane's boyhood memory on p 152. All the elements – the boats under oars, the small net stretched to the very shore (where even trees and rocks had names) and the old men talking in Gaelic – could belong to a millennium ago.

A hundred-and-five years on from that night in Bight Lucky, there are no herring-fishermen left in Kintyre or Ayrshire or anywhere else on the Clyde, though there are still herring. The advance of technology – beginning simply with the tiny 7-9 hp engine – has destroyed the herring-fishing industry and all but destroyed the communities which, for generation after generation, made their living from it.

The wisdom of hindsight is all too easy to apply and I shall resist the temptation. One thing, however, is certain: there was never a fishery more satisfying than the herring. It was exciting, clean, highly skilled, engaged the senses, and, often, for the most successful practitioners, highly lucrative – fortunes could be made in a night. There wasn't a ring-net fisherman I talked with who didn't regret the method's demise and there were many who openly despised the alternatives they were forced to adopt.

In the stories which follow may be glimpsed, I hope, something of the traditions of herring-fishing by which the men of Kintyre and Ayrshire made their names and their boats' names known on diverse fishing grounds around the British Isles, and if anyone should ever doubt, in the distant future, that fishermen were ever other than carpet-slippered screen-watchers or shelter-deck labourers, then perhaps this book will help dispel that doubt. If, however, a century from now, there is any fishing industry left on the Clyde against which to measure the substance of the men who made this book possible, I should be very surprised.

Acknowledgements

Most obviously, I have to thank the informants themselves, who gave their time and their knowledge freely. I haven't forgotten them, nor have I forgotten what they represent to me – a way of living and a system of values that have gone forever. Sincere thanks go to the following, who read and commented on the penultimate draft or parts of it: Jim Tarvit, Anstruther (who also helped immensely with the compilation of the appendix of boats); Lachie Paterson, Carradale (who also gave invaluable assistance with the provision and selection of photographs); Tommy Ralston, Lundin Links; Bob Smith, Linlithgow and Moira Burgess, Glasgow. Thanks also to Bob Miller, Peninver, for information on herring steamers, and to Ian A Fraser and Cathlin Macaulay, School of Scottish Studies, Edinburgh. I have eliminated all the errors I could find, but have no doubt that hawk-eyed readers will spot survivors and pounce on them.

Angus Martin, Campbeltown. August, 2002.

Fishermen Contributors

An asterisk denotes that the informant was deceased at the time of this work's completion.

T Andrew Alexander*, b 1928, Maidens
Dugald Blair*, b 1889, Campbeltown
Duncan Campbell, b 1926, Campbeltown
Jim Campbell, b 1938, Carradale
John Conley*, b 1886, Carradale
Robert Conley*, b 1896, Carradale
Hugh Edgar, b 1940, Dunure
John Galbraith, b 1951, Carradale
Grieve Gemmell, b 1925, Dunure
Iain Gemmell, b 1934, Dunure
Archibald Graham, b 1923, Peninver, Kintyre
Thomas Hughes, b 1924, Pittenweem
Neil Jackson, b 1926, Tarbert
Thomas Kelly*, b 1932, Campbeltown
Peter Laing, b 1948, Campbeltown
John McConnachie, b 1932, Carradale
James McCreath*, b 1897, Girvan
Andy McCrindle, b 1924, Maidens
T Angus McCrindle, b 1924, Maidens

John 'Jake' McCrindle*, b 1888, Maidens
J Turner McCrindle*, b 1902, Maidens
Thomas 'Wee Tam' McCrindle*, b 1897, Maidens
James Macdonald, b 1925, Campbeltown
Matthew McDougall*, b 1909, Carradale
Neil McDougall, b 1940, Carradale
David MacFarlane*, b 1895, Tarbert
Hugh MacFarlane*, b 1884, Tarbert
Robert McGown*, b 1902, Campbeltown
John McIntyre*, b 1911, Campbeltown
Denis MacIntosh*, b 1899, Carradale
Donald McIntosh*, b 1893, Carradale
David McLean*, b 1888, Campbeltown
David McNaughton, b 1926, Campbeltown
Hugh McPhee, b 1941, Alloway
Duncan McSporran*, b 1888, Dalintober
Francis McWhirter, b 1927, Campbeltown
John McWhirter*, Campbeltown, b 1886
Angus Martin*, b 1895, Dalintober
Angus Martin Jr, b 1920, Dalintober
Angus Martin*, b 1910, Dalintober
Henry Martin*, b 1891, Dalintober
Robert Morans*, b 1891, Campbeltown
John Munro, b 1922, Dunure
Mungo Munro*, b 1907, Dunure
George Newlands*, b 1902, Campbeltown
Archibald Paterson, b 1925, Carradale
Robert Ross, Tarbert, b 1926
Neil Short, b 1917, Campbeltown
Matthew Sloan, Maidens, b 1917
Thomas Sloan*, b 1892, Maidens
Archibald Stewart*, b 1889, Campbeltown
James Wareham*, b 1900, Campbeltown
Wareham, John 'Jake', b 1929, Campbeltown
John Weir*, b 1895, Tarbert
George Wilson*, b 1902, Tarbert

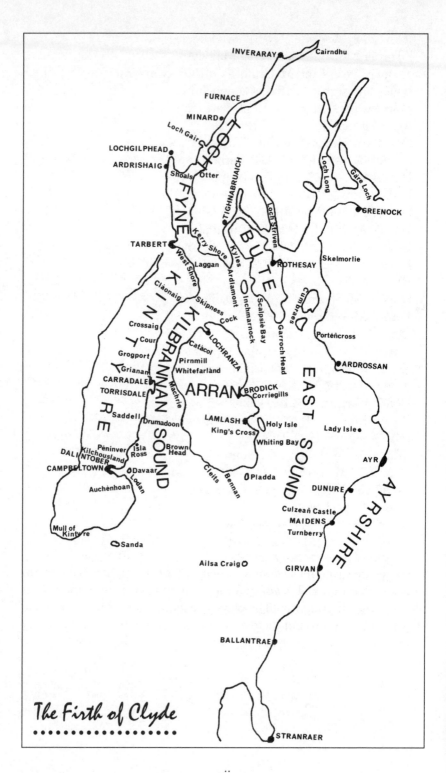

The Firth of Clyde

Origins
·············

The 'trawl', from which the ring-net evolved, evidently made its appearance in Loch Fyne in the early 1830s, when drift-nets were stretched across a bay to enclose a shoal of herring. From that, some Tarbert fishermen began to design small nets specifically for hauling to the shore. The concept was scarcely novel, beach-seines having been used the world over for centuries; but the phenomenal success of the 'trawlers' rapidly generated a wave of opposition from the traditional drift-net fishermen and the herring-curers, with claims that the new method destroyed herring fry and spawn and interfered with the working of drift-nets. As a result of that opposition, trawling was made illegal by Act of Parliament in 1851 and remained so until 1867. In the intervening years, much strife ensued as the full weight of the Government's preventive measures fell on the trawl-fishermen. In 1853, Colin McKeich of Tarbert was shot and wounded off Skipness by a crew from HMS Porcupine, and in 1862 Peter McDougall of Ardrishaig was shot dead at Otter Spit by a gunner and marine from HMS Jackal. In all, some 26 Tarbert fishermen were imprisoned in Campbeltown, and the general repression brought the Tarbert fishing community to a very low ebb.

The beginning

There was an abundance of herring in Loch Fyne the year trawling started. All the fishermen were using drift-nets, but the herring were 'lazy' and weren't going into the nets. Although the fish would 'come up tae play', they weren't swimming when they came up, 'jeest goin up an down – what they call *lochin* – an they couldn't get them in the nets at all'. So, when herring would be playing inshore, some crews 'started tae shot the drift-nets round them an draw them intae the shore. An they wir gettin the herrin that wey. That wis the start o the ring-net'. [John Weir, 1974]

The first trawls comprised two or three pieces of drift-net sewn together with a weighted sole-rope attached. 'Ye wid cerry it under yer erms for all the weight that wis in it.' The herring were so thick along the shores that only one boat was needed to work the net – a man would be landed with an end of the net and then the net would be shot in a circle from the boat, which would return to the shore with the other end, for the crew to begin hauling on both ends until the net was dragged ashore.

One Tarbertman, Johnny MacQuilkan, was hauling his net from a flat rock north of Lub Dhubh and there was so much herring in the net he was crying, *Tha mi beartaich gu bràth*! – I'm wealthy forever! 'Well, they call that place, tae this day, Craig Johnny MacQuilkan. An they're tellin, the mark o his heels is on the rock yit – ye winna pierce the rock wi wan o the modern drills.'

As time passed, the herring got 'cuter' and weren't coming so close inshore, so crews paired off and instead of hauling the net directly to the shore would haul it to the boats, anchored offshore. [David MacFarlane, 1974]

Conflict

Tarbert was the place trawling started and though the Ardrishaig men 'went in wi it all right', the drift-net fishermen north of Otter Spit 'wirna in favour o it'. Their small boats – crewed perhaps by a father and two sons – operated from all the lochside communities 'right up tae Cairndhu', at the very head of the loch. There were 'some battles up the Loch' between the trawlers and drifters. 'They wid go tae Inverara an the Inverara men wid pitch them ower the quay. But they got thir own back. They come doon here, some o the Loch Fyne men, for the Fair in July. The Tarbertmen wid kick two or three barrels asunder an get staves an half-kill them, chase them away.'

A cruiser was stationed on Loch Fyne and when her pinnaces would be seen going out to watch the fishermen, a 'good swanky crew' of paid oarsmen would proceed from Tarbert. Guns would be fired into the air and torches waved on dark nights to warn of the cruiser's presence. 'They wid row them upside-doon an jeenk them through all the wee corners.' In Tarbert itself, where the fire-station now stands, a big building – called the Barracks – was erected to house the fishery police.

Trawl-nets would be concealed before the crews returned to Tarbert with a few pieces of drift-net on board to avert suspicion. The fishermen had certain places where they would sink the nets with stones, and in the back end of the year they'd put branches of the red-berried rowan on top of the nets, the easier to locate and recover them. 'Aye they had all the tricks. Needs must when the Devil rides.'

Tarbert fishermen camped at Skipness, and, on one occasion, a policeman who was preventing trawling appeared there. The police and trawlers fraternised at that time, so the trawlers took him to the pub at Claonaig and they all got drunk. Coming back, one of the fishermen would say, 'A'll cerry yer musket', and another, 'A'll cerry yer sword', until the policeman was disarmed. Back at Skipness, 'they made a pure cod o him'.

On another occasion, a spy was seen ashore, watching the trawlers. Two or three fishermen landed and crawled up to where this 'big black man' was hiding. They jumped on him and disarmed him, which put him into an 'awful state – what an insult tae take the arms off him!' After a while, they returned his cutlass, with which he 'started makin passes roond thir heids, an then they bolted'. [David MacFarlane, 1974, 1975]

Ayrshiremen adopt trawling

Although 'trawls' had been worked in the mid-19th century by fishermen from Irvine and Saltcoats and, on a more casual basis, by a few Ayr and Dunure crews, the method was not established on the Ayrshire coast until the early years of the 20th century. Many of the Ayrshire fishermen started out with second-hand nets purchased on the Argyll side of the Firth.

John Ritchie

The following account cannot be substantiated and remains very doubtful. MacVicar was not a Tarbert surname, but belonged farther north on Loch Fyneside. Similarly, fisherfolk – Ritchies among them – colonised Newton-upon-Ayr from Pitsligo in Aberdeenshire, not Rosehearty, in the late 18th century.

Mungo Munro was given the tradition, 'which causes a bit o controversy', that a great-grandfather of his, John Ritchie, came from Rosehearty with a very small ring-net and settled about a mile north of Dunure. He wasn't allowed to use the net, however, and sold it to a Tarbert man by the name of MacVicar, who then pioneered the method; but the Tarbert fishermen had no knowledge 'o gettin it fae this side. We've no proof, ye see; no records tae show; it's just that it's been handed doon'. [Mungo Munro, 1976]

'Jeely Jock'

The Tarbert ring-net fishermen 'never used tae pay any heed' to the Ayrshiremen. 'They wir at the drifts. We'd hear about them gettin two or three baskets away down on the Track thonder. We never paid much heed. But, by hokey, when they did start, they came on.' 'Jeely Jock' McCrindle acquired his first ring-net second-hand in Ardrishaig 'and the Ardrishaig men showed him how tae lay it on the stern'. [David MacFarlane, 1975]

Hughie Anderson

John McWhirter maintained that the first Ayrshireman at ringing was Hughie Anderson, who stayed on Arran and had 'a wee boat, the *Peggy Prim*'. [1974] Tam McCrindle in Maidens recalled Hughie living in a big shed in a wood at King's Cross, whence he would row to the south end of the island to work lines. Tam reckoned that Hughie was among the first – if not the first – to use a ring-net winch. [1976]

'Plenty RVO'

The three Anderson brothers, Hugh, Jimmy and John, lived at King's Cross on Arran, but their mother belonged to Dunure. They were line-fishing from Arran, but had acquired an old ring-net from Campbeltown and made an agreement with the Gibsons in Dunure to go into part-nership at ring-netting if the chance arose. One day, a telegram from the Andersons arrived in Dunure. It said: 'PLENTY RVO. WHITING BAY.' 'RVO' represented 'Russian Vaporising Oil', the paraffin on which the early engines ran, and was a code for 'herring'. [Mungo Munro, 1976]

Uncle Stewart

Mungo Munro understood that ring-netting was adopted earlier in Dunure than in Maidens, because Stewart Gibson went up to Maidens from Dunure to 'set up' (assemble) a ring-net belonging to his Sloan nephews. These Sloans were once watching a man setting up a net some-where and one of them remarked: 'Well, that's naw how Uncle Stewart* sets up the net.' [Mungo Munro, 1976]

*Stewart Gibson's wife, Mary Andrew, was a sister of Matthew Sloan's wife, Isobel.

Sloans and McCrindles

Tommy Sloan recalled the purchase, c. 1911, of a 42-score-deep (p 58) ring-net from Kilbirnie, which Stewart Gibson came up from Dunure to set up, assisted by Johnny and Jimmy Roy McCrindle of Maidens. The Sloans at that time partnered Tommy's uncle Tam McCrindle's *Seagull*, but Tam had no net of his own at first. He later bought one second-hand from Campbeltown, but it was already 'done' and every time the *Seagull*'s crew rang with it, the netting would tear away from the sole-rope. [Thomas Sloan, 1976]

Jimmy Edgar

Tommy Sloan believed that Jimmy 'Eggart' (Edgar) in Dunure was among the first on the Ayrshire side to work a ring-net. Edgar got a 'traal' – possibly from Kilbirnie – and had that net between the two boats – square-sterned Nabbies – one of which was the *Osprey*. [Thomas Sloan, 1976]

Herring

It has been written that: 'The herring has no friends. Every living thing in the water, in the air and on the land preys upon its race ... and will do so, probably, for all time to come.'

Symbolism

These symbols were shown to Turner McCrindle by an East Coast fisherman, William Donaldson.

Place a herring end-on and look at his head – a drifter with her mast lowered can be seen. Turn him up and look at the top of his head and a lighthouse or a coffin is visible. Scrape the scales off him and the meshes of a net appear. Take the *thrapple* – or throat – out of him and you have a gannet in your hand. Further, look at his tail – if it's very frayed, he was one of a big shoal, because the tail becomes ruffled when herring swim close together; if it's nice and tidy, that denotes a small shoal. [Turner McCrindle, 1976]

Glasgow Magistrates

When Davie MacFarlane was young at the fishing and a skiff with a catch aboard would go alongside a herring-steamer, the buyer would be shouting: 'What kinna herrin? Good herrin?' If the herring were big, the skipper might reply: 'A've got sixty boxes o Glasgow Magistrates!'* [David MacFarlane, 1975]

* *The expression is variously explained in reference books, but the linking of plump fish with well-fed magistrates might be preferred.*

'Deukers'

Turner McCrindle recalled ringing in the Shoals in 18 fathoms of water one evening and 'the herrin rose an played black – ye could've heard them half-a-mile away'. The net was torn and only one fish 'marked'. A southerly breeze came away and the boats made for Loch Gair. The next morning, rain came on and the wind checked to the west. The Ayrshire pair didn't venture out, but the Ardrishaig boats did and got fishings – as high as 400 baskets – in the Shoals. The herring were there, Turner said, 'but they were only the *deukers* (duckers)'. [Turner McCrindle, 1976]

In September, the herring would 'go tae lie'. Hugh MacFarlane saw herring playing from Inchmarnock to Ardrishaig and 'ye winna sink through it; ye cou'na catch it'. The herring were 'playin the water dry', and the 'roar' of the fish – 'lik a breeze o win' – could be heard half-a-mile away; but although the fishermen would shoot round the herring, the nets weren't going 'near the bottom' and hardly a fish would be marked. They went out the next night and the herring were gone. 'There wirna another herrin-tell (tail) from that for three solid month afore it wis got up in the Showls. Lyin on the bottom.' The first night that fishing resumed off Ardrishaig, some 35,000 baskets were taken. [Hugh MacFarlane, 1976]

The moon and darkness

Herring will not leave the Clyde with the moon. Say they're up by Skipness, they might shift as far south as the Brown Head, but they'll not go away. They'll go away with the dark, though. On a dark night, if a 'big play' of herring was heard, fishermen would say: 'Oh, that's them – they're shiftin away somewhere clear o that or they're goin tae lie doon.'

They might go and lie down for weeks, down in the deep, without rising at all. [Donald McIntosh, 1974]

Migrations

Davie MacFarlane heard the old men say that the herring used to start 'away doon above Campbeltown' at the beginning of the season – the drift-net fishing – and by Tarbert Fair, in July, would be off Tarbert harbour, 'workin up all the time'. [David MacFarlane, 1975]

Henry Martin, when young, heard older fishermen say that 'if ye heard a wild play o herrin on a good mornin, ye could say goodbye'. That was the herring 'on a passage'; but when individual herring would be heard jumping here and there, the shoal was 'stationary'. One night, the Martins were at the mouth of Tarbert harbour on a shoal; by daybreak, they were near Skipness. The older men said: 'Them herrin'll naw be lang till they're awa.' Several days later, fishing in Whiting Bay, on the east side of Arran, the older men maintained that it was the same herring. The ring-nets were 'gan flat' with the herring swimming out; buoys and cork-rope were sinking and even the winch was of no benefit until the herring 'wid clear the net an then everythin wid come up. They wir travellin hard when we loast them doon at Pladda; then it wis away home an pack the bag an go away for Ballantrae Banks'. [Henry Martin, 1974]

Spawning grounds

The two main winter spawning grounds of herring in the Clyde are the Ballantrae Banks, off the Ayrshire coast, and the Brown Head, off the south-west coast of Arran. But there were other areas where fishermen believed that herring spawned.

There is ample evidence, from fishermen in the 19th century, that herring once spawned in Loch Fyne, particularly in the narrow upper reaches. The belief was that, in late spring or early summer, herring shoals came around the Mull of Kintyre and passed up through the Kilbrannan Sound to spawn in Upper Loch Fyne in August. There was also supposed to be a herring-spawning ground in Scalpsie Bay, off the south-west coast of Bute.

Off the east coast of Kintyre, herring were said to have spawned off Smerby and in the Lodan, between Davaar Island and Auchenhoan Head. But these spawning grounds were not regularly used by herring, it would seem, because fishermen would find 'spawnies' there only in certain years.

For two years, John McWhirter saw 'spannie herrin' north of the buoy at Ardnacross and from that almost up to Isle o Ross, to a breadth of about a mile. In another year, there were small herring – about the length of a man's hand – came to the Lodan to spawn. They were 'native herrin', he said, and 'nane o them any bigger as the other'. At the back end of the year, when otter-trawling there, big sheets of spawn would be lifted in the net. [John McWhirter, 1975]

Henry Martin recalled getting spawn in ring-nets in March at the Brown Head. The spawn, which was stuck to shingle, would come up in lumps. He too recalled herring spawning in the Lodan, between Ru Stafnish and the Waters. [1974]

Hugh MacFarlane heard old men say that herring spawned along 'the East Shore', in Scalpsie Bay, Bute, but he had never seen it himself. The Smerbies, 'Broon Heid' and Ballantrae were the other spawning grounds. [1974]

Bob Conley in Carradale was told by his father that in the month of July a small spot of herring spawned 'on the hard ground, up at Grogport an Grianan'. These were 'lazy, big herrin', called 'groundkeepers' because 'they wir always on the bottom'. [1975]

Abundance

There were years when there were few herring, but in 1938 'the place wis alive wi herrin – the whole o the Clyde wis full o herrin'. Fish were being got in tidal pools at Lochgilphead. All the boats were fishing at the 'Broon Heid' in 1938 and 'ye could get as many herrin as ye liked'. There was a quota – of 30 or 40 or 60 baskets per boat – imposed. 'I seen us,' said Robert McGown, 'workin a whole week an dumped oor quota every day.' The buyers were taking only so many herring and some crews had to dump their catch if they couldn't sell it. Even selling their quotas daily, the most that a crew could expect to make for a week was three or four pounds. [Robert McGown, 1975]

Bob Conley recalled coming out of Ayr one day in a stiff south-westerly breeze. The boat was plunging after she left the bar, and, with one of the dips she took, two or three herring landed on the deck. 'That shows ye how thick the herrin wis then,' Bob remarked. They couldn't shoot there, because the ground was foul, but continued south a bit to where the ground was clean, and shot there. They got the fill of the net and shouted for help. The herring were 'spannie' – close to spawning – and were making for Ballantrae Banks. They were heavy, and after the sole of the net was taken aboard the net would go down. 'Well, ye cou'na move them, 'cause the herrin wis wantin the ground.' Sometimes the net – 'up an doon' – would burst; at other times the herring would be manageable. [Robert Conley, 1976]

Extra-large herring

The 'Desperates' – Archibald Mathieson and Duncan Wilkinson in the *Perseverance* and the *Ellen*, respectively – kept a record of extra-large herring by notching the length of each fish on a deck board. [Turner McCrindle, 1976]

Herring and Light

The use of light as a means of attracting herring was never seriously experimented with by Kintyre fishermen, but lamps were so employed in pilchard and other pelagic fisheries. The main uses of light in the ring-net fishery were in detecting herring in the beam of a strong electric lamp, directed over the bow of a boat; in scaring herring off the shore by flashing and in repulsing herring from the soles of an unclosed net by the flashing of an outrigger light.

The Lodan

John McWhirter was crewing with Archie McKay in the *Noel* one night in the Lodan when he first saw herring 'ryse tae the light'. They'd had a shot and were hauling the net aft again, into shooting position, by the light of a *flambeau* hung on a stand in the boat's side. Their sail was up and the neighbour-boat was sailing ahead. Suddenly, Archie McKay, sitting aft steering, called out: 'My God, look at this!' A ball of herring was swimming along after the boat, following the light. They 'shot back', but caught merely 15 baskets. As John McWhirter speculated, however, 'there mightna have been any merr as that'. He saw the same sight on another occasion, going out to a herring-steamer from the Gull Rock. Herring were all around the boat, drawn by the glow of the torch. [John McWhirter, 1975]

'Stealing' herring

John McWhirter 'stole' 230 baskets of herring one night, when neigh-bouring Hugh McLean. The fishing had been about Fairlie and up along Wemyss Bay, but they left Rothesay and kept south by the Cumbraes. Both boats had a ring and caught very little, so it was decided to steam out 'atween the Fairlies' and lie. Later in the night, at flood water, they saw a Dunure boat approaching, working with a lamp over the bow, and could hear the man with the lamp calling repeatedly: 'A hope ye see them here, faither. They're awfy thick here.' To which the reply was: 'Whaur's yer neebor?' Then there would be quietness for a while, and a voice would be heard again: 'A dinna ken. The last time we seen him he wis away doon off Portencross.'

John McWhirter said to one of his crew, Tommy Finn: 'Tommy, away you doon tae the engine.' When John heard the urgent cry, 'Oh, faither, they're thick here!' he gave the order to Tommy Finn: 'Start her an shot.' They shot down to meet the Ayrshire boat and netted 230 baskets, and, as John McWhirter remarked: 'The poor man never got a shot yit.' There were two sons aboard the Ayrshire boat, 'wild men' who were 'on tae thir fether, blamin him for everythin. If they'd tae ken what we did!' John speculated. His neighbour went across to Rothesay with the catch and got four shillings a basket. The incident never ceased to vex John with feelings of guilt, and he admitted: 'A tell that tae some, but A don't tell it tae very many.' [John McWhirter, 1975]

'Jumpin in the grass'

Hugh MacFarlane recalled *redding* (clearing) a net offshore and 'the water wid be rid wi shrimps comin up wi the ray o the torch'. Fish too would rise to torchlight. Discussing searchlights, he recalled working one night off Kilfinan, looking with a 'spotlight' for herring and seeing the ground too. Four boats were being filled that night when the Sloans came in and enquired: 'How did ye see them?' Big Johnny Murray told the Ayrshiremen: 'We seen them wi the light. They wir jumpin in the grass.' The light, Hugh explained, was 'puttin them in an they wir jumpin ashore'. The Sloans were critical of the strategy and one of them warned: 'Ye'll pit the herrin awa aff the shore.' Hugh was inclined to agree with the assessment: 'A studied on what he wis sayin. If you wir in, it wid put them oot.' [Hugh MacFarlane, 1975]

Sgeir Bhuidhe Grianan*

The Carradale fleet was working the shore north of the village one summer night in the early 1960s. By the time the *Maid of the Mist* and *Harvest Queen* arrived on the scene, the other pairs had already moved south. Johnny McMillan in the *Maid of the Mist* had a ring in the Minister's Sloc at Grogport for 50 baskets of herring. After that, the two crews continued south, following the rest of the fleet, but without any real expectation of finding herring because rock-faces characterise that coast, which lacks bays into which herring could have gone to escape the earlier crews' attentions. In the ironic words of Archie Paterson, who skippered the *Harvest Queen*: 'That wis wiped clean, by the way.' There was, however, a surprise in store for Archie and his crew: 'We wir jeest throwin buckets o water on the deck, goin doon past Sgeir Bhuidhe, close in, an there the herrin wir, swimmin alongside us, between us an the rock, wi the light. Ye wid hardly believe it. An we got a good puckle herrin. It shows ye how tight in they'll go, right enough. So, we had a good night there – the boats had gone away doon an it wis left tae us. Now, we knew that we had tae be tight in tae get anythin.' [Archie Paterson, 2000]

* Gaelic, 'Yellow Reef', directly on the north side of Grianan Island. There is another Sgeir Bhuidhe that fishermen spoke of on that coast, known as Sgeir Bhuidhe Crossaig.

The Morning Star

For countless generations it has been known that, generally speaking, as night begins to fall, herring leave deep water and seek the shores; and that the reverse happens as day breaks. The following story, however, suggests that subtler influences might also affect the shoals' responses to light. The Morning Star is, of course, Venus, which rises three hours before the sun. Whether that star, or the combined light of all the stars in a clear sky, produced the minuscule increase in light intensity to which the herring reacted, or whether some other coincidental factor was at work, the account provides an insight into the acutely nature-attuned mind of a fisherman of the old school.

On a visit to James Campbell Sr, several weeks before his death in 1967, Jim Campbell acquired a gem of knowledge. 'What's happenin at the fishin?' was the old man's first question, for he had little interest in any other subject. Jim reported that the Carradale fleet was seeing herring in the evening along the Woods of Machrie, but when they'd ring all they'd get would be a 'lift aboard', i.e. a basket or two of fish that could be lifted aboard by hand. The boats would then go to an anchor until morning, when they'd return to the Woods; but there were no herring to be seen there at daylight. His father turned to him and asked: 'What sort o moarnins is it – are they clear, the moarnins?' – 'Aye, they're quite clear, some o the moarnins,' Jim replied. 'What time have ye been there at?' his father continued. 'Six o' clock, quarter tae six,' Jim replied. 'Well,' said his father, 'the next time ye see them, if it's a clear night, be there aboot four o' clock in the mornin.' *For God's sake,* Jim thought, *what's this?*

He gave no more thought to his father's advice until the conditions they'd discussed recurred. He'd seen herring in the evening along the Arran shore and he and his neighbour, John McConnachie in the *Florentine*, went to an anchor at Rudha Darach to sleep until daylight. But Jim couldn't rest, so he got up and was pacing the deck, wondering if he should risk waking the crews and incurring their annoyance. Finally, just before four o' clock, he shouted John McConnachie and put it to him: 'Dae ye want tae go oot for a wee look?' John had no objection, but when his crew were roused, one of them, a cousin, was less than enthusiastic and enquired of Jim: 'Is there anythin wrang wi ye – can ye naw sleep?'

They lifted their anchors quietly, slipped away from the other boats, crossed to the Schoolhouse in Machrie and proceeded north along the shore. By the time they had gone half-way along the Woods with still no sign of herring, Jim had begun to despair. *What am I gonny say this time?* he thought. *This is it agane. What will A tell them this time?* These thoughts had scarcely passed through his mind when, just north of the Long Dyke, a spot of herring appeared on the echo-meter. He shot and netted 180 baskets. John McConnachie took the catch aboard the *Florentine* and headed for the market at Ayr. By the time Jim returned to Carradale, the rest of the fleet was out, but finding nothing. Jim went to see his father the following day and asked him directly: 'How did ye know I should've been there at four o' clock?' – 'On a starry moarnin,' his father replied, 'the herrin's gan off wi the Mornin Star.'

'The wey they used tae go off wi the moon, the moon gettin up over Beinn Bharrain,' Jim theorised years later, 'they'd go off wi the big bright Mornin Star.' A fellow-skipper, Archie Paterson, queried the 'wile droll oors' (eccentric hours) Jim and John were 'prowlin aboot at', but by and large the star apparently remained his secret, though an older crewman, Tait Rennie, asked him once, when on passage to Ayr: 'Did yer Ould Fella ever mention a star?' – 'Naw,' Jim replied, 'never mentioned a star.'
[Jim Campbell, 2001]

Appearances

· · · · · · · · · · · · · · · · ·

An 'appearance' was a sign of herring, sometimes so minute or subtle that none but an expert fisherman would notice it.

Gannets

The gannet was an important sign of herring, and the surest indication that it was feeding on sizeable herring was when it would plummet vertically from a height. Low, angular strikes usually – but not always – signified the presence of mackerel or small fish close to the surface. The granite dome of Ailsa Craig, which rises 1,114 ft (339 m) from sea-level off the south Ayrshire coast, is, after St Kilda, the world's second-largest gannetry.

The skiff *Fame* of Dalintober was in Machrie, Arran, one evening in June. Some crews had earlier rung small quantities of mackerel and these had 'kept them goin'; but the *Fame* and her neighbour *Renown* decided to try the Kintyre shore and set their sails to cross in a northerly wind.

A couple of miles into the Kilbrannan Sound, Henry Martin remarked to his father: 'Look at them gannets aheid o us there. That's herrin – they're up on the surface.' The birds were *skitin*, or skimming, into the sea after fish. Such gannets would ordinarily be ignored, and, at that time, too, fishermen were reluctant to shoot a ring-net in a depth of water that exceeded the reach of the net, believing that the shoal would likely sound to safety before the sole could be closed under it. Regardless of these considerations, Duncan Martin decided: 'We'll try it.' There was 'a bit o growsin' when the sail was lowered to shoot the net, but: 'Be God – we got a fine fishin.'

'Well, we got herrin every night that week, gan oot intae the channel lookin for wan o them kinna gannets – wan! Ye know, it's naw up above, it's jeest skitin – that wis good enough. The neebor winna shot on that … Now, we had a good week that week. I think we had therty poun a man, an that wis good in them dehs, an that wis aal through gan oot intae the channel. We done well that month o June an there wir nae herrin at aal har'ly bein got apart fae anybody that wis gan ootside, an there wir very few o them wid dae't.' [Henry Martin, 1974]

The gannet that never struck

There was a scatter of boats off the Sanny Point, Arran, cruising up and down looking for gannets, one evening in July of 1933. Among them were the *Nulli Secundus* and *Nil Desperandum* of Campbeltown, their first time out since returning from the Minch spring fishing, which hadn't been a success that year.

The skipper of the *Nulli Secundus*, John Short, suddenly stuck his head out the wheelhouse, remarking: 'Look at that bird there – it's in two-ply' (both head and tail pointing downwards). The bird was also, significantly, flying at the right height for striking on herring. 'We'll naw wait for it,' he decided. 'It's seein somethin good. We'll jeest take it.' He shot the net at once and rang in 500 baskets of herring.

The catch wasn't apparent, however, until the very end of the haul. None of the usual indications – cork-floats bunching or the flotation buoys semi-submerging with the strain of the herrings' weight – were seen; but a Marconi technician aboard a nearby ringer, the *Nobles*, was aware of the catch and remarked to the *Nobles'* crew: 'There's herring in that man's net.' He was at sea supervising trials of the echo-sounder (p 41) which had disclosed the catch.

Neil Short described gannet fishing as a 'frustrating' business. 'Ye could be ringing on gannets for long enough an draw a blank every time.' For that reason, the crews weren't surprised there was no sign of herring in the net until they started to 'dry the middle' and, at the very last, the herring surfaced. [Neil Short, 2001]

Gulls

David McLean and his neighbour were lying at anchor with about 20 other pairs of boats in Saddell Bay one morning in a northerly gale. At about five o' clock they got under way, and, heading south, saw gulls 'pickin'. Since there were no boats ahead, they knew the gulls couldn't be feeding on refuse thrown overboard. Judging that the birds must be at fish, they shot and had such a meshing of herring in the net that 'she wis goin down, an that's wi Davaar Light through the Sound o Isla Ross. That's eight fadom o water there an a grand run; ye know ye'll no tear a net'. [David McLean, 1974]

Gulls could reveal herring when darting down and 'walking on the water', as fishermen described the motion when the birds hit the surface to peck at a fish. Turner McCrindle recalled, in his 'early days', going across to the Arran shore in partnership with his cousins in the *Ocean Bride*. He had been fishing whitings because the herring-fishing was slack, but the herring shoals were now leaving Loch Fyne and a Tarbert pair had got a good fishing off Arran the morning before. The Ayrshire crews prowled about and, in the 'dead evenin'', as they entered Brodick Bay, a gull suddenly 'just pounced right out of the heavens'. They went over to the spot and found a 'nice round black lump' of herring and shot, netting 200 or 300 baskets, 'away out off bottom too'. This, said Turner, was the herring 'on the move south', ready for spawning on the Ballantrae Banks. [Turner McCrindle, 1976]

One February morning, c. 1941, the *Golden Sheaf* and *Maireared* of Maidens came 'north-aboot fae the Cock' and began searching south along the Arran shore. In the south end of Whiting Bay, at daylight, there was an 'appearance o gulls … dartin on the herrin', which were playing as they came off the shore, except the fishermen hadn't heard the play, owing to the 'nesty jabble' the east wind was throwing up. Both boats were filled, and when Hughie McCrindle of Girvan appeared in the *Verbena*, looking for some bait for line-fishing, he was given the couple of hundred baskets left in the net!

When the two boats arrived in Girvan to discharge their herring, the other Maidens crews were already going ashore to catch a bus home. At that time, crews normally finished the week's work on a Friday morning; but, having seen the *Golden Sheaf* and *Maireared* arriving loaded, all the Maidens crews returned to their boats and crossed to Whiting Bay that night with several of the Girvan crews. They 'got a spoilt night,' however, having to shelter in Lamlash Loch when the east wind strengthened. The crews of the *Golden Sheaf* and *Maireared* had discharged their herring and gone home. [Andy McCrindle, 2001]

Putting up

This phenomenon, which was very useful to fishermen, is caused by the expulsion of gas from the swim-bladders of herring, enabling them to maintain their natural buoyancy.

'The herrin,' said Davie McLean, 'give themselves aweh even when they're on the bottom, puttin up.' Bubbles released from herring tend to come to the surface in 'bunches', whereas those from a seabird swimming underwater will rise individually in a constant stream. He took a

big fishing once from a surface patch of 'old' putting up, on the calcula-
tion that, 'There's been herrin here or there is herrin naw far aweh.'
[David McLean, 1975]

The 'ould fellas' called it *fryin*. The *bells*, or bubbles, would come up and
burst and, when the shoals were 'enormous thick', a haze would form
over the sea's surface.

One of the biggest hauls Hugh MacFarlane ever saw was in the Kyles
of Bute at Kames. The herring were moving away and all that he saw
was 'wan string o fry'. He said to his skipper: 'Here a string o puttin up.'
– 'Well,' Neillie replied, 'come doon an we'll try it.' The bridle-ropes on
the ends of the net were no sooner aboard than the catch was 'dry', so
the neighbour-boat went to the back of the net to load up there, and after
both boats had been filled, the crews 'backed the net oot it'.

'We left it livin. The Campbeltown men – "Dry them up, boys." Ye
know, the herrin smothered themsels. We never killt a herrin but what
we took. Went aweh tae Rothesay. That's all we took oot, an there wis,
aye, six thousand baskets, aye, an more. An there wir no fleet in't – not
a boat.' [Hugh MacFarlane, 1975, 1976]

A calm patch

The McLeans were out one night off Ayr. John Short's boats were the
only others out; the fleet was away for harbour. The McLeans 'took a
shot on chance' and netted 20 baskets. Short was north of them and they
saw him shooting. They went up and established that he had about 100
baskets in the net, and as they were going out by him they found themselves on a 'flat-calm bit o watter' – perhaps 100 acres in extent – outside
of which was broken water. 'An I thought,' said Davie McLean, 'this is
a phenomenon. And so it wis – it wis a mass o herrin, an we dinna know
that.' [David McLean, 1975]

Lumps

One time up Loch Fyne, the herring were 'floating in black lumps'.
These black lumps, with gulls attending them, could be seen ahead, but
when the fishermen got up to where the appearance had been, all that
was left was scales – the fish had 'made right for the bottom'. The fishermen were 'sick' of ringing for nothing. The only successful boats were
a Tarbert pair that rung in the mouth of Loch Gair after dark and got
300 baskets. The herring were 'by the thousand ton', but were *deukers*

(p 6) and went 'straight to the bottom and lay down that night'. [Turner McCrindle, 1976]

'Red Mines'

In the autumn of 1939, Archie Paterson was a boy of 14 cooking on the *Rolling Wave*, in company with the *Maid of Honour*. They were the only Carradale boats in Campbeltown, having, the previous Friday, left Loch Fyne because the fishery there was slackening. They were preparing to go to sea that evening when a puffer came into Campbeltown harbour. Her crew was shouting about having seen 'red mines out there at the Light'*. There was something of a panic on, owing to the outbreak of war, but the older hands understood what the puffer crew might have been seeing.

They went out and, sure enough, there were the herring, in two or three red scudding balls. Johnny McMillan in the *Maid of Honour* shot at the back of Davaar Island. He got a score of baskets of herring and a bit of a tearing. The breeze was freshening, so they went back into Campbeltown, sold the catch and loaded it on to a lorry. The lorry-driver stopped briefly at Ardrishaig on his way to the market at Glasgow, and it so happened that several of the Carradale boats were lying in Ardrishaig, having had no success out on the loch. When the crews discovered that there were herring on the lorry from the *Rolling Wave* at Campbeltown, they set off south and had good fishings on the shore between their home village and Campbeltown before morning. [Archibald Paterson, 2000]

Davaar Lighthouse.

A 'triangle' of herring

The colour of herring shoaling close to the surface depended on the state of the day – if a dull day, they showed 'dark' and if a sunny day 'purple'. The *Sea Flower* and *Silver Spray* of Maidens came out of the Kyles of Bute one day and went into Scalpsie Bay. The gulls were 'by the thousand' and the herring could be seen quite plainly in the form of 'a big triangle'. It was a sunny day and they were almost on the surface, but there was a breeze of north wind and fishing was impractical. The two boats went into McCallum's Hole and lay there until break of day, when they ventured out and had a ring, but the tide was 'thrawn' (perverse) with 'the north breeze an the spate after the rainy weather', and the strength of the current broke the bridle of the net. Only one boat had a fishing that morning, the *Hawk* of Dunure. She went out near break of day and her crew rung without the assistance of a neighbour. [Turner McCrindle, 1976]

The colour of the water

Tam Hughes's father, Jimmy, spent some 18 months, after the First World War, crewing on Charlie McKay's *Marjory* of St Monans. Tam described Charlie McKay – who was his great uncle – as 'anointed', on account of his phenomenal success. Charlie had predicted that Jimmy Hughes would make enough money with him to buy a boat of his own, and he did. While at the Buchan fishery, the *Marjory*'s Gardner engine broke down and an engineer had to be despatched from Manchester to repair it. Consequently, the boat was tied up all week until Friday, by which time the St Monans crews – which had averaged £140 – £150 a boat for the week – decided to return home for the week-end and had hired buses.

Charlie McKay had also decided to go home, but his crew, having earned nothing that week, prevailed upon him to go out that night. Under pressure, he agreed, and they set off for the fishing grounds. They had gone only 12 miles off when the crew, who weren't long turned in, heard the engine slow down. Jimmy Hughes went on deck and enquired testily: 'What's this? Is there somethin wrang, Charlie?' – 'Naw, Jimmy,' the skipper replied, 'A like the colour o the water.' There was not a bird or any other sign to be seen and Jimmy Hughes was sceptical, to say the least, of the older man's judgement. They ended up with their biggest shot of the summer – £180 for the night's work! [Tam Hughes, 2001]

Jim Tarvit (letter, 15 Nov 2001) offered the following comments on water-colouration, a set of phenomena in which West Coast ring-net fishermen, incidentally, had apparently no interest: 'Good colour in the water was gener-ally a shade of green and was quite noticeable; also, water showing oily streaks was a good omen. These oily streaks were more evident if there was a breeze on the water. Clear water was not a good sign, nor was white water. If nets were shot in white water, when dried the next morning they were almost white as if they had been dusted with flour or something similar. If white water prevailed (off Peterhead) fishing was always light the next day, whereas, if the prevalent colour was green, good landings could be expected. Naturally, of course, the water could be patchy.'

Herring dirt

When the herring were going away from Loch Fyne, they left their excreta behind. That was a sign that they were leaving to spawn on the Ballantrae Banks. The old men called it 'herrin durt', and, where gathered by the tide, it would appear red, very nearly like the feeding, or *croy**, only 'the wan's alive an the other's the leavins-behind'. This was always before Christmas. 'As soon as the week o Christmas came in, ye'd be seein plenty o the herrin durt there. That wis a sure sign it wis makin tracks.' [Hugh MacFarlane, 1975]

* Gaelic *crò*, 'blood'.

Herring were sometimes seen with a 'great big poke in them, a great big bag o lice, wee shrimp things'. One or two years in Loch Fyne they were very bad that way. The bellies would burst with the soft poke and the buyers would hardly take them. When the herring would 'clean', the red dirt would be seen on the surface of the water. 'A've seen us steamin up Loch Fyne ... och, it wis solid nearly, that stuff, an that wis the herrin cleanin. The next herrin ye wid get, they wid be quite clean. The poke wid be away.' [Robert McGown, 1975]

The Herring Wave

When the herring were going away, they would make a wave in the water, and a boat with an 8-10 hp motor could 'hardly keep tae it'. In the Sound of the Inch, Hugh MacFarlane said to his cousin, Davie MacFarlane: 'Gie her the full speed till we get aheid o it.' They shot and 'never seen a herrin'. They were thinking they were ahead of the shoal when they got ahead of the wave, but, no, the shoal had left the wave well behind. This was in 10 or 12 fathoms of water, and they didn't mark a herring. There was another pair there – the 'Swallowers'* – and they had a go too: nothing. The sea was dead-calm and the wash from the herring was 'two or three inches off the level o the surface'. The herring were 'too quick' for them. [Hugh MacFarlane, 1976]

**Properly 'Gold-Swallowers', from their success. One of the pair was named the* Maggie McDougall.

The Hoppers

For two or three years, in the early 1900s, the Campbeltown fishermen fished a spot of winter herring which they called 'hoppers', from the herrings' leaping on the surface. They would set sail about 10 o' clock in the morning, and if there was any sun at all, that was what they wanted. The sun brought *sil doo* – a red shrimp-like creature on which the herring fed – to the surface, and the fishermen would watch for gulls and when they'd get among where the gulls were, they'd see 'an odd herrin jumpin at the sil doo'; but 'as soon as the sun got low', the feeding, and the herring with it, disappeared.

The McKays went out one Monday to the hopper fishing with a brand-new net. They crossed with a 'nice wee *sar* (breeze) o win', but saw no gulls and decided to head in the direction of Ailsa Craig. The wind fell away and they were becalmed. While lying thus, they heard the puffing of a whale between them and Pladda and managed to make their way there. There were actually two whales, rising and then submerging with surprising rapidity – hardly a minute between their appearing and disappearing – and blowing all the while. John McWhirter thought they must be 'drinkin at herrin'. The herring were certainly there, 'puttin up' bubbles like lemonade, a 'dose' of herring. They shot, and the neighbour-boat caught the end, but with the creaking of the blocks as the neighbour's sail was lowered, the shoal suddenly rose out of the water in the middle of the net and all that was left to the fishermen was 10 or 15 baskets. [John McWhirter, 1976]

The Whale

Those whales – collectively known as 'herring-whales' – that fed on herring were a valued sign, particularly when one would surface to blow and throw the herring off its back.

Willie 'Tarry' Martin in the *Renown* of Dalintober shot one evening off Dougarie, Arran. There were signs of herring there, an 'odd gannet' and whales, and one of these whales found itself surrounded by the net. One of the crew 'kept harpin' that the whale would burst through the net – which was afloat with herring, 'wan in every mash' – and that the catch would be lost. Another crewman, however, declared that the whale 'wid dae nothin o the sort – he could keep there tae the last, but he wid get oot through the openin. An so he did'. The crews were agreed that it was through the whale that the herrin 'wis *breengin* (darting) aweh aa roon' and meshing in the soft, tanned net. Tarred nets, which didn't mesh so readily, were coming into use at that time, but 'Tarry', ironically, 'dinna believe in the tar'. [Henry Martin, 1974]

One night a Carradale fisherman shouted to a Dunure crew: 'Did ye see the whale?' – 'Naw,' was the answer, and quick as a flash: 'Did ye lose wan?' [Hugh Edgar, 2000]

A pessimist

One night the Carradale ringers *Rolling Wave* and *Maid of Honour* were between Skipness and the Inch. There was nothing doing, so the boats were brought alongside each other. The *Maid*'s skipper, Johnny McMillan – young and as 'keen as mustard' – was intent on persevering, but old Angus Paterson on the *Rolling Wave* had other ideas: 'There naw enough burnin tae see them in the water; there too much burnin tae feel them on the wire, an there too much o a *sar* tae hear them playin, so what the hell can a body do but go away an let go the anchor?' [Archie Paterson, 2000]

Herring Playing, Jumping and Breaking the Water
. . . .

Listening for herring was one of the main methods of detection on quiet nights, particularly in winter and spring when 'burning' (p 26) had left the water. Some fishermen were so attuned to their environment that even the merest indication of fish on the surface would not escape their notice.

A bleeng

One of the biggest shots of herring George Wilson of Tarbert ever saw was taken opposite Helensburgh. They had left Gare Loch and were listening for 'the morning play'. George was standing on the bow and heard, but quite distinctly, the merest of sounds. This, he said, 'wis jeest wan [herring] that came tae the surface an sort o gasped'. The skipper said to him: 'Did ye hear anythin there, George?' – 'Aye,' George replied, 'there a *bleeng** astern o ye.' They shot and had to call for help, filling, in the end, the two skiffs and also one of Robert Robertson's big boats. All, as George put it, 'wi wan bleeng – ye might describe it as a gasp'. [George Wilson, 1978]

*Gaelic *blian*

A 'spittle'

When George Newlands was aboard the Blairs' *Glad Tidings*, she and her neighbour were lying in the Kyles of Bute one moonlit night. They heard what George described as 'like a spittle in the water', and, more to pass the time than anything else, decided to have a go. They hauled a big catch and had to call for help. That netful of herring filled almost four boats, and all from 'one spittle'. [George Newlands, 1975]

At the Cock of Arran

Lying off the Cock of Arran one calm night, James McCreath called to his brother Jock: 'Is there anything playing wi ye there?' – 'An odd fish,' Jock replied. 'Well,' James said, 'there's an odd thing here jist breakin the watter lik a fly landin on't, an A've seen big herrin workin this way. Jeest stan by an we'll try it.' They rang and got about 70 baskets of 'great big herrin'; but, as James said, 'if it hadnae been as calm as that, ye wouldn'ta heard it.' [James McCreath, 1976]

Ripples by starlight

John McWhirter was in the Lodan one dark, calm night. They'd been 'up an doon a wheen o times in the evenin', without detecting herring. On their last run, off the Guns, they encountered 'wee spittles in a spot … jeest breakin the watter, har'ly makin a sound at aa', and couldn't understand what it was. They continued south and found no herring, so turned about and returned north, only to come on that same spot again. 'Ye could see them wi the stars,' John McWhirter recalled, 'jeest wee rings, but that's the only thing that drew oor attention – they wir in a spot. There wir nane on eether side o that, so we came to the conclusion: well, if it's herrin we've a chance o gettin them.' Still they debated the appearance, baffled, because had herring been the cause, one or other of the fish should have disclosed itself by a more forceful motion, 'a breakin or jumpin'. Finally, some one suggested: 'Ach, A think we'll try a haal.'

Not wishing to steam through the spot and risk disturbing it, they shot 'the wrong way'; in other words, the net, instead of streaming out clear over the port quarter as the boat circled to port, was being shot on a starboard cant. This was always a risky operation, seldom performed. In this case, the accident which the fishermen most feared happened – the sole-rope went over one of the buoys and hung up the net. They got only 16 baskets of herring – fine herring – out of the fouled net, and were 'mad at wan another' for passing the spot the first time. 'Dammit,' said John McWhirter, ' it wis big herrin, great big herrin, jeest puttin thir noses above the watter!' [John McWhirter, 1976]

Giving the net the benefit of the doubt

Davie McLean lost his neighbour one night, after discharging a catch into the herring-steamer *Good Design*. Approaching four o' clock in the morning, the engine was stopped and the crew took a cup of tea. When Davie came on deck, smoking his pipe, there were fish, 'jeest lik flies', breaking the surface. He said to his uncle: 'A think we'll have a go at that.' – 'Ach,' his uncle replied, 'that's *sile* or *lice*.' – 'Well,' said Davie, 'this is the thing that'll test it,' and the net was shot.

Despite having no neighbour to assist with net-hauling, the crew got 50 baskets of big herring, 'an us right ower the top o the net'. The herring 'rose to play' while the net was out, and Davie speculated that, had their neighbour been there, they'd have netted thousands of baskets; but there was no towing boat to keep a strain and preserve the net's shape. He described the phenomenon as a sound 'lighter' than a pot boiling, adding: 'But, ye see, there plenty men widna put thir net out on that. They wid say, "That's naw herrin", an they wid go away an leave it. But I aalways liked tae give the net the benefit of the doubt.' [David McLean, 1975]

A distant play

In the earliest years of ring-netting, fishermen would 'hardly think on shootin a ring-net outside o where the net wid touch the ground – they thought it wis hopeless, but what they didna know at that time was that sometimes herrin are apt tae stay up'. Davie McLean, one night off the Coves, Arran, heard herring playing about four miles distant. The rest of the fleet was farther north, at Iorsa, so Davie, wishing to maintain secrecy, called to his father, Neil, retired by that time, but 'oot for a holiday' on the neighbour-boat: 'A'm hearin herrin away between us an the Cruban Buoy an don't move tae I give ye a signal.' His father asked what the signal would be. 'A'll strike a match over the boat's quarter,' Davie replied, reasoning that the crews to the north would never see that.

The two boats steamed off in the direction of the play and stopped. The herring were west of them. Ten minutes' more steaming and Davie called to his father: 'We're in the heart o a sea o herrin playin.' – 'We're in the middle o herrin here, jumpin,' his father replied. 'Well,' said Davie, 'that's the herrin tae shot on.' Herring jumping here and there were considered to be 'steady' and not so apt to plummet, whereas playing herring were liable to disappear with the slightest noise. They netted 270 baskets, and his father remarked that he had 'never seen bigger herrin'. [David McLean, 1974]

At Machrie

One night the *Silver Spray* and the *Twin Sisters* of Maidens got 180 baskets of mackerel along the Woods of Arran and were leaving to go to Girvan. The boats were brought alongside each other and the two John McCrindles and Tom Sloan had a discussion. 'What about goin out an havin a wee listen for herrin afore we go?' one of them suggested. This was agreed, and the boats went off Machrie a bit, to where a whale was, and there heard 'an odd one jumping'. They rang and netted about 120 baskets of herring, which they stowed on the boats' decks, the holds already containing mackerel. The Sloans' *Twin Sisters* went to Ayr market and got 10s a basket for the herring, while the *Silver Spray* landed at Girvan and received 7s or 8s a basket. The mackerel sold for 6s or 7s. [Turner McCrindle, 1976]

Dancing in the moonlight

Close inshore, in Lady Bay, Stranraer Loch, a Maidens crew 'heard herrin jumpin an went in an they wir jumpin round the sandbank, lik dancin – ye could see them wi the moonlight'. They shot the net to haul off the shore, which was 'against the rules', but it was the only way they could get round the shoal. The shot encircled some 2000 baskets, but when discharged next morning, the herring were red around the gills. 'Ye thought they wir a week old.' [Turner McCrindle, 1976]

Too many

At Corriegills, Arran, in the winter of 1940 or '41, 'the herrin came off the shore jeest lik a gale o win at daylight in the mornin'. 'Wee Tam' McCrindle, who skippered the *Golden Sheaf*, shot the net 'across the shore in the face o the herrin comin off' and trapped too many. 'Och,' Andy McCrindle recalled, '[we] couldnae dae nothin wae her. She wis foo when we started tae lift the soles, absolutely boilin wi herrin.' The crew let the sole of the net back out and tried to release part of the catch, while the neighbouring crew, in the *Maireared*, gripped the cork-rope on the opposite side of the bag to prevent its sinking; but after just 120 baskets had been discharged from the net – which Andy McCrindle reckoned might have held 2000 or more baskets – it burst and the rest of the catch was lost. The sea was flat-calm and there was a keen frost in the air. Andy's father, Jake, then a man in his early fifties, was hanging on to the cork-rope, his hands turned blue, and fainted with the cold. [Andy McCrindle, 2001]

Enhanced hearing

Johnny Munro, as a teenager, was in the crew of the *Night Hawk* of Dunure when she was 'commandeered' for wartime service, so he went with his uncles on the *Columbine III*. One of these uncles, Tommy Munro, had eye trouble and was losing his sight, so much so that he shouldn't have been at sea at all; but the ailment seemed, in compensatory fashion, to enhance his sense of hearing. 'A've seen us stannin – A wis jeest a teenager at that time, comin up on eighteen – at the heid o the boat. He wid say: "A can hear fish jumpin." God, he could hear them before anybody else.' At that time, the practice was to stop the engine, listen; restart the engine and then steam two or three hundred yards before listening again. [John Munro, 1999]

Pan-shells

Turner McCrindle was told of a Tarbertman shooting off Meall Dubh 'on a play'. It wasn't, however, herring that he'd heard, but queen scallops, which the Ayrshire fishermen called *pan-shells*. These dainty bivalves are known to swim in multitudes, by the repeated opening and closing of their shells, and the Tarbert crews had a 'wile job' getting the net aboard, because the shellfish would 'get clipped' – fasten themselves – on to the meshes and have to be smashed to clear the net. [Turner McCrindle, 1976]

•

Burning

*The expressions 'burning' and 'fire in the water' described that most beautiful
and startling appearance, the phosphorescence that lit the sea with its greeny bril-
liance in late summer and autumn. During that period, a man or two men would
be stationed all night on the bow watching for signs of fish and intermittently
'chapping', or knocking, the anchor-stock on the gunwale or tapping with a bolt
or thumping the foredeck with the side of the leather seaboot. The sound-wave
thus transmitted would cause herring to start with a flash, a response which was
known as 'answering the anchor'. The organism most likely to produce phosphorescence, when disturbed by the movement of fish, or anything else, is the
multitudinous dinoflagellate* Noctiluca, *a member of the phytoplankton, which
are minute drifting plants; but quite how the glow is generated remains uncertain.*

A shot in Sgolaig

On the night before Tarbert Fair, about 1906, the Tarbert fleet was in
Sgolaig. Hugh MacFarlane was forward (probably on the *Mary*) and saw
a flash very near the bottom in 12 fathoms of water. The fellow beside
him said: 'What dae ye see?' – 'Are ye naw seein it?' Hugh replied. They
were over bad ground and Hugh said to his brother Sandy, who was
steering the boat: 'Jeest turn her in the wey ye're goin.' The end-buoy
was dropped and the skiff drawn 'right up tae the rock'. When the neighbour-boat came in, the operation was immediately questioned: 'What
are ye doin?' – 'Come on in wi the en,' the doubtful crew was instructed.
'Gie her a wee chug an come on in wi the en.' When the net was lifted,
there were 130 baskets of herring in it.

There had been no other herring caught that night and the market
was starved. Nine or ten herring-steamers came in to bid on the catch,
which went to Murray in Saltcoats for 23s a basket, a remarkable price
at the time. That week-end, Hugh – who wasn't a drinker at the time –
was walking through the fair and encountered an elderly fisherman,
Dougie Smith, who had 'a bucket in him'. 'Come on,' said Dougie.
Hugh, baffled, asked him: 'Where are ye goin to?' – 'A'm gonny gie ye
a drink,' Dougie replied. 'A'm no takin it,' Hugh said, adding: 'What
for?' – 'The whole fishin fleet was in Sgolaig an there wirna a man seen
a herrin but yersel,' Dougie said. 'A seen wan stroke,' Hugh explained.
'Well,' Dougie repeated, 'there weren't a man …' and, breaking off,

announced to Hugh's embarrassment: 'Ye're the best fisherman in Tarbert!' [Hugh MacFarlane, 1974]

At the Wee Herbour

John McWhirter once saw herring respond to anchors being struck about a mile distant. He was off the Wee Herbour, below Ardnacross farmhouse. It was a windless night and there was burning in the water, but only a few herring to be seen in it. He went as far into the Wee Herbour as he could – it lay behind a reef, but had 'plenty watter' in it – and could see the herring inside and hear 'an odd yin jumpin'. So, he and his neighbour lay perhaps 50 or 100 fathoms off as morning came. There was another pair of boats coming round Isla Ross and with every *chap* (knock) these crews gave the anchor, bunches of herring could be seen going out past the waiting boats, heading off to sea from the Wee Herbour. At 'the hinner en', when the bunches of herring seemed to get a little thicker, John shot and netted 40 baskets. [John McWhirter, 1975]

Small in the burning

Good-sized herring could sometimes, for reasons unknown, appear small when sighted in the burning. The *Watchful* and *Wistaria* were in the Kilbrannan Sound one night, while the Carradale and Tarbert fleets were working about the Bucks and Portavadie in lower Loch Fyne. There was, at the time, a quota on small herring, and most of these crews, having caught their quotas, were in Tarbert by 10 o' clock, finished for the night. The Carradale crews, whose neighbours had gone to market, were returning home, and one of the skippers, Ronnie Brownie, came on the radio and announced, for the benefit of any of the Carradale men who didn't yet have their quota, that there were plenty of wee herring at Skipness.

The Sloans heard this information and took a turn down along the Iron Wharf at Skipness. Andy Alexander was on the bow of the *Watchful* and called to his skipper, Matt Sloan: 'There a good lot o herrin here. They don't look very big.' – 'Ach, well,' Matt replied, 'it doesnae matter; we huvnae got wir quota o wee yins anyway. Dae ye think it's worth a go?' – 'Oh,' Andy said, 'it's worth a go.'

They shot and rung 800 baskets of big herring. 'An ye want tae've heard the Carradalemen the next day!' Andy recalled. 'They'd run ower the top o them. They wir goin away home; they'd got thir quota o wee yins. An they aw thought it wis wee herrin – it wis great big herrin.' Andy himself admitted that he would have sworn it was just 'rubbish in the watter'. But, he said, 'ye could be deceived', and speculated that the shallowness of the water might have been a contributory factor. [Andy Alexander, 1976]

Stars in the water

Phosphorescence is rarely seen in wintertime, and when seen is likely to be minimal, a few sparks in shallow water, which Tarbert fishermen described as 'stars in the water'. Herring were said to 'make their own burnin' in winter. One dark winter's night on the West Shore, Dugald Johnson – skipper of the *Little Flower* – came up from the forecastle after a cup of tea and, instead of going straight to the helm, lay forward 'tae get his eyes', i.e. accustom his sight again to the darkness. The boat was 'going down through the white sand at Sgolaig' with her neighbour, the *Silver Spray*, when Dugald came off the bow, instructed the helmsman to 'Keep her hard off', and, without saying another word to anybody, dropped the *winky*. He'd seen 'stars in the water' and these few sparks, casually responded to, yielded a couple of hundred baskets of big herring. 'Dugal wis that canny,' said Robert Ross, 'he never did anythin in a hurry in his life.' [Robert Ross, 2001]

'A scatter o sparks'

Matt Sloan reckoned that within most pairs of ring-net crews there would be a man or two truly expert with burning in the water. Johnny Sloan, an uncle, and Turner McCrindle, were two such men, and both were involved in the following account, which can be dated to the early 1930s, because it involved the McCrindles' little *Margarita* BA 117, which was replaced in 1934 by *Margarita* BA 56. The neighbour-boat was the Sloans' *Virginia* BA 66.

Matt was just a boy at the time and the two boats were lying at Saddell. The wind was westerly or north-westerly and he didn't recall any other Clyde boats being out that night. It was autumn and the burning was fading. The boats ran across the Kilbrannan Sound to Machrie and searched up through the middle of that wide bay. The *Margarita*'s crew located herring, shot, and got about 200 baskets, which, owing to the weather, were taken aboard without the *Virginia*'s 'passing round' to lash up to the bag of the net. The *Margarita*, with only her skipper Johnny McCrindle and the engineer aboard, was then sent back across the Sound to Saddell, the remainder of her crew transferring to the *Virginia*.

After 'two or three turns' around the north end of Machrie, another spot of herring was located and the net was shot and hauled in a single-boat operation, which again yielded about 200 baskets. As the *Virginia* headed back across the Sound to rejoin her neighbour, supposed to be at anchor, 'here was the *Margarita* comin running to leeward because they wondered what had happened when they hadn't seen or heard from [us]'.

The boats found a herring-steamer, the *Norman*, lying at Port na Cùile, Carradale, and the *Margarita* sold her herring there, for about 8s a basket. The steamer's skipper, Davie Woods, told Tommy Sloan: 'If ye go up tae Loch Ranza, ye'll probably find the *Watchful*.' This was another herring-steamer, skippered by an Ardrishaig man, Davie Bruce. The *Watchful* was indeed there, and shifted across the Sound to Claonaig to get a lee shore for loading the *Virginia*'s catch.

Both catches were secured from just 'a scatter o sparks', as Matt described the appearance. It was, he said, a case of 'getting a good result from what had been seen'. [Matt Sloan, 2001]

Men on the bow

Jim Campbell of Carradale – who skippered first the Irma, *while still in his teens, and then the* Bairn's Pride *– considered it vital to have a reliable man on the bow and offered two contrasting accounts of the burning fishing.*

In the first, he and his neighbour, John McConnachie in the *Florentine*, were going down through Carradale Bay one night, the first pair on the scene. An elderly man on the bow was shouting: 'Slow her doon!' – 'What are ye seein there?' Jim enquired. 'Oh, there a braw light here,' was the reply. Since the water was shallow – no deeper than three or four fathoms – and the echo-sounder was ineffective there, he probed further: 'Are ye sure?' – 'Ye canna pass it!' was the emphatic reply. As Jim remarked: 'Well, that's you in a box right away.'

He canted back a bit and 'rounded up' to shoot. His neighbour had just caught the *winky* when the older man came aft and opined: 'Aw, A think ye wir too far past them.' – 'Naw, A wisna too far past them,' Jim countered. As the net-hauling proceeded, 'naw a cheep oot o anybody' until the old man began shouting: 'There they're showin at the corks!' But the phosphorescent flash at the back-rope was coming from a 'great big ball of burning' that wasn't herring at all, but perhaps *sil doo* (shrimp-like plankton). A 'wile shine' – or angry dispute – ensued!

Duncan McIntosh*, conversely, was a master on the bow, and the last time he practised his skills there, on the *Bairn's Pride*, the pair was coming south along the shore by Sunadale. By that time, Duncan was well up in years and Jim was reluctant to expose him to the rigours of lying forward on cold nights. They went into Grogport Bay, by which time Jim could see the fleet starting to shoot to the southward. As they skirted Barmollach Rock, Duncan began shouting: 'Slow her doon!' Jim duly slowed the boat. 'Aye, right, try this,' said Duncan. 'The boats are shootin, Duncan, sooth o the Cruban. A think they're seein herrin well sooth o the Cruban,' Jim remarked. 'Aye, ye're all right – try this,' Duncan persisted. Jim checked the echo-meter. 'A canna see … there's nothin on the meter, mind.' – 'Naw, ye're all right – jeest fire away.' They fished 180 baskets. 'Ye could never question him,' Jim concluded. [Jim Campbell, 2001]

Jim's neighbour of 20 years, John McConnachie, concurred. Going aboard the Campbell boat to haul a ring, to the question, 'What did ye see here, Duncan?', the answer would be specific: 'Aw, there wir a scatter – maybe thirty or forty baskets.' 'He could tell what ye wid get. Other men, if you went aboard: "Oh, a big thing here." Ye maybe winna get anythin. They dinna know.' John heard older men talk of seeing herring 'blue in the watter', but never himself saw such an appearance. At night, the old men preferred to put out the fire in the forecastle in case the smoke would blow over the water and 'spoil them for seein herrin'. [John McConnachie, 2001]

*The Campbeltown Courier *of 20 October, 1966, reported the retirement of Duncan McIntosh after 47 years' continuous service on Campbell-owned boats, first the* Flora Campbell, *then the* Irma *and finally the* Bairn's Pride.

Lighting the sky

When Grieve Gemmell first went to Whitby, in 1946 or '47 – his father had been before then – the herring shoals were so vast, the light from their motion was illuminating the sky. 'Look at that – they're lightin the sky!' the men would say. 'Ye could read the name o the boat when ye steamed in among them,' Grieve recalled. 'It wis pitch-black an ye wir steamin along an then, all of a sudden, ye went intae a big spot – ye could read the name.' [Grieve Gemmell, 1999]

It was said that in the first year at Whitby you'd see the herring from the wheelhouse; the next year you'd need to be at the break of the deck; and the year after that, you'd be lying over the bow. [John McConnachie, 2001]

Nocturnal light

There was a night at the Cock of Arran when the entire sea was aglow as though moonlight was shining on it; yet there was no moon and nothing but phosphorescence by which the phenomenon might be explained. The crews were hunting mackerel and the general opinion was: 'Ye'll no be gettin mackerel wi that.' Hugh MacFarlane saw that manifestation only once in his long experience of fishing. [Hugh MacFarlane, 1976]

Chancer and Bad
●●●●●●●●●●●●●●●●●●●●●●●

Both the 'chance-haul', or 'chancer', and the bad *– which is simply Gaelic for 'a piece', i.e. of the end of the net – were resorted to when conditions were unfavourable for locating herring by the usual means – seeing, hearing, smelling, etc. The advent of the feeling-wire and, later, the echo-sounder, enabled fishermen to locate herring no matter the prevailing conditions, and the 'chance-haul' and bad fell into disuse.*

The West Shore

Before motor-power came in, the Tarbert fishermen engaged routinely in summer 'chance work' along the West Shore 'right tae Skipness'. Each pair of crews had their own spot, and if they shifted they'd have to go miles away because every other beat would be occupied. Night after night they'd go through 'the drill', shooting the net and hauling it shorewards to anchors. The crews were lucky if they could have two shots in a night. In the morning, they'd 'light the torches for the screws. That's the only time o the year, if ye wir lucky, ye wid get a pound a basket – great big herrin'. [Hugh MacFarlane, 1974]

Robert Ross was never at that fishing, but he experienced chancers on *peuchkies* (saithe) along Skipness Point, where a crew would always be sure, at the least, of 'a basket o flounders'. [2001]

The Long Point

Davie McLean and his neighbour were lying off the Cuilleam, at the back of Davaar Island, one night. The rest of the fleet, Davie said, had gone 'away for the quay'. About three o' clock in the morning, he felt the boats touching ground and hurried on deck. The wind was southerly and the boats were 'on a dead lee shore by this time, an it's rather a dangerous thing tae be lyin on a lee shore'. One of his crew was already on deck and Davie remarked to him: 'A see there a change o win.' – 'Aye,' the man agreed. 'Will we go over tae Porter's Glen?' – 'Whoot are ye gonny do over there?' Davie responded. 'Oh, we'll get an anchorage on a weather shore,' was the reply. 'Well,' said Davie, 'there's another shore I know that we might go an see if we can get some herrin.'

They went straight to the Flat Rock in Kildalloig Bay, and, as soon as they got in there, canted north till they came to a haul at the Long Point, and shot there. They got 'a fine ring o herrin'. By this time – between four and five o' clock in the morning – the fleet was beginning to leave Campbeltown, but Davie's crew, he said, was the only one that got a fishing.

The Flat Rock was a 'famous spot for a chance haul, for it's clean ground'. On the south side of the Long Point, 'ye've got tae waatch in the dark that ye don't go too far up … if ye go right up over the point, ye'll get yer net badly torn on that side. So, ye'd jeest tae judge'. [David McLean, 1974]

The Flat Rock

Some nights there would be 'a race' to reach the Flat Rock and some crews would shoot their net in daylight, even before the herring had come in at all. The McLellans and Gilchrists were 'great han's for tryin that'. Even if there were no herring caught, a 'male o fish' could be expected. [Henry Martin, 1974]

The Back of the Geelot

'Upside o the Geelot' – the rocky gullet or gut at Peninver – was a 'great place' for Angus Martin's father, John. 'That's the wey I know so much aboot it,' Angus said, 'becaas A learnt aal aboot it when A wis young.' The Campbeltown fishermen wouldn't go near it, maintaining that the ground was all bad; and, certainly, north of the Geelot, in the middle of Ardnacross Bay, 'it's aa rocks thegither, an A've seen them comin up there an shottin on gannets, an me fether winna look at them. Aw, haulin thir nets aboord in strings, ribbons'.

If the Martins didn't locate herring, they 'chanced it'. At the back of the Geelot, the ground was rather rough, but they'd get herring there.

John Martin ordered a flax bag purposely for the winter fishing, and put that into the net. At the back of the Geelot, the net would snag on big stones and tangles, but when they hauled it the damage would be insignificant, 'jeest wee bunches o't away'. That flax bag was as tough as nylon, Angus maintained. They used to go up there every night in winter and had herring nearly every morning, though maybe not many, because they weren't getting right round the spots of herring. 'It wis chancers.' [Angus Martin, 1974]

'Chasing each other ...'

'That used tae be the fishin when we went tae the ringin in the early spring. We'd be chasin each other along the shore tae get intae a certain ring. That's where they congregate, the herrin, at a certain time o the tide. If ye went wi the ebb, ye got nothin. Flood tide ... they're a wise fish, the herrin; they just knew when the tide wis comin in.' [Thomas McCrindle, 1976]

The Washinghouse Rock

The Washinghouse Rock took its name from a laundry on the shore below Culzean Castle. The rock was immediately offshore in 12 fathoms.

One winter night the crew of the *Twin Sisters* of Maidens – Tommy, Bill and Jimmy Sloan, John and Davie Andrew and Jimmy Girvan – went out without a neighbour to the Washinghouse Rock to try a chancer with a ring-net 50 score of meshes deep. They had no idea whether there were herring there or not, but they took over 100 baskets out of the net and went to Ayr with the shot. One of the herring-buyers was at 'the pictures' and bidding was delayed until he returned. The buyers that night put the herring up to 31s a basket, and when the crew was discharging the catch, basket by basket with the halyards, the successful buyer remarked: 'Noo, then, fill them up tae the cran-hooks.' These were the hooks which caught the handles of the basket for hoisting the catch ashore, and he wanted to be sure that the baskets were as full as could be. [Tommy Sloan, 1976]

Waiting for the moon to set

One night Jake McCrindle and his crew dropped anchor in the Maidens to wait for the moon to go down, for herring are hard to catch in bright moonlight. Jake was keeping an eye on the moon – 'it gets kinna red before it goes doon' – and when it set, he woke the crew and they went to Turnberry Lighthouse, where there was a chance haul. They shot there – without a neighbour-boat – and got 400 baskets, but they were nearly swept on to the rocks and had to let go their anchor and chain to hold the boat. [John McCrindle, 1976]

Sunday fishing

Jake McCrindle recalled going out before midnight one Sunday to try a 'chance haul'. He knew, of course, that what he was doing was illegal, but the Maidens fishermen, when returning home on the Saturday, had seen 'the signs' and knew there were herring about. When his and the neighbouring crew assembled at the harbour at the agreed time, there were no signs of any other crews appearing. 'Ach,' Jake said, 'we'll go away out anyway.' Off Culzean Castle, they had a 'chance ring' and netted 200 baskets of herring. The catch was divided between the two boats, 100 baskets into each, so that they 'wouldnae show too much weight', and sold secretly at sea. [John McCrindle, 1976]

A smelting

Coming from the Kyles of Bute and making for Tarbert, a Dalintober crew encountered a *smeltin*, a slick of fish-oil on the surface. *Stanelock* – big saithe – were very often the cause of that smoothness and the associated fishy smell. One of the crew remarked: 'It'll naw dae any herm tae put the en o the net oot.' They did that and didn't wait very long until they hauled it in, with a herring 'marked' on the end. So they tried a 'chancer'; went to windward a bit, shot and got a good fishing. 'That happened very of'en. Ye wid put oot the en o the net an if ye marked wan or two at aa, ye wid haev a go tae see if ye wid get anythin.' [Henry Martin, 1974]

A *bad* at the Isle of Ross

On a quiet night, with nothing doing, fishermen would 'try the end o the net, the half o the end'. They'd take a 'weather gauge o the tide', drift with it and then lift the *bad*. 'Aw, as sure as the eye in the needle,' Hugh MacFarlane remarked.

As a 'stated instance' of that practice, he told of one night he was down off the Isle of Ross with 'the whole fleet', Campbeltown and Carradale boats too. They were lying listening and Hugh suggested: 'Come on we'll throw oot a bad.' They 'put on the two oars an put oot the half o the net', giving it 10 or 15 minutes to drift. When they hauled back, there was a *strag* – a thick meshing – of herring in the end. They didn't shake the fish out at all, but just hauled them on board, put on the oars again and shot. They got a fine fishing.

'Then there wir torches; then they wir throwin away bi chance, ye know, when they got close. But if they wid put oot a bad, they wid mark it the same as us. We wir lyin there all evenin, aye, tae we wir tired, ye know. Not a breath o win an a bit o moon. The sea wis lik gless. The whole fleet wis there. Aye, we got a fine fishin.' [Hugh MacFarlane, 1976]

Feeling for Herring

The feeling-wire – up to 100 fathoms (183m) of snare-wire or fine-ply twine, with a lead weight on the end of it, wound on to the side of a fish-box – was in regular use by 1932, but its origins are obscure. The Fishery Board claimed to have introduced the device to select Ayrshire and Kintyre crews in 1925, without success. Robert McGown of Campbeltown maintained that he received the equipment from Swedish seine-net fishermen in 1928, but neglected it until about 1930 or 1931. Its secret and successful use by certain Ayrshire crews in the late 1920s and early 1930s, may well be the key to its eventual general adoption.

Whatever the truth of the matter, the wire became an indispensable tool in identifying the nature of the seabed and in locating herring when conditions were unfavourable for detection by natural means, and it continued in use, electronic aids notwithstanding, until the very demise of ring-netting. The feeling-wire on display in Campbeltown Museum was in use aboard Skipper Donald McMillan of Carradale's boats the Marie *and, subsequently, the* Mairi Bhan, *until 1971.*

Experiments

It was Donald McIntosh's belief that fishery officers gave one wire to McGown in Campbeltown, another to Smith in Tarbert and a third to Sloan in Maidens, and that 'Sloan wis the only wan that worked it'. The

Sloans' secret – and successful – use of the wire was only discovered, according to Donald, when they got a netful of herring at Knock Castle, north of Largs, and another Maidens pair, the *Maireared* and *Golden Sheaf*, went alongside to assist. The feeling-wire thereafter was in general demand and snare-wire sold out in all the shops. Donald McIntosh managed to obtain piano-wire, which was dearer, but rejected it after an experience in Loch Long. He was out in the middle of the loch when the wire-man reported: 'Oh, there plenty o them here!' Donald shot, but the wireman couldn't reel in the wire quickly enough and there was 'a pile near as big as a haystack o the wire on the stern'. [Donald McIntosh, 1974]

Matt Sloan, who was a boy on the family ringer *Veronica* when 'the wire was first worked with', was 'not too confident' about the Sloans being credited with its introduction. By his recollection, it was one of the crew of John Gemmell's *Mary Sturgeon* of Dunure – possibly his son, Sammy – who got the credit, on the Ayrshire side, anyway, for pioneering the wire. Matt's uncle, Jimmy Sloan, however, was an expert on the feeling-wire and offered Matt peculiar advice: 'Listen, son, ye've goat tae be awfully keen in the touch. Sometimes ye've almost goat tae listen for the herrin hittin the wire.' That, Matt affirmed, 'wis his expression'.

Certainly, in Matt's own later experience, there were times when herring could be felt by a gentle 'touch' rather than a 'knock'. There were occasions, too, when herring would register steadily on the wire, and other occasions – the fishing being 'slack' – when if perhaps three or four fish could be felt along 'the length o a net … ye could sometimes get a nice pickle oot o that'. Some men, however, 'could go to the wire an they would hardly have felt them although they wir jumpin up against it'. [Matt Sloan, 2001]

The Swedish experience

Robert McGown was given a feeling-wire around 1928 by Swedish hake-fishermen who were based at Campbeltown. There were herring in Campbeltown Loch that spring and three Swedes asked if they could go out on the *Faustina* to see the ring-net worked. They asked to be taken alongside their own boats, which were moored at the New Quay, and came back aboard the *Faustina* with a feeling-wire. The Swedes were 'puttin out this wire an trailin it astern o the boat', but the ringers were watching for gannets striking, and, when someone would report, 'There a gannet struck', the wire would have to be hauled in. The ringers were not impressed. Nevertheless, the weighted coil of wire was left aboard the *Faustina*. 'Nobody bothered about it. It just lay. Goodness me, when ye think on it back, what ye could have been doin with it. Ach, it wis too slow a way tae be goin about, dead-slow, trailin a wire. This wis no good. Goodness, what it turned out tae be after that!' [Robert McGown, 1974]

The wire validated

Davie McLean had tried and 'condemned' a reel of 15-ply twine with a net-lead attached to its end. They had been 'steamin full-bit' when experimenting with it, and the man entrusted with the device 'wis feelin oceans o herrin – jeest the *jabble!*' In the *May Queen* one night off Ayr, however, when confronted with the 'very curious phenomenon' of a patch of calm amid broken water (p 16), Davie retrieved the line and gave it to young Norman Brodie*, who drowned on the Arctic Patrol during the subsequent War. 'When we keep her round this time, you put that oot, an if it's really as they say it is, we'll maybe feel somethin,' he told him. Norman had hardly let the wire over the side when he called Davie over. 'Ye'd think it wis somebody playin the piano,' Davie recalled. 'Well,' he decided, 'if there wir ever herrin on the wire, this is them.'

The pair got so much herring that the *May Queen* was more heavily loaded than she'd been for years and began to sink. Davie called to the boy to light the *flambeau*, which he took aft. He found where the water was pouring in, stopped it with a screw-driver, then smeared butter around the plug. Off the Heads of Ayr, on their way to market, they met Jimmy Edgar of Dunure, who asked where they'd got the herring. 'Wi the leadin lights off Ayr bar,' Davie told Dan Black to answer. Edgar got the spot too and put the rest of the boats, coming out in the morning, on to it. The McLean boats received the lowest price in Ayr market that morning, owing to a crew member 'mouthin aboot watter in the boat', an indiscretion which reached the buyers' ears. [David McLean, 1974]

*Actually Neil Brodie. Most of the boat's crew were named 'Neil', so by-names were necessary to distinguish one man from another, and Neil's by-name was 'Norman'. He was lost from H M Trawler Stella Capella, in March 1942, after she was struck by a torpedo fired from U-Boat 701 off Iceland.

Some men better than others

Some wire-men would rub their hands with the rough side of a matchbox, believing they would thereby enhance their tactile sensitivity; yet it was a demonstrable truth that certain fishermen were just naturally more adept than others at feeling herring.

Of Fred Rennie on the *Glen Carradale*, Davie McNaughton remarked: 'He wis wan o the finest wire-men ever I wis wae. If there wir two herrin there, Fred wid feel wan-an-a-half o them.' A wise skipper would invariably take the word of a trusted wire-man, though, as Davie McNaughton admitted: 'Ye could feel wan or two an jeest say: Ach, well, ye're stannin here frozen anyway. Ye might as well get a shot an maybe get a puckle.' [David McNaughton, 2000]

Some men, Grieve Gemmell recalled, 'wirnae too sure o what they wir feelin'. His father Sammy told him about a young cook he had on the boat. They were going up Loch Long, which is remarkably deep, and the boy had the wire. 'Are ye feelin onythin?' Sammy said to him. 'Na, no feelin a thing, Sam, but the ground's hell of a bad here.' – 'The ground's hell of a bad?' said Sammy, incredulous. 'Aye, aye.' All the other boats round about had big rings of herring. 'It wis the bloody herrin he wis feelin!' Grieve explained. 'The wire winnae go tae the bottom o the loch, ye know. A'm no kiddin ye – they wid shake yer han if ye wir goin through them thick.' [Grieve Gemmell, 1999]

A faithless skipper

Davie McNaughton, as boy aboard the *Lily*, had a sound training in wire work from Jock 'Glindy' McKinlay. Years later, Davie was wire-man aboard a Campbeltown ringer whose skipper manifestly – and unwisely – preferred the evidence of the echo-sounder to that of the wire. They were searching for herring one night in Poll Gattan, on the south side of Otter Spit, Loch Fyne, when Davie 'got a good feel on the wire'. He at once alerted the skipper – 'Here ye are' – but the skipper referred the matter to his son, who was watching the echo-meter: 'Are ye seein anythin on the machine?' – 'Naw, A'm naw seein anything, Fether,' was the response. 'Aw,' said the skipper to Davie, 'Junior's naw seein naethin on the machine.' – 'Are ye naw shottin?' Davie asked. 'Naw,' was the skipper's answer. 'We're naw shottin if we're naw seein naethin on the machine.'

A few nights later, 'upside o Claonaig', the boat was heading south – the right way for an immediate shot – and Davie again felt herring on the wire. 'Here ye are – a good scatter o herrin here. Are ye seein anythin on the meter?' Davie called to the skipper. 'Naw,' was the answer, 'Junior's naw seein anythin, so there canna be anythin.' With that, the two Blair boats – *Bengullion* and *Seafarer* – appeared from the south and enquired what was doing. Davie informed them: 'A good scatter o herrin astern o us there. If ye go doon oor wake ye'll come intae them.'

The Blairs took his advice, rung back and netted 40 baskets; but, as Davie reasoned, 'that doesna mean tae say we mightna have got a couple o hunner baskets, because we wir gan sooth tae take the shot'. Seeing the Blairs with herring, Davie caught the wire and threw it overboard, announcing: 'My name's Walker!' He returned to Campbeltown that night with the neighbour-boat and secured a berth on Robbie McKellar's *Royal Burghs*. [David McNaughton, 2000]

Caught by surprise

A fishing on *peuchties* 'caught the whole fleet by surprise' in December of 1945. The Campbeltown fleet was at Tarbert, except for the *Shenandoah* and *Crimson Arrow*, which were operating close to home, in the Lodan, and landed the fill of the two boats of peuchties in Campbeltown. The crews had a 'big, big week' – in excess of £100 a man. They'd been regularly feeling just an odd tap on the wire as they hunted for herring up and down the Lodan. Finally, somebody said: 'The next time we feel a couple o taps on the wire, we'll shot on it an maybe get the price o a bottle for the New Year.'

They filled the boats with saithe, and inevitably the fleet arrived from Tarbert to capitalise too on this fishery. Their hopes of success, however, were unrealised. The newcomers, feeling 'big lumps' on the wire, were shooting and getting nothing, while the *Shenandoah* and *Crimson Arrow* continued to land good fishings in Campbeltown every morning. 'Nane o the rest o us wis gettin them,' Davie McNaughton recounted, 'because we wir waitin for the big feels. When we shot on the big feels we wid get naethin oot o it. Heaven knows how that worked – I do not know tae this day whether it wis them on the move.' [David McNaughton, 2000]

Jim Campbell of Carradale had similar thoughts on the frequency of taps. With 'maizy' herring – fish that were ready to spawn – the wire-man might feel only an odd fish because, although perhaps 'as thick as the grass', they were full of spawn and heavy. Spent herring, on the contrary, would be 'flyin everywhere' and easy to feel. [Jim Campbell, 2001]

A dual role

Jim's father, 'Wee' Jamie Campbell, though himself in the wheelhouse of the *Irma*, chose to combine steering the boat with the operation of the wire, a remarkable and perhaps unique dual responsibility, particularly when working close inshore on the darkest of nights. 'He had the wire himself an nobody knew what he wis feelin,' John McConnachie remarked. When he decided to shoot, he'd hand the wire to one of the crew and that man would go to the 'breist o the daik' and start winding in. Nothing would be said.

A Tarbert skipper, Ronnie Johnson, once asked Jim if he had a photograph of the coping-iron along the rail of the *Irma*'s starboard quarter, for it was there that Jamie would combine wiring with steering, and the iron was notched here and there along its length, as though cut with a hack-saw, where Jamie would shift to the wheelhouse, dragging the wire with him, to turn the wheel through an open window.

'Wan thing,' remarked Jim, 'ye can only make the mistake yersel.' The vast majority of skippers, however, left the working of the wire to a 'wire-man'. Jim continued: 'See, ye could ask somebody footerin at the wire, "Are ye feelin any there?", an they'll come back an say tae ye, "The ground's bad". Ye never asked them that. That's the first thing they'll say. They're naw waantin tae take a risk.' [John McConnachie, Jim Campbell, 2001]

'Rubbish'

Even to the very end of the ring-net fishery, the feeling-wire had its value, as the following story from John McConnachie illustrates.

With both echo-sounder and fish-loop installed in the *Florentine*, he was in Catacol Bay looking for herring. As soon as he rounded Church Point, he saw a spot of fish register simultaneously on meter and loop, and switched on his winch-light in readiness to shoot. As John took the *Florentine* through the spot, however, his cousin Donald McConnachie unwound the wire, and, on the basis of what he felt, pronounced the spot 'rubbish, sprats'. They carried on by that spot until Donald, still wiring, shouted: 'Aye, there a scatter o herrin through them now.' John canted, shot, and rung 200 baskets of herring. 'But, if we'd tae shot the first time, we wid have got sprats.' [John McConnachie, 2001]

Fouling trammel nets

The wire was always used on the Ballantrae Banks, more to feel the bottom than to feel for herring. The wire-man had to be extra-alert when working among trammel-nets*. If he felt the wire touching a trammel, he'd to slack it out straight away, because, if he held on, the lead-weight would give a turn and snag the back-rope of the trammel. In latter years, the combination of unyielding piano-wire and equally unyielding nylon trammels often resulted in the nets being pulled almost to the surface in the attempt to free the lead weight. Some trammel boats would have half-a-dozen feeling-wire leads lying on their decks when they returned to harbour in the morning and would 'sell them back tae the ringers'. [Andy Alexander, 1976]

*Actually ground-nets, as described on p 100. The trammel – from French trois mailles (three meshes) – is a more complex instrument, consisting of a central large-meshed net hung on either side with slack, fine-meshed netting.

Echo-Sounders
* * * * * * * * * * * * * * * * * * * *

The echo-sounder, which electronically records the depth and nature of the seabed and detects fish-shoals, was experimented with briefly, in the 1930s, aboard the Nobles *of Campbeltown (p 14) and later the* Golden Sheaf *of Maidens, but was not adopted generally until about 1950. Thereafter, the 'meter' became indispensable, and during fishing operations was always watched for the ink-strokes, between keel and seabed, which indicated fish.*

A saving

While the *Margaret Rose* of Campbeltown was 'in the build' in 1947, a Kelvin-Hughes salesman approached the boat's owner, Archie Graham, and said to him: 'You've got a new boat building in St Monans. Can I save you fifty pounds?' – 'You'll need to explain that,' Archie replied. The salesman took out his company's catalogue and showed Archie the information on echo-sounders. 'They're going up fifty pounds next week,' he said, explaining that it would be much cheaper to order the sounder there and then and have it installed before the boat was launched. 'When he opened the first page or two,' Archie recalled, 'you could see what a tremendous advantage a Kelvin-Hughes echo-sounder was, not only as a navigation instrument, but also for detecting herring and [determining] the depth and density of the shoals and the nature of the bottom.' He did order one there and then, and believed that the *Margaret Rose* – launched in September of 1947 – was the second boat on the Clyde to have a Kelvin-Hughes echo-sounder installed. Two or three years later, the instrument had been adopted generally throughout the fleets. [Archibald Graham, 1999]

Disbelief

When the *Endeavour* of Campbeltown, launched in 1948 for Angus Martin and his three sons, had an echo-sounder installed, Angus refused at first to believe that the instrument could locate fish. 'He couldn't get it that strokes on a piece of paper were herring,' his son Angus recalled. The old man, accustomed to fishing in skiffs and to locating herring with his senses, had a traditional cast of mind, but when it came to telling the nature of the sea-bottom along familiar coasts, using marks on the land to judge his position, he was perhaps as accurate as the machine itself. 'My father knew every rock along the shore an he jeest lifted his eyes so high when we were goin into the land an he wid say: "Ye're in nine or ten fathom."' [Angus Martin Jr, 2001]

Fallibility of echo-sounders

'You had such confidence in your echo-sounder that you thought it would detect herring if there was herring there,' Archie Graham remarked; but that confidence was occasionally misplaced, as Archie himself was to discover. He was over at the Brown Head one night looking for herring. A few Carradale boats were lying there at anchor. There was nothing to be seen, so his *Margaret Rose* crossed back to the west side of the Kilbrannan Sound, where herring had earlier been got; but they 'missed out' there in the morning. The Carradale crews, however, all had good shots at the Brown Head, and one of the skippers, John 'Nonna' Campbell of the *Queen of the Fleet*, later remarked to Archie: 'A see yer echo-sounder has got nae sense o smell. If ye had tae use yer nose instead o yer echo-sounder, ye might have got a shot along wi us!' [Archibald Graham, 1999]

David McLean was working in Loch Fyne one week, going up and down and seeing nothing on the echo-sounder. Sometimes, in the morning, he said, 'ye'd see somethin on the bottom that wisna there before an ye knew that must be herrin'. Other times, however, 'ye wouldna even see a pin-head'. One night, off St Catherine's, they saw a few herring, shot and netted 30 baskets. Another pair of boats was seen coming up the loch, so they put out their lights and took the herring aboard in darkness, then headed north to Shira. In the morning, coming down off Strachur, three tiny marks – 'lik dots wi pencil' – were noticed on the echo-meter paper and attributed to *sile*, or immature herring. They carried on down to Crarae then canted back up and, in the same place, again saw the same three marks. David's son Neil said to him: 'I think we'll have a go at this.' They shot and started to tow the net and the herring were 'playin the sea dry'. They got a fine shot of big herring, and, all the time the crews were boating the catch, the herring played around the boats as day came on; then they went to the bottom. 'See, if ye had them herrin on the shore, it's aa wan whether they dook or no – they're trapped,' David remarked; but the point of the story for him was: 'The echo-sounder's no infallible.' [David McLean, 1974]

The compact spot

The marks appearing on an echo-meter required interpretation, and jargon evolved, some of the terms – such as 'scatter' and 'spot' – being carried over from the traditional systems of herring-detection, while others – such as 'white-lining' – arose out of the new technology itself. Fishermen advanced their expertise at echo-sounding in the usual ways, by personal observation and the advice of others.

Jim Campbell recalled a mass of herring on Catacol Bank one winter, but he and his neighbour John McConnachie were getting just 20 or 30 baskets each ring and gathering perhaps 80 or 90 baskets for a night's work. He noticed, however, that the McCrindle brothers, Angus and Willie, in the *Saffron* and *Minicoy*, were managing 150 and 160 baskets nightly.

One morning, after John McConnachie had left for Tarbert with herring in the *Florentine*, Jim decided to take the *Bairn's Pride* into Loch Ranza to mend a net. He was moored alongside Willie McCrindle and the two skippers got talking. The Ayrshireman asked how Jim was doing, and Jim told him that they were seeing plenty of herring, but failing to secure any bulk. 'Away an get yer meter-paper,' Willie said. Jim tore off the previous night's length of paper and gave it to Willie. 'Show me where ye had the rings,' Willie said. Jim pointed out the marks. 'Aye,' said Willie, 'there plenty o colour there, but that's no use.' – 'Wait a minute,' Jim put in, 'there plenty on the meter.' – 'Aye, but it's the same thing ye're maybe seein every night. Never mind that stuff. Look for the compact spot. Look for the short, sharp thing in among the scatter – jeest two or three strokes. Never mind that stuff – it's movin.'

That evening, when Jim was steaming across for Skipness to meet his

43

neighbour returning from Tarbert, he saw two or three 'wee strokes' appear on the meter. John, by this time, was close at hand and Jim called him on the radio and announced: 'A'm gonny shot here.' – 'The boats,' John replied, 'are seeing a loat o herrin on Catacol Bank.' – 'We'll try this anyway,' Jim affirmed.

'What did ye see there?' John queried as the boats began towing. 'Oh, A don'know,' Jim admitted. 'A jeest seen a hair (fine stroke), catchin yer end,' John reported. 'Jeest a hair?' was Jim's uneasy response. By this time he was 'startin to sweat', but when net-hauling commenced the signs were promising – herring meshed in the wings – and the result was 120 baskets. 'It wis the compact spot,' Jim remarked. 'The more ye see, the more they're movin.' [Jim Campbell, 2001]

Shedding off the boat

Matt Sloan, discussing the few 'sparks' that herring themselves generated in winter when phosphorescence proper had left the water (p 28), believed that shots on that appearance occurred less frequently once fishermen got accustomed to the echo-sounder as a fish-finding instrument. 'I'd be the first tae confess,' he said, 'that there wasnae the same attention paid by a man lyin on the bow once the sounder came into being, because if ye wir goin over them wi the sounder goin, ye wid see some indication underneath; but A'm quite certain there were occasions when herrin wir high up – perhaps sheddin off the boat – they might've been seen by this sparks in the water in wintertime. And yet if they wir sheddin off the boat, often an often ye wir goin along an ye wirnae seein anythin underneath on the sounder at all.'

From time to time, a 'tick' would register on the echo-meter paper and that would be all that would be seen, but if the skipper slowed the boat, 'a continuous wee thing about a fathom in depth' might appear 'right up at the keel', and if he 'took the chance', that sign often turned out to be herring. 'If ye wir goin too fast, ye widnae see anythin because they wir jeest sheddin off the boat; the boat wis disturbin them.'

'A wid be the first tae say there wir certain people – and A wid like tae think that A wis included in that group – who had experience o wee things lik that happenin, an if it happened once ye could ascertain an look for it happenin again.' [Matt Sloan, 2001]

Fishing Grounds

The emphasis here is on the knowledge that fishermen had of the seabed, invisible but none the less charted in their minds – the clean patches of ground where nets would 'run' unobstructed, and the tight corners where submerged rocks and reefs lurked to snag and destroy gear. That knowledge was mostly won by bitter experience – the damage to and loss of nets – and, once won, was preserved by bearings on the land. The old fishermen had a vast store of place-names, including names for the smallest of features, such as rocks and trees. As Neil Short remarked, 'If ye moved a net-length, ye wir in a different [named] place.'

The West Shore

The West Shore, from Tarbert to Skipness, and the bay at Skipness, Craig Aornigh as the fishermen called it; and bits on the Kerry Shore. 'Ach, they had it all taped off. They knew all about where the net wid run. An tae this present day, that's the knowledge this men have got. Och, ye needna ridicule the old men. The old men forgot more than ye ever learned. All ye do now, ye owe it tae the old men. They passed it on tae ye. Ye hivna improved – ye've got bigger nets, but on the same principle. We knew every shot lik yer han there, a name for every place a net wid come.' [David MacFarlane, 1975]

At Lub Dhubh

'A've seen me sittin on the herrin, rowin tae the steamer, at Lo Poo (Lub Dhubh) doon there. Ye winna do wi a sprappal*. The boat wis fuul jeest lik that. She cou'na take another herrin. A wis sittin rowin on the herrin. Aye. But that wis in the bays. Ye cou'na dae thon ootside, no.' [Hugh MacFarlane, 1975]

Obscure Gaelic, likely meaning 'choppy sea'.

Poll Gattan

The *Lily* of Campbeltown neighboured the *Fionnaghal* of Tarbert during the Second World War, and one of the Campbeltown crew, Davie McNaughton, recalled that the *Fionnaghal*'s skipper, Donald 'Tom' McDougall, had a particular haul in Poll a Ghattan, which was ringed with bad ground; 'but Donal could jeest put the net in there. We tried it wance or twice an got a teirin, but naw him. Great marks on it'. [David McNaughton, 1999]

Robert Ross described Poll a Ghattan as 'a wee sandy hole' at the north end of Poll Gattan proper. A 'gut' ran into a small harbour inside Otter Spit, and the hole was there. All the Tarbertmen knew it, he said, and the old Ardrishaig fishermen knew it even better, perhaps. It was a good spot for *peuchky*, though there was 'hardly room tae shot a ring-net'. The net was best shot with flood water, so that, if either boat would touch on the ground, the tide was making. During the Second World War, a lot of saithe was taken out of there. It was a lucrative fishery because saithe, being classed as white fish, had a 'controlled price' of 32/6d a basket, compared with 24/6d for herring. The Campbeltown fishermen, for the duration of the War, referred to saithe as 'goldfish'. After the War, however, Robert saw saithe landed at 5s a basket. Poll Gattan Island, at the south end of the bay, had been a herring-curing station at an earlier period and its ruins remain there. [Robert Ross, 2001]

Dearg Uillt

'A could tell ye nearly every spot fae MacRingan's Point tae Skipness, everywhere,' John McWhirter said. There were places other crews wouldn't come near, especially about Jerdigal (Dearg Uillt). At the White Rocks, south of Cour Island, you could go in till you almost touched the rocks and the ground was 'nice and clean'. Jerdigal was different and the mark for that was two hills inside. You always kept the farther hill open on the nearer one, and if you continued in until that farther hill went out of sight, you were far enough – the ground was coarse. 'But ye wid get that left tae yersel. Ach, I've seen us in July wi John McKay there, straight there on a Monday an there aa week. Nobody wid hardly disturb ye. But of course they had aa wee spots o their own.' [John McWhirter, 1974]

The Minister's Head

The Minister's Head was a favourite place of the Campbeltown men. Davie MacFarlane remembered Neil 'Teedlety' McLean telling him of how they lost a net there one night. The tide was so strong it broke every-thing, and they got the net in the morning on the *skair* (reef) at Grogport. [David MacFarlane, 1975]

During the Second World War, Henry Martin was crewing on Johnny Galbraith's *Cluaran* of Carradale, neighbouring the *Dusky Maid*. They shot at the Minister's. He doubted the decision, but wouldn't comment because the Minister's was home ground to the Carradale fishermen. After the net was out, however, one of the crew asked him: 'How do you think we are here, Henry?' – 'Ye're too close in,' he replied. 'Nothin o the sort,' came the response. 'You look aheid o ye there – the rock's in there,' Henry countered. 'Aye, well, what depth o watter? Get the leid-line.' A sounding was taken: four-and-a-half fathoms. 'Aye, aye, ye're right – we are too close in.' It was a case of shouting to the tow-boat to throw the engine into neutral every now and again until the net was lifted. The man forward on the boat had said there was a ball of something, which he couldn't name, whether mackerel or herring, but Henry reckoned that he'd been seeing tangles, which make, not a proper flame but a lightness when they wave in the *burning*. Henry had seen that lightness often on the top of submerged rocks. 'The fella spoke aboot it efterwards. He says: "I think I made a mistake." We wir shot roon a rock, up there aboot the Minister's. Things look closer wi northerly wind.' [Henry Martin, 1974]

Aorainn Mhór

In the winter of 1959, herring were thick in and around Carradale Bay. It was standard thinking that herring would 'drain in wi the flood watter', but in November of that year boats were going down to Rudha Darach at dead low water and ringing 800 baskets, or two quotas. John McConnachie remembered the year – not always an easy matter – because it was also the year that he and his brothers, James and Walter, bought the Oban-registered *Mallaig Mhor*, later renamed *Florentine*.

One night that November, the *Florentine* and her neighbour, the *Bairn's Pride*, went into the High Rocks, north of Whitestone, to have a look. John's brother James and his cousin Donald McConnachie were on the bow with a searchlight, and, as the *Florentine* 'went though the haul', John was shouting to them: 'Are ye naw seein anythin?' They were in shallow water – a fathom or two – where echo-sounding was ineffectual. The response was negative.

They were now at the rock-face of Erin Vore (*Aorainn Mhór* – Big Foreland) – a haul with just enough length to get a ring-net clear of the rocky bottom – and, as John lifted the throttle to go out again, Donald suddenly saw, in the beam of the searchlight, a shoal of herring swimming below the boat, and shouted: 'Aye, there some there – we'll try it!' They rung about 1200 baskets. 'What A'm thinkin wis,' John recalled, 'they must've been lyin lik cement on the bottom an [when] A lifted the throttle the engine must've disturbed them.' Years after the ring-net fishing ended, and the McConnachies were reluctantly clam-dredging for a living, John had a look at Erin Vore, the old ring-net haul, and saw that its grey face was overgrown with ivy. [John McConnachie, 2001]

Machrie

When Henry Martin went to the fishing first, and for long after that, the family boats, the *Fame* and *Renown*, went over to Machrie Bay and were there for the week. (The Black Head had been their traditional spot during the long ropes fishing, p 51.) Their crews 'never bothered aboot anybody else' unless, in latter years, they went to the East Sound and 'wir muxed up amang the rest'. 'But I've seen us for weeks an weeks jeest crossin tae Machrie and waitin there, an when ye wid come home on Seterday ye'd find oot ye wir as good (financially) as the rest, if naw better.' [Henry Martin, 1974]

The Woods

Among Carradale fishermen, 'The Wuds in the mornin' was a time-honoured destination, convenient to their home port for a run across.

The wooded Arran shoreline between Dougarie and Imachar was a favourite fishing-ground of the Carradale ring-net fishermen. Herring, with darkness, would seek the shore and remain there until daybreak, when they'd come off again 'in bunches, here an there'. [Robert Conley, 1976]

The Geelot and Ardnacross

Davie McLean got word of herring in Machrie and went away one morning about half-past eleven. Going off at the Otter Ard buoy, 'two big heavy gulls in the water' were observed. Davie went forward and saw 'a mass o herrin there, puttin up'. They crossed to Machrie and found nothing there, so returned across the Sound to Isla Ross and spoke to Dunky Martin up at Mecky's. Then they went down to the Geelot, inside of where the herring had earlier been seen, and found 'a mass o herrin' there. They shot and got a badly torn net. 'Now,' said Davie, 'A've seen us shottin there of'en an naw breckin a mash. Depends on the tide. If you get a tide that's liftin ye off, ye'll shoot nearly anywhere, unless ye're in a very bad grip.' They got 50 or 60 baskets of herring and went into

Campbeltown with the bad net. Dunky Martin must have seen the McLean pair's lights and come south. By that time, it was 'dead' – or slack – water and he shot at Ardnacross. 'It's a bad place, Ardnacross, wi rocks,' Davie remarked, 'an it's naw a place ye can footer much about wi ebb watter in case ye go on a rock an the win comes on ye.' As the McLeans were heading back out to sea, the Martin pair, the *Fame* and the *Renown*, were heading in, with 400 baskets. [David McLean, 1974]

MacRingan's Point

The first week John McWhirter had the skiff *Elizabeth*, he was neighbouring Charlie Cameron. There were herring being got about Davaar Island and when the pair came out in the morning there were two or three other pairs there. It was a quiet morning and they went 'in roon aback o' MacRingan's Point. John knew there were rocks there, but remembered one time, when he was crewing with Archie McKay, they had a 'wee haal' in there. 'Heavens,' said John, 'we went away in roon this wee point, right enough, an, God, there they wir! They wir jumpin away, an we got fifty boxes.'

There was just room for the net and no more, for they had a look at the haul in the spring of the year, when, with north wind, the bottom can be seen clearly, and there were big pinnacles of rock here and there. They just happened to shoot in the right place, and were in clear of tide. John saw bottom in 14 fathoms off the Isle Slip, Davaar, one day when the water was clear, and he remarked that it was wonderful 'the bottom ye seen goin up that shore in the spring'. [John McWhirter, 1974]

Checking the hauls

Jim Campbell remembered, as a boy growing up in Waterfoot, Carradale, that in springtime, when the boats were on the beach cleaning, his father would 'go away in the punt', with an outboard motor, to 'look at the hauls'. He'd go as far south as the Pluck, 'checkin them over', for sandy seabed was visible through the clear water. [Jim Campbell, 2001]

'Yer fether wid've shot there'

Jim Campbell hadn't been long in the wheelhouse of the *Irma*. Just 18 years of age and, by his own admission, relatively inexperienced, he was steering south along the shore one night. An old hand, Davie, was on the bow, looking for herring in the water. His practice was to bang the deck with his leather sea-boot to start the herring into showing themselves in the phosphorescence. Off Mecky's Point, near Ugadale, Davie called from the bow, 'Slow her doon'; then, 'Aye, right – we'll try this.' But Jim was unsure of the ground and unwilling to risk damage to the net. *A don'know where we are here*, he thought to himself, and, lifting the throttle, carried on. With that, Davie walked aft and said: 'Now, yer fether wid've shot there.' His parting remark was: 'Well, don't ask me tae go up on the bow agane.' [Jim Campbell, 2001]

Far enough off

When, in 1949, John Short withdrew from the successful consortium of skipper-owners to which he had belonged since 1927, he took with him one of the company's boats, the *King Bird*, and a cash settlement. John asked his son Neil to 'go into the wheelhouse' of the *King Bird*, but Neil demurred, feeling that his knowledge couldn't compare with that of his father and other men of that generation. Ultimately, however, he relented and enjoyed a spell neighbouring the 'very pliable and very willing' Mathieson brothers, Dugald and Daniel ('Dainky') in the *Falcon*.

One night, c. 1953, having seen herring on the echo-sounder off Morrison's*, Neil was reluctant to shoot, because the ground there is foul and it was 'wan o these places ye jeest lifted the throttle an steamed past'. His father and old Jock Brodie, however, had other ideas and queried: 'Can ye see the Light?' – 'Aye,' Neil replied, 'the Light's there tae be seen.' – 'Aye, well, ye're all right – ye can shot away.' The older men's sight had deteriorated and they weren't 'pickin up the light so far away', but they knew that, with Davaar Lighthouse 'open' – or unobscured by land – they were far enough off the bad ground to shoot, and a good haul of herring resulted.

Curiously, Neil's father, despite having been at the forefront of modern ring-netting in the 1920s and '30s, was never comfortable in a wheelhouse, which he felt restricted his vision and, consequently, his control of the fishing operation. 'He was all right on the skift, sittin at a tiller,' Neil explained. 'He could see everythin then.' [Neil Short, 2001]

A stretch of shore, north of Pluck, Saddell, named after a family of crofter-fishermen, headed by John Morrison, which inhabited a cottage there in the mid-19th century.

Fishing

Until the general adoption of motor-power just before the First World War, 'trawling' was fundamentally a method of the shores. The later term for the method, 'ring-netting', applied to deep water work, when engines allowed the boats to successfully surround and catch herring offshore, without the necessity of anchors and long hauling-ropes. This dependence on the shores generated an immense and intimate knowledge of the coasts and a proliferation of place-names, much of which was gradually lost as 'ring-netting' assumed pre-eminence.

This collection of anecdotes in part attempts to illustrate both the complex skills and the hazards of ring-netting. The reckoning of where a spot of herring lay in relation to the boat, once she had run by the spot and was being got into a shooting position; the assessment of wind and tide; the position of the neighbour-boat, and of any other boats round about; the nature of the seabed; if the net was likely to 'take top and bottom' and thus be exposed to damage ... these and many other factors all required to be judged in mere minutes, before the net was set. Soundness of judgement, indeed, was what made a top-class skipper.

A tramp on the anchor

On certain parts of the coast, if the holding ground was bad, the anchor would be taken ashore and secured in a rock crevice or behind a rock, 'that it winna slip or drag', thus causing the boat to 'fall over the net' and the catch to be lost. The Tarbert fishermen used to put their anchors ashore at Camus na Ban-tighearna to haul the net to the shore. One night, the net having been boated, one of the crew went ashore to recover the anchor and found a man sitting on it. This was a tramp who had seen lights from the hill. When he descended to the shore and found the anchor, he 'had an idea' and sat on the anchor. He was going to Tarbert, so the fishermen took him aboard and landed him there. [Hugh MacFarlane, 1977]

Deep-water ringing

Ring-netting in deep water began about 1910. The Campbeltown, Carradale and Tarbert boats were working 'oot in the middle', in the Track, between the Ayrshire coast and Arran, all July, August and September. The crews waited until they heard herring jumping or playing, then shot away. 'If the herrin wid stay up, ye had it; if naw, if the herrin wis gan doon, ye winna get it,' Hugh MacFarlane recalled. He saw two, three and four hundred baskets in a ring out there. [Hugh MacFarlane, 1974]

Ring-nets were shallow, 45 score of meshes deep, when John McWhirter went to the fishing in the early years of the 20th century. Crossing from one shore to another, herring might be seen all the way, but fishermen then were all of the opinion that it was useless to try ringing in deep water. 'It wis when the Ayrshiremen came so much on the scene they began tae ring mair,' John reckoned. In his last years at the job, and thence until the end of ring-netting, most of the fishing was in deep water, except for certain times in spring and summer when herring could be got on the shore. [John McWhirter, 1976]

Wind and tide

Sometimes the tide isn't true. John McWhirter was 'roon the other side' – out off Brodick, Arran – one evening. Jock McGeachy with the *Waterbird* was there too and shot. There was a 'wee breeze doon fae the norrid' and Jock shot with the wind and rung down. He was boating his net when John McWhirter went to the other side of him and located herring. Going by the time given in his nautical almanac, flood water should have been running, so John 'turned roon an shot for flood'; but unknowingly he'd shot against the tide, for, as the fishermen would say: 'The tide wis goin the opposite way.' All he got was two or three baskets, while Jock McGeachy got 80 or 90 baskets.

Working out the times of high and low water was all very well, but, as John said, 'when ye came tae corners lik Cock o Arran ye dinna know hoot's flood or hoot's ebb'. In Loch Fyne, the tide could be going up the loch – flooding – but fresh water coming down 'lik mad', and that's when crews would 'get intae proper rinkles'. [John McWhirter, 1976]

A phenomenal tide

There were times when the tide ran 'very strange'. One night at the Garroch Head, there were several pairs ringing, but the nets wouldn't sink below the surface with the ebb. 'Ye wid seh it wis incredible. The net could not go below wi the tide. If we'd got the net tae fish, we'd have got the fuul o the boats.' There wasn't a ripple on the water and herring were jumping everywhere. Such was the force of the current, the fish should've been taken away by it, 'but then they do put their nose tae the tide; they're jeest paidlin – they'll stay in the wan place'. The crews had 'two or three goes at it' before deciding: 'Ye may go tae an anchor till the tide'll change.' And that's what they did. [Hugh MacFarlane, 1976]

A big moon

One night, when the moon was full and too bright for fishing – herring are flighty then and hard to surround – a fleet of ringers went to anchor and the crews turned in. An old Carradale man, who had risen through the night, saw that the moon was down, and in his excitement – he was prone to muddling his speech – called out: 'Hurry up an get up – all the stars are at anchor an no a boat in the sky!' [John McConnachie, 2002]

Shooting over the weather

Shooting over the weather described the practice of setting the net on a starboard rather than a port circuit. It was unorthodox, risky and resorted to only when absolutely necessary.

During John McWhirter's 'last days at the fishin', he was in the Lodan one very dark night. Two or three pairs had been 'up an doon', but there was 'nawthing tae be felt'. Just before daylight, John and his neighbour were down off the Guns and 'felt' a fine spot of herring playing ahead of them. John wanted to 'gie her a tip on an shot back the right wey' – that is, on a circuit to port – but one of the crew, Daniel Morans, opposed that strategy. 'Ach,' he said, 'if ye start yer engine an go doon there, them herrin'll be away.' So they shot over the weather, so as not to risk disturbing the spot by manoeuvring into position, and, just as the last of the net was going overboard, to their consternation another boat was seen coming out and shooting across their bow.

This was Robert Robertson – 'the Hoodie' – who had been lying, unobserved in the quiet of the night, below Auchenhoan Head, and had emerged to take the same spot. The convention of the time was that the boat shooting 'the right wey' was entitled to the shot, so John aborted his effort, but had to run over Robertson's cork-rope and into the middle of his net. John didn't make a move until Robertson's net had been shot, then began hauling back on his own net. There was a 'nice mashin' in each wing, but that, of course, was all. The 'Hoodie', for his part, netted 120 baskets. 'We might've done all right if he hanna tae shot there,' John speculated. 'But he wis comin in the right wey, he could keep inside o us aal the time.' [John McWhirter, 1976]

Tearings

Shooting across tide on the shore was liable to cause tearings on coarse ground, because the net was 'comin up sideyways all the time'. Sometimes, when the net snagged ringing with the tide, and the sole-rope held, a crew could haul up on the net until abreast of it and it might jump and free itself. The only thing then was that, though the sole jumped, the net itself might be caught and that's when a bad tearing might ensue, because a snagged net generally left a bit behind. [John McWhirter, 1976]

Hauling end-on

On one occasion, a little south of Dunure, Davie McLean shot and the net snagged. It was a mass of rocks where they'd shot, but they hadn't known that. They couldn't get the net in, so they started to haul it end-on, in other words the fore side was released, thus breaking the circle of the net. At the very end, 100 baskets of herring were taken out of a pocket in the net, which led Davie McLean to believe that the net – though effectively disabled for fishing – must have been 'packed tight wi herrin'. He heard his father say that the same thing had happened to him in a corner at the Bight of the Struthlag, north of the Pluck. 'If yer net's badly fast,' Davie concluded, 'ye've got tae take her end-on or stan the chance o gettin a bad teirin.' [David McLean, 1975]

The *Mhairi*

Denis MacIntosh went to the fishing in 1913 and when war 'came on' joined his father's crew, but his father said to him: 'Well, A think we'll put ye in another boat because A don't want too many tae be in the one boat from the same family.' His father was referring to the drowning of his brother and three nephews a few years earlier in the skiff *Mhairi**. 'An it's a funny thing,' Denis recalled, 'but [with] the last boat I had, the *Maid o Morven*, we shot off Bunlarie an, dash me, the net went fast an then it jumped, oot in twinty fathoms, an a bit o that boat came up, aye a bit o that boat came up, the *Mhairi*.' [Denis MacIntosh, 1976]

The Mhairi *of Carradale foundered in a squall about a mile-and-a-half off Bunlarie, Saddell, on the morning of 8 March 1911, with the loss of the entire crew: Walter McIntosh (60), skipper-owner; his sons Dugald (26) and Walter (19) and nephew Johnny McIntosh (19), son of John McIntosh.*

Snagged on an anchor

One morning, in Stranraer Loch, a Maidens pair came out and found the *Lady Edith* and *Lady Charlotte* of Campbeltown with about 400 baskets netted from a 'daylight ring'. Herring were coming off Lady Bay in 'black lumps ... wi the gulls on them', and one of the Ayrshire crews shot; but the net came fast on a big anchor lying abandoned on the seabed and the sole-ropes were 'up an down'. The net wasn't badly torn, but had merely 15 baskets of herring in it. [Turner McCrindle, 1976]

Jellyfish

Off Furnace, an Ayrshire pair had so many big white jellyfish in the ring that, once the soles of the net were aboard, all hands had to haul in the 'bottom sheets' and run the jellyfish over the corkrope. At the Isle of Man, smaller 'white scalders' were so abundant one night that it was feared the net would be lost with the weight of them, 'but we managed ultimately tae get them over the corks'. When herring were mixed in with large quantities of jellyfish, they became soft and descaled and were spoiled for the market. [Turner McCrindle, 1976]

Shooting single-handed

James McCreath recalled having 16 rings one night in the Kyles of Bute, neighbouring Jock 'Lowe' Forbes, and the two boats hadn't a dozen baskets of herring between them. There were no winches on ring-net boats at that time, so the work was entirely manual. During that sixteenth ring, below Kames, James was alone on the tow-boat as Jock's net was being hauled. The sun was just 'looking over the hill' when herring 'started tae play the sea dry'. He cast off and, entirely alone, shot his own net. That audacious effort yielded 460 baskets, 'in daylight, after ringin all night and gettin none', and the whole fleet by then had left the fishing grounds. [James McCreath, 1976]

Single-boat ringing

Angus Martin and his crew on the *Fame* used to go out unaccompanied, and did very well. They'd shoot the net round and catch the *winky* themselves; then they'd run inshore, let go the anchor and make the cable fast in the middle of the boat, and that kept her broadside to the net and allowed it to be boated. They were out one night and saw a 'wee whale' off MacRingan's Point, so they stopped there. Herring started to play in the evening and they shot round the spot and went in to let go the anchor. There was only a short cable on the anchor and, while they were winching back on the bridles of the net, the cable-end 'slipped over the bow'. They lost anchor and cable and 'blew right ower the top o the net'. They had a 'wile job' getting the net aboard and got only 11 baskets out of it.

Angus and his crew dropped the spare anchor at MacRingan's Point, *redd* (cleared) the net and had a cup of tea. Just as daylight was coming, herring began to play again. They shot and netted over 200 baskets. About 170 baskets was ample for the *Fame*, so a Carradale pair came alongside. Robert Paterson in the *Fairy Queen* shouted: 'Angus, ye've too much – ye'll naw be able tae take all these herrin.' – 'Naw,' said Angus, 'A don't think we will.' – 'Well,' Robert suggested, 'what aboot runnin them for ye, tae Ayr?' Angus agreed, the *Fairy Queen* came in alongside the net and took all the herring aboard, plus the 11 baskets in the *Fame*'s hold. The catch fetched 17s a basket and Angus and Robert split the money equally. [Angus Martin, 1974]

One night, off Inchmarnock, Jake McCrindle was three times at herring-steamers discharging catches, 'a bit o work' as he remarked. The last time they left the steamer, day was breaking and the crew said among themselves: 'A wunner if it's worthwhile goin away back oot tae aback o the Inch an hae a go?' They did that and shot, with a jib-sail set to keep the boat out of the net if wind would come; when wind came, however, it came 'the opposite way' and they were blown into the net, which went away round the boat. The crew thought they had nothing, but the corks began to dip and, as the sun was getting up, they took 90 baskets of big herring out of the net. They set off for Rothesay with the catch, Jake observing the bizarre sight of small East Coast boats 'goin roon aboot chappin thir anchor in broad daylight'. [John McCrindle, 1976]

A collision at the Brown Head

When a big fleet of ring-netters would be working in a confined area, mishaps – involving both boats and gear – inevitably occurred. The 'spawnie fishin' at the Brown Head was one such trouble-spot. Neil Jackson recalled shooting there one night and taking 400 baskets of herring aboard the *Village Belle*. He put the lights out and began steaming about looking for more herring. He was seeing another boat coming towards him and, even at a distance, recognised her as Duncan 'Moora'

McAlpine's *Maryeared*. A curious – and ultimately ineffectual – series of evasive manoeuvres then ensued. When Neil would turn the *Village Belle*, Duncan would choose to alter the *Maryeared*'s course identically. The boats were closing on each other and one of Neil's crew called to him: 'Here, dae ye see that boat comin?' – 'Aye,' Neil answered, 'A'm seein him, but how am A gonny get oot his bloody road? A'm bloody sure A'm no turnin this boat side-on tae him!' The *Village Belle* was low in the water with the weight of herring aboard her. Seeing that collision was unavoidable, Neil put the *Belle* full astern, but the stock of his anchor struck the *Maryeared*'s shoulder and penetrated a top bunk, in which one of Duncan McAlpine's crew was lying. The man got such a fright, he jumped out the bunk and on to the forecastle table, then scrambled out through the skylight. 'That wis the quickest he ever moved in his bloody life!' [Neil Jackson, 2001]

Catching holidaymakers

The *Golden Dawn* and *Frigate Bird* 'caught' two holidaymakers one evening in Douglas Bay, near Inveraray. The *Golden Dawn* shot round a gannet that struck in the middle of the bay. There were a couple of men from a caravan site out in a dinghy – perhaps line-fishing – and when they saw the sudden activity in the bay they rowed out. They approached too close to the back of the net, however, and when the herring suddenly rose and 'blew up' the bag, as the net was being 'dried', they found themselves afloat on a mass of fish. Francis McWhirter, who was a crew-member on the *Golden Dawn*, vividly remembered 'the fright on the men's faces when they saw the herring'.

Panic-stricken, they called out: 'What'll we do, mister?' The *Golden Dawn*'s skipper, John Conley, was no less agitated, because there was the imminent danger of the dinghy's keel or oars 'nicking the net' and the weight of the catch bursting the bag wide open. John at once told them not to move or touch the oars, and, as the bag was dried to the boat's side, the dinghy slipped harmlessly off the net. The two holidaymakers were taken on board the *Golden Dawn* once the boats 'squared', and they watched the catch being brailed aboard, after which they were given a good rasher of fish to take back to the caravan site. They had never, they said, seen so many fish in their lives before. In fact, there were about 500 baskets taken aboard and landed the following morning in Tarbert. [Francis McWhirter, 2000]

Meshings
······

Whereas drift-net fishermen looked for heavy meshings of fish – that was how their nets functioned – ring-net fishermen did not. A few herring stuck in the wings of a ring-net were often a welcome indication of a catch to come, where they wanted a catch to be – in the bag of the net – but excessive meshing bedevilled the hauling of the net and invariably necessitated hours of effort to get the net clear and ready for further use. Netting was reckoned in 'rows to the yard' (0.91m), therefore '34 rows-to-the-yard', for example, represented 34 rows of meshes contained in a yard of netting. The more rows to the yard, the narrower the meshes, and vice versa.

The Hole of the Isle o Ross

'It used tae be a great thing when the wings wir thirty-four rows,' Davie McLean reminisced. '"Aw, here they come!" Ye wir happy tae see them comin – ye knew ye had herrin in the net – an yet it wis creatin a lot o additional work tae get the net in.' He remembered a shot, 'on gulls pickin', in the Hole of the Isla Ross, and the net – which was absolutely loaded with meshed herring – was going out of sight as his crew was shooting it. There were about 150 baskets of herring meshed, more than was swimming free in the net. Had the herring been larger, they wouldn't have meshed and the whole catch of 250 baskets would have been loose. As it was, the loose herring sold for 30s and the meshed herring for 10s or 15s. 'It wis brutal work.' [David McLean, 1975]

In Kilchousland Bay

John Short's *Mary Graham* and the *Lady Edith* were fishing in the Kyles of Bute one winter, but there wasn't much doing and they headed home. Going into Kilchousland Bay, 'Baldy' Stewart, who was forward on the *Mary Graham*, could hear 'a bing o them … a bloody sea o herrin playin', but no one on the neighbour-boat – including Jock 'Takins' Carmichael and Willie Galbraith – could. The *Mary Graham* shot and 'never marked wan'. The neighbouring crew was dismissive: 'There fuck aal herrin there' … 'There nae fuckin herrin – where's the herrin ye heard?'

Short's crew hastily bundled the net aft again as wintry showers swept across the bay from the west. Off Isla Muller, on the north side of Kilchousland Bay, there are good hauls and there are bad ones, and it was there that Baldy again heard herring playing. 'We'll be chancin this again,' was the verdict, so the *Mary Graham* shot once more and this time the net snagged, the ring had to be aborted and the net hauled end-on. They'd been 'jeest that wee bit off the good haal' and on to a nasty rock on the south side, but as soon as the lugs were lifted there were the herring, 'hingin lik cannles'.

Baldy was exultant: 'There yer fuckin herrin now!' he shouted repeatedly. Though glad that herring had been marked, he reckoned that a netful had been lost owing to the fastener. The net could hardly be taken aboard with the meshing, and both crews spent the entire day picking out herring – 50 baskets in all – at Campbeltown Quay. Of the neighbouring crew, he remarked: 'They wir hellish. They wirna worryin aboot herrin – it wis the bloody showers they wir worryin aboot.' [Archibald Stewart, 1974]

A new net in the Lodan

During the First World War, when John McWhirter 'wis wi Gilchrist neeborin' – probably William Gilchrist in the *Mary McLellan* – his neighbour's net was useless and he told him not to shoot it at all. They were working close to home, in the Lodan, and fishing nicely. Gilchrist said that he had a new net in the house, below the bed, so one week that net arrived at the quay on a barrow. She was duly soaked so that she'd sink and the two boats went down through the Lodan that night. Gilchrist 'felt a spot o herrin' out off the Guns and shot his new net; but she was the same size of mesh from end to end, there being no narrow bag in her.

It was mid-day before they got the net aboard, and they took only 60 baskets of herring out of her – the herring were 'mashed the whole bloomin wey'. The net being soft and fine in the twine, herring coming off the shore just stuck in her. It was solid herring the crews were hauling over the rail, the same as hauling drift-nets, or trammels on Ballantrae Banks. 'It wis bad enough when we'd tae sen a man doon an make a cup o tea, an when ye got a chance ye wid run doon an hae a drink wan at a time.' [John McWhirter, 1974]

A flattened winky

Bob Conley recalled steaming down along the Kerry Shore one Monday, making for the Kyles, and the boats ahead were shooting as they went. The neighbour came into herring on the upside of Ardlamont and shot, but there was such a heavy meshing in the wings that by the time the crew Bob was with got to the end, it was sinking with the weight of fish, and sank to the very bottom. They had to catch the back-rope and run along that until they reached the bridle, secured it and were able to give the net a 'wee tow'. The metal *winky* on the end of the net, however, had been flattened on the seabed with the pressure. They managed a good fishing, however, despite the problems. [Robert Conley, 1975]

Wide wings

The idea of wide-meshed wings was to eliminate heavy meshings in the tradi-tional 34 and 36 rows-to-the-yard wings and the consequent labour involved in clearing nets. John McWhirter, below, assembled his first wide-winged net in 1914, the year after he married, but wide wings were not generally adopted until the late 1920s. The initial wings of 29 rows-to-the-yard proved too conser-vative, and meshes expanded progressively until the wings in use would mesh nothing.

The first time John McWhirter worked with wide wings, he was at the Coves of Arran and got 'a chap or two o herrin in the watter'. The net was shot, and, 'Dammit! – the wide wings, they wir afloat wi machrel'. Mackerel never meshed in narrow wings. Every one had to be picked out, because if a mackerel was 'scutched' – beaten out of the net – it broke the mesh. 'A mind that night well enough. The first shot, an we jeest tried this shot tae wet her in case we wid come across somethin better, an that's hoot we got'. [John McWhirter, 1974]

Wide wings were set up at 20-and-a-half rows-to-the-yard at first, but weren't 'plain enough' and were bad for catching dogfish. They were later 'stretched more' and ended up at 14 rows-to-the-yard. [Turner McCrindle, 1976]

'Ye grow older an ye learn by yer mistakes,' Davie McLean remarked. When wide wings began to be discussed, some fishermen maintained, 'Och, ye'll lose an aafu herrin', believing that the fish would go through the wide meshes; but Davie McLean never considered how many herring were going through because the herring that would have been meshed in the traditional narrow wings were more or less useless. 'Ye wid hardly get a market for them, they wir mutilated that bad'. Ring-nets were initially 34 rows-to-the-yard with a top bag of 42 rows. When

Davie McLean was fishing in the North with 29-row wings, he shot one night at Canna and got a meshing of 'big North herrin ... it wis jeest solid herrin comin in'. Wee 'Dina' Wareham was hauling aft on the boat and the net was heaped higher than his head with the meshing. In the Kilbrannan Sound, too, when working among big herring, the 29-row wings were 'pure murder'. These were eventually discarded and replaced with 16-row netting and 'ye wou'na see a herrin hardly till ye came tae the shoulder net'. [David McLean, 1975]

Boating Herring

In the earliest days, herring were discharged – or 'boated' – from the bag of the ring-net using quarter-cran baskets dipped over the boat's side and pulled aboard manually; later, a pole was added to the basket to reduce the crews' labour and eliminate the soakings they were prone to when stooping in rough seas; finally, the 'brailer' – a winch-operated discharging-net – was introduced in the 1930s, enabling much greater quantities of herring to be removed at a time.

'Tie a bonny soogan ...'

A 'soogan' – Gaelic sùgan, *a rope of twisted straw or heather – was, among other things in fishing terminology, a short rope, or bicket, used for lashing the bag of a ring-net to the boat's side before discharging a catch.*

The fleet was at the head of Loch Fyne one Monday. There was a quota in operation and Archie Kerr from Tarbert had a big ring of herring in broad daylight. Matthew McDougall and his neighbour were among the later arrivals on the fishing ground and got their quota from Archie's net. He had a couple more quotas left and Ayrshire boats were coming. A crowd from Dunure – 'real hard cases' – appeared and Archie shouted to them as they came alongside to take the herring out of the net: 'Now, ye'll tie a bonny soogan there.' – 'Whit the fuck's a soogan?' was the response. [Matthew McDougall, 1978]

Losing a bag off Rudha Leathann

The point of this story, which is rather obscure, is that Archie Kerr, the skipper – probably of the Jessie *of Tarbert – became exasperated with the struggle to retain his grip on the net and flung it from him in disgust, with the result that the weight of the netted herring took the bag clean out of the net.*

With herring enmeshed in 34 and 36-rows-to-the-yard nets, 'ye cou'na haul it', Hugh MacFarlane said. 'Well, I seen the four men bate tae take it aboard – wan in every hole ye looked, a wall o silver.' He saw Kerr 'lose his rag' one night off Rudha Leathann, and 'whatever wey he did it, the whole bag drapped away'. Kerr was getting a grip of a bit of the net, but when he would try to take up another bit, the bit he had aboard was out again. 'The meenit ye wid slack, ye wir oot as far as ever,' Hugh remarked. Kerr hadn't a piece of net with which to replace the lost bag, but he spoke with Dan Conley in the *Frigate Bird* on the fishing grounds the following evening. 'How did ye get on last night?' Dan asked. 'Dan,' said Kerr, 'we lost the bag last night. We got a big ring above Rudha Leathann – lost the most o the bag wi bulk mashed herrin. We hae'na a bit.' As Hugh remarked: 'It wis himsel that did it.' Dan, 'a dacent man', said to Kerr, 'Come alongside here', and gave him 'damn near a new bag'. [Hugh MacFarlane, 1975]

A ripped bag

A similar reckless action cost the skiff *Fame* of Dalintober part of a valuable catch of herring in Loch Fyne, c. 1925. Her crew had shot close inshore, 'dried' the catch and was basketing it aboard when wind 'came away'. The neighbour-boat – 'squared' alongside – had an iron-belted rubbing-strake which extended aft and ended at her quarter, where the wood of the strake was worn, leaving a jutting end of metal. One of the *Fame*'s crew advised: 'Watch that beltin there or ye're gonny burst the net.'

The old neighbouring skipper responded by gathering up the threatened netting and holding it clear; but at last he wearied of sitting in the wind and rain and let the handful of netting drop away. With that, his boat took a roll, the net caught on the metal and in an instant the bag was ripped open. About 130 baskets had been removed before the rest was lost, and these herring fetched the fine price of 14s a basket, fishing having been light that night. [Angus Martin, author's father, 1974]

Halyards on the cork-rope

One night, the *Silver Spray*, neighbouring the *Twin Sisters*, netted 100 baskets of herring in the Kilbrannan Sound and got the buying-steamers alongside. The Maidens crews wanted 10s a basket, but the buyers wouldn't give them that price, so the *Twin Sisters* went away to Ayr and the *Silver Spray* headed down the Sound to look for mackerel. They rung on a spot at the Kirk Point*, but the mackerel were so heavy that the crew could do nothing. There's a bad swirl of tide there and boat and net were 'goin round and round'. The crew saw a pair of boats coming and waved torches. This was the *Harvest Queen* and *May Queen* of Campbeltown, and while the pair was still a good bit away, the Maidens crew heard big Dan Black shout to his neighbour: 'There's a man on the rocks'. At that, the *Silver Spray*'s crew waved their torches the more. When the Campbeltown skiffs came alongside, their crews put halyards on to the cork-rope of the net and hove it up. Then the Campbeltown men came aboard the *Silver Spray* and helped fill her with 280 baskets of mackerel. These fish fetched 7s 6d a basket at Ayr and 'we wired the half o the proceeds tae Campbeltown that mornin'. [Turner McCrindle, 1976]

Church Point to most of the Kintyre fishermen. It is at the south end of Catacol Bay, Arran.

Mungo Munro saw half-a-bag of coarse salt tipped into the bag of a ring-net off Ettrick Bay in an attempt to stir up heavy herring. In the end, however, it was the efforts of a pair of Campbeltown crews – the *Sweet Home* was one of the boats – that saved the catch. 'A could never believe this – A'd heard them talkin aboot liftin the net wi the long halyards,' Mungo recalled. 'But that's what happened – the old done skiffs came alongside and the halyards were hooked on to the cork-rope and the net lifted, herring and all.' One of the Ayrshiremen fell in among the fish while this was going on. He was pulled out of the bag and withdrew to the den. When he came back out, somebody remarked: 'Have ye changed yer clothes?' – 'Aye, A've a dry bunnet!' he replied. [Mungo Munro, 1976]

Brailing with an extra-long pole

Turner McCrindle was up Loch Fyne at the sunk-net fishings* when the herring were moving out the loch. They shot at the Stallion, above Furnace, but the middle-buoy jammed on the boat's stern going over and was torn away. They got 40 baskets of herring from the net and were heading down the loch when they saw lights in Loch Gair and went in. This was Eddie 'Tarry' McCrindle, of the Girvan *Alipeds*, with a netful of herring which the crews couldn't raise. Eddie shouted the Maidens crews alongside and they attached longer ropes to the brailer and an additional length of pole to the handle, and, with the extra reach, filled two boats. The tide was low when they started the operation, but with flood they could no longer reach the herring in the bag and had to get 'all the men on to the middle' and run the remainder over the corks. The boats then left for the market at Gourock, 'so Loch Gair wid be a braw smell a fortnight efter that'. [Turner McCrindle, 1976]

*Nets were weighted and sunk to the bottom, using extra-long sweeplines, to reach herring in deep water.

Dredging herring

The *Silver Spray* and *Twin Sisters* of Tarbert* went alongside a Girvan pair – James McCreath was skipper of one of the boats – in Ayr Bay one winter night. They had a big netful and couldn't get the herring up. The water was just about four fathoms deep, but they couldn't extend the handle of a pole-basket sufficiently to reach the fish, which they could see. The Tarbert crews 'manipulated the net' and showed the Ayrshiremen how to 'drag' the herring using fathoms of chain lashed to the sole-rope of a portion of free net, which was repeatedly passed across to the opposite boat, raising 100 baskets at a time. 'The Tarbertmen wir expert at that,' Turner McCrindle remarked. 'We wir only learners.' By that method, three pairs of boats were loaded with herring. [Turner McCrindle, 1976]

*Skippered respectively by Donald 'Tom' McDougall and Archie Kerr.

A tumble in the bag

When John McWhirter in the *Elizabeth* was neighbouring Johnny McAulay, they were out off Tarbert at break of day and got a nice ring of herring. The boy on the *Elizabeth* was Archie McIntyre, whose mother was one of the Irish McKays and kept a shop in Kirk Street, Campbeltown. With the *skiddoag**, Archie was fending off the neighbour-boat while the catch was being basketed aboard. There was a southerly roll on the sea and Archie's *skiddoag* slipped and he fell into the net. He was down among the herring but there was no sign of him and the crews thought that he was gone. Luckily, however, someone noticed a bit of his oilskin showing through the herring, and his shipmates got hold of his jumper and lifted him on to the deck, where he lay squealing 'lik a wee pig'. He finally came to and was none the worse of the experience, but there were no dry clothes for him. 'That,' said John McWhirter, 'wis the worst fright A got – A thought he wis never gonny come up.' [John McWhirter, 1975]

Cutting the bag

Hugh MacFarlane heard of the old men cutting the bags out of ring-nets and leaving them tied while they went to discharge herring at the steamers. Donald 'Nondy' McDougall of Tarbert was 'among it'. One night at the Battle Isle, the McDougalls cut the bag out, tied it and let it go with a buoy on it and came back and loaded the boats twice more, taking every herring out of it. 'Aye,' Nondy told Hugh, 'they never lost a herrin or brock a mash. Oh, they had some patience.' Of course, as Hugh observed, 'the nets wirna as big'. [Hugh MacFarlane, 1976]

Stranraer Loch

The same practice was resorted to in Stranraer Loch in December 1906. The date is known, because the episode was mentioned in the annual report of the Fishery Board for Scotland for that year.

John McWhirter was in the *Annunciata* with Denis McKay, who was working four boats with his brother Archie in the *Noel* and the McGeachy pair from Dalintober, the *Isa McGeachy* and the little *Nemo*. The McKays had been fishing in the Gareloch, taking hauls on chance and getting baskets of herring. Word had reached Campbeltown that there were herring in Stranraer Loch and 'Greasy Water' (Neil McKay) and 'The Junk' (John McIntyre) went down and had two or three fine fishings there. The McKays, back in Campbeltown, heard the report and got a tow south from Neil Hyndman, skipper of the herring-steamer *Rob Roy*.

In Stranraer Loch, on the Monday morning, the McKays met four pairs of boats, whose crews told them that they were too late: 'The herrin's naw tae be felt this while.' They were 'quite downed' by this news, because there was 'any amount o herrin' in Ayr Bay, but prospects there were doubtful owing to the westerly wind and the bay's exposure. They carried on down the loch, the sail catching a southerly breeze, and near the Winky Buoy they saw one, then two herring leaping; but the fish were in the tideway, so the boats continued to the mouth of the loch, where the earlier fishings had been.

They decided to run back up the loch with flood tide and weren't long by the Winky Buoy when they saw a *flambeau* being lit. They went in to look and there was McGeachy, 'jeest wi the ends aboard an her dry, nearly the whole net dry o herrin'. The McGeachys were relieved to see the McKays arrive, having feared they were about to lose the net. The *Annunciata* and *Noel* got alongside and the four crews together managed to boat the net; but, even without getting the ends or the bottom of the bag, the net was dry, 'fine herrin an spread oot dried lik that'.

The crews basketed and basketed until they reckoned they had plenty aboard. The question then was: what was to be done to get the net clear of the remaining herring? There were no other boats nearby to come in and take a share. Somebody suggested that they cut the bag, so the crews evened up the net as best they could and secured it with a good rope hauled tight. The corks were gathered into a bunch and then the bag was cut out the net and two big buoys attached to it and the whole thing allowed to sink away.

There were four herring-steamers in Stranraer harbour, Carmichael's *Louise*, Gordon's *Talisman*, Reid's *Asia* and another small vessel. The *Annunciata* went alongside the *Louise* and discharged 293 baskets. The *Noel* had 282 baskets, the *Isa McGeachy* 290 and the *Nemo* 220. The price was low: 6s a basket. When the boats had been discharged, they put on the sail and headed for the Railway Quay, only to discover crews with netfuls of herring there too. They went into the *mush* of boats and – 'noise or no noise' – came on herring playing, shot and got a fine ring. The Gilchrists from Campbeltown, in the *Mary McLellan* and the *Janet*, came in and were filled, then all the boats went to the quay, by which time it was daylight. The whole of the next day was occupied with the discharging of herring, and few boats ventured out.

By the following morning, the wind had freshened from the south-west and was blowing stiffly. The fleet left the quay and kept to the weather side of the loch going down. The McKays dropped anchor in what they thought was three or four fathoms of water. The McGeachys arrived later and lashed alongside them as the gloaming was coming on. John 'Buffs' McGeachy had come aboard the *Annunciata*, whose crew was about to eat. 'Ach,' said he, 'A'll go ower an see if that kettle o oors is boilin.' He went up on the stage to cross to the *Nemo* and was heard to call out: 'Aw, for God's sake, come up here!' – 'The herrin wis dry at wir stern, playin away, playin away good-o,' John McWhirter recalled. The outside boat shoved off, shot, and another fine ring was secured. The *Isa McGeachy* was filled and her crew was working at the net when it was discovered that she was aground, so legs were put out to hold her upright as the tide ebbed.

The next day was spent discharging herring, and when that was done the crews had a badly-needed sleep. The following day, Friday, it was decided that the deposited bag would have to be attended to or else it would be lost, so the crews went to it, got a grip of the buoys and raised and spread the bag between two of the boats, in the usual way. Discharging then began, using baskets lashed to the loom of oars, with a rope attached to the baskets for hauling up. Some 320 baskets of herring were removed from the bag before the tide fell and the crews began to take up mud and worry that they might not get the herring sold and that the bottom of the net was being torn by the oars. They did sell the herring, for the same price as before: 6s. There were still fish swimming in the bag when the crews returned to it, but 'when the tide got low they began tae settle tae the bottom so that feenished it'. [John McWhirter, 1974]

Markets and Money

Markets – or lack of them – have always bedevilled fishermen. When fish are abundant and catches high, prices generally plummet. The ideal is a hungry market and a good catch with which to supply it, at a better-than-average price.

'The Floating Market' was the collective name for the herring-carrying steamers, or 'herring screws', which accompanied the fleets on the fishing grounds. By the mid-1870s, specially chartered steamers had begun buying herring on the Clyde grounds. Catches were bid on and bought at sea, and then conveyed at speed to Glasgow or to the rail-head at Fairlie. The steamers' market was purely a fresh one, and herring caught at, say, 3 am in the Kilbrannan Sound, could be on sale in the streets of Glasgow, and beyond, that same morning. The extent of the steamers' share of the market is not always easy to quantify, but it undoubtedly accounted for the bulk of herring caught in Loch Fyne and the Kilbrannan Sound. In 1900, for example, 69,719 cwts of herring, valued at £31,305, were shipped aboard steamers in Loch Fyne, and in the following year the figures were 89,039 cwts and £29,578.

Screws were normally crewed by six men – skipper, mate, engineer, fireman, cook and deckhand – and could carry up to 1000 boxes at a time. Some had been built as steam-drifters, others were specially built for herring-carrying, such as the Rob Roy *and the* Marie. *The main requirement in a herring steamer was speed. One steamer, the* Good Design, *was known to have landed at Fairlie no fewer than three times within a 24-hour period, and from the same Tarbert skiff, during a heavy fishing off Inchmarnock in the 1920s. The greatest* number of herring steamers recorded on the Clyde fishing grounds at any one time was 21, in 1885.

Until the arrival, between the wars, of Davie Woods from Portsoy in Aberdeenshire – who bought herring, first in his own Roseacre and then in the Norman for James Alexander – the steamers carried a skipper and a buyer. Davie – who was somewhat sarcastically known to the Tarbert fishermen as 'the Wise Man from the East' – economised, however, by combining the two roles and set a precedent which other operators followed. The last of the herring steamers was the Dutiful, which operated until 1947.

When, in the 1920s and '30s, fishing-boats became bigger and their engines more powerful, fishermen realised that they no longer needed the herring-steamers – they could run their own catches to market. And when lorries came into use, in the late 1940s, for the transportation of fish, shore-markets no longer had to be served by rail. On one morning in 1948, during a heavy fishing in Loch Fyne, no fewer than 100 lorries were crammed into the village of Tarbert awaiting the fleet's arrival. By then, the screws had disappeared.

In 1924, sea-going herring-carriers of another kind appeared on the scene. These were the Klondykers, vessels of about 250 tons which shipped loads of herring to Altona in Germany. The herring would be bought on the fishing grounds and iced and salted for the trip. In the winter of 1925-26, there were 12 sailings of Klondykers from Loch Fyne with a total of 5,500 crans, and 50 from the Kyles of Bute with 30,000 crans.

Until the Klondykers arrived, the fishermen had been catching mixed herring in Loch Fyne and were forced to pick out the larger fish and dump the smaller ones – a labour that often took a whole winter's night – or else pass the catch through a wide-meshed net, called a 'riddle', so that the small fish were able to escape. The buyers in the Klondykers, however, were willing to take small fish as well as big, which saved the fishermen much labour. This market led, however, to the destruction of immature herring on a large scale, as did the later markets for pet-food and fish-meal. The Klondyking market continued until about 1935 on the Clyde.

The name 'Klondyke' comes from an area of Canada which saw a 'gold rush' in the 1890s, and that was also when German steamers began coming to Shetland and North East Scotland to buy herring and rush them, boxed with salt and ice, to Hamburg.

The herring-screws

If a crew 'got a puckle herrin', the signal to the sea-going buyers was two torches lit and waved. The steamers might be lying at Skipness and the successful pair of skiffs at Imachar or Grogport, but when the torches were waved there would be perhaps four or five steamers 'comin doon full bit' to the signal. A dinghy would be launched from each steamer and the buyers would come aboard the boats to inspect the catch, 'dried up' in the net, and offer a price. Once negotiations were completed, the herring would be discharged from the net and into the steamer whose buyer had bid successfully. In Bob Conley's time, there were 'sixteen herrin-steamers on the ground oot there every night waitin tae be loaded up wi herrin an away tae Fairlie'. [Robert Conley, 1975, 1976]

All the way to Kilchattan Bay

The skipper-buyers of the herring-steamers had to secure loads early in the night to catch the trains that left the rail-head at Fairlie at 6.45 am, and there were times, when the 'mornin wis gettin on', that a crew along-side a steamer would be told to 'put out an extra rope'. The steamer would then head for Fairlie, with the fishing-boat lashed alongside.

One night, in the mid-1930s, Willie McIntyre in the *Nil Desperandum* shot off Cour and secured about 280 baskets of herring. There were a couple of herring-steamers close by and one came alongside the *Nulli Secundus* – into which the catch was being discharged – and bought the herring. The steamer's skipper, satisfied with his load, set off for market, and the crew of the *Nulli Secundus* discharged the herring all the way to Kilchattan Bay, Bute, being borne along slowly at first and then, 'as the night went on', with greater speed. Her crew went into Kilchattan Bay and dropped anchor there. [Neil Short, 2001]

A comedian

There were two brothers from Rothesay, Willie and Jimmy O'Neill, who bought herring on the fishing grounds, and Jimmy was 'a bit of a come-dian'. The *Nulli Secundus* had 40 baskets for sale one night. 'What kinna quality have ye got?' O'Neill asked. 'Och, they're kinna mixed,' one of the fishermen replied. 'Well,' Jimmy said, 'come away alongside – A'll give ye a kinna mixed price.' [Neil Short, 2001]

Bob Miller, who was born in Fairlie in 1922 and who is an authority on the 'Floating Market', had a similar example of Jimmy O'Neill's wit. Surveying a skiff's catch one night, Jimmy remarked: 'A'll gie ye a packet o Woodbine for them.' 'Woodbine' was a cheap brand of cigarettes. Jimmy O'Neill was buyer on the *R. McKay* and his brother Willie was on the *Titania*. [2001]

Fraud

There was an Arran herring-buyer, Sandy, who had a small steamer, and he was 'a very honest man'. In those days, it was all boxes – baskets weren't in use – and 'consequently, the fellows on the steamers robbed the fishermen'. The box was supposed to hold the equivalent of one-and-a-half baskets, but instead of that, the steamer crews would have two baskets to a box. Sandy, however, wouldn't allow his crew to 'steal a single herrin on the fishermen', and, 'if you had two or three herrin-screws alongside ye, biddin for yer herrin, as they did quite of'en, ye'd be better off if Sandy got yer herrin, ye saved that much'. If, for example, a crew had 100 boxes of herring to discharge, going alongside Sandy 'ye wid've twinty more wi him, or eighteen anyway'.

Davie McLean's crew put 200 boxes aboard the *Gael* on the 'upside o Pladda' one night. The steamer's skipper asked Davie up on to the bridge to take a telegraph message, which Davie agreed to despatch at Whiting Bay. 'Mr McLean,' he remarked, 'I'm ashamed looking at this boat.'

'Ye wouldna know she had a box aboard,' Davie said, recalling the stacks of boxes filled to overflowing. 'Ye'd think she wis jeest a mass o solid herrin. Aal this wis *scran* for the crew. Ye see, whenever you could close the lid an tie it, that wis a full box, but they never did any o them things while you wir there.'

Another trick the steamers' crews had, when there was a crew the worse of drink alongside … if there were two or three tiers of boxes already stacked on the deck, they would put a chalk-mark on one of the boxes and say: 'Now, you start from here.' But, after a while, 'when things wis goin merrily, when ye had a few tiers goin', the chalk-mark would be rubbed off and another mark made a tier up. 'Took a tier off! Well, that wis approximately therty boxes they wir whippin off, but they widna dae that tae the like o me or men that had aal thir wits about them. But they often did it wi men that wis quite sort o fuddled, especially on a Monday. I've seen them tryin tae do it wi us, an naw a man on the boat ever touched drink.' [David McLean, 1974]

'Ye wanted them for nothin'

Davie McLean rung 100 baskets of mackerel off Grianan Island one night. The tea was ready and he went below for a cup. There were always two men left on deck, and one of these men put his head down the scuttle and reported: 'The machrels' jumpin here yit.' – 'Ach,' said Davie, 'we've plenty o mackerel.' He was desperate for his supper – hungry –

but thought to himself: *Wouldn't it be an aafu thing if that's herrin?* It was herring and he shot and got a fishing. The Carradale men were coming up along the shore, shooting as they were going; nets were coming up – nothing, nothing, nothing.

Two Ayrshire steamers appeared, Murray in one and Reid in the other. 'What have ye got?' Reid enquired. Davie told him. 'Will ye take five shillins for them?' That was a good enough price at the time, but fishing that night had been slack, so Davie rejected the offer: 'Naw, we're naw takin that money.' He shouted to his neighbour to give him an extra torch; he was going to go away. He passed close to Murray's steamer. 'What dae ye want for the herrin, Davie?' Murray shouted. 'A want ten shillins for the herrin an eight for the mackerel,' Davie replied. 'Right,' said Murray, 'come alongside.' But Reid was shouting: 'Are ye naw comin wi they herrin.' – 'Oh,' Davie shouted back, 'the herrin's sold.' – 'That's a bonny trick ye play on folk,' was Reid's response. 'Ye got a full chance tae get the herrin. They wir there for the buyin. Ye wanted them for nothin,' Davie replied. [David McLean, 1975]

A worthless venture

There were years when 'there wir herrin anywhere ye wid go – ye dinna know where ye wir goin wi them'. Hugh MacFarlane was out one year on the 17th of March for bait for lines. The skiff was over at Bagh Asgog on the Kerry Shore and had a ring of 'great big herrin', far more than was needed. One of the crew suggested: 'Take aboard the herrin – we'll go tae Rothesay.' An old fellow by the name of MacNeill, however, was sceptical. 'Man, ye'll no get anything,' he warned. It was decided to take 60 baskets, in addition to the baiting requirement, and Slaven in Rothesay gave them 2s a basket. 'Now,' he told them, 'don't come back here, boys, wi any more o that. No market.' If, said Hugh, 'wan o thon years wid come back, [the present-day fishermen] wid be wealthy in a short time.' [Hugh McFarlane, 1974]

Dumping herring

The year (1936) the *Noss Head* came to Carradale, they were fishing up Loch Fyne and there were 'tons o herrin'. They had a big ring off Strachur and filled the boat to the hatches. There was a Klondyking market at Gourock at the time, and that's where the *Noss Head* went with the catch. The sample was taken up to the market and placed at the end of a long queue of samples. The buyers were very particular about 'pokes' – bellies full of feeding, that softened the herring – and one of them, 'Big

Ivor', was going through all the samples, pulling out the gills and taking out the guts to find long pokes. The herring were big enough, but the buyers didn't want them. There was, as Bob Conley put it, 'buggar all tae do but jeest go away back oot'. South of the Cloch, the *Noss Head*'s crew began emptying the hold. They were at it all the way through the Kyles and until they arrived back at where the herring had been caught the previous night. They had just finished dumping the 400 baskets when their neighbour, who had been lying waiting for their return, began blinking his lights, signalling his intention of shooting. He'd been 'lyin above any God's amount o herring' and rung another netful. They went to Ayr with the catch and got half-a-crown a basket. [Robert Conley, 1975]

Picking herring

The picking of herring began in Loch Fyne. Crews with the fill of the boats would go into Loch Gair and sit, every man, all through a winter's night, picking herring into three selections – extra-large, large, and the rest – each of which was segregated on a different part of the deck. The extra-large fish were fetching 11s at the herring-steamers, the large 8s, and some of the buyers would pay 5s or 6s for the rest, but others didn't want them at all. [John McWhirter, 1974]

Tommy Sloan was up Loch Fyne one prolific year and filled the *Twin Sisters* with 280 baskets of mixed herring. The crew picked all the way from Loch Fyne to Maidens, and out of these 280 baskets they were left with 18 baskets which sold at 15s to a local fish-buyer and 33 baskets which sold at 3s for salting. The buyers on the herring-steamers were taking only drift-net herring and giving very little money for them, though selected big herring were fetching 15s a basket. [Tommy Sloan, 1976]

Riddling

Duncan McSporran saw herring discharged at 1s a basket 'many's the time' and 'many's the time put them ower the side for naethin'. At other times, fishermen would be 'pickin good herrin oot o smaller herrin … Ye wid haev a hell of a job, aal night pickin maybe fifty or sixty baskets oot o over a hunner'. Then the riddle was devised. [Duncan McSporran, 1974]

Leaving early

One night Jake McCrindle was in the Kilbrannan Sound at Crossaig. He got 600 baskets in a ring and some one said: 'Dae ye think we'll wait an have another ring?' – 'Naw,' Jake replied, 'go for Ayr as hard as ye can an get in for the furst market.' They did that and got the top price. As the rest of the boats came in, the price dropped and dropped steadily until the buyer of the McCrindles' catch approached Jake and said: 'Will ye naw reduce it a bit? Look at the prices noo.' Jake rejected the man's plea. 'That's the wey we came away early,' he replied. 'We coulda got more herrin, but we left tae come here and get the furst o the market.' [John McCrindle, 1976]

Klondyking

Donald McIntosh was in Loch Fyne – 'up inside o Otter' – one night. The fleet was there and killed 40,000 baskets of herring off Loch Gair. The sea was black with herring, but there was no demand for them. A curer came, but he wanted all the herring a foot long and gave the fishermen a measuring stick. Donald had the skiff *Victoria* at that time – about 1922 – and her capacity was 220 baskets. He remembered picking the fill of her and getting just 30 baskets of marketable herring which sold at only 4s or 5s; the rest was dumped.

Such were the conditions that led to the start of the Klondyking market. A fellow Craig in Aberdeen 'got wind o this lot o herrin that wis gettin dumped an he came wi trawlers an then he buyed them up'. One night, in the week that Donald was married (in January, 1925) there was a gale of wind and the boats were crossing about the Inch and had to go into the Bootack, in the Kyles of Bute, for shelter. In the morning, Jamie Wilson of Tarbert went up into Loch Riddon and not long afterwards came back with the fill of the two boats. The Klondykers were there by this time. Then the whole fleet went up and filled four Klondykers that day.

'So that wis the start o the Klondykin ower the heid o them dumpin the herrin in Loch Fyne. But A seen us trevellin all night an ye cou'na sail clear o the herrin – solid black below ye all the time. A thing ye'll naw see nowadays.' [Donald McIntosh, 1974]

A doomed Klondyker

The Hoheluft *left the Clyde in December, 1924, heavily laden. She was so overloaded that fishermen who saw her feared for her safety. Their fears were realised, for on Christmas Eve she was wrecked on the Mull of Oa, Islay. Only one man of her crew of 12 was saved.*

Henry Martin remembered a German trawler leaving the Kyles round about Christmas, 'an ye never seen a boat such a shape in yer life – the top o his whaleback wis nearly flush wi the watter an his stern wis up in the air'. The herring hadn't been boxed aboard her, but poured down chutes into the hold until it was filled to the deck. All the fishermen who saw her leave were both appalled by the look of her and puzzled as to why her crew hadn't opposed the overloading. [Henry Martin, 1976]

An astute buyer

Neil Jackson came home from the North with the *Village Maid* one Thursday, but instead of 'calling it a week', after his stint in the Minch, he decided: 'We'll go doon tae the Rock* an see if we'll get a start for Monday.' On the Friday night, he and his neighbour – brother Willie in the *Village Belle* – secured a big ring of *podlies* (saithe) 'with an odd big herrin through them'. With 400 baskets in each boat, they steamed for Ayr. They were in such a hurry to get home on the Saturday, they didn't bother to separate the herring, but the buyer who secured the catch – at 10s a basket – kept out the herring and ended up with perhaps 20 baskets, which, by his own admission, were worth more than the amount he paid the fishermen for the entire shot. [Neil Jackson, 2001]

*Erines Bank in Kilbrannan Sound.

'A flash an a half'

It was the habit of the Dunure fishermen, when passing their home port, to flash their lights as an indication of their success or otherwise. There was one night a boat was going up by Dunure with 150 baskets of herring on board. The skipper enquired what he would indicate for 150 baskets and his brother replied: 'A flash an a half.' [Iain Gemmell, 2000]

The 'beauty' of ring-netting

There were 'plenty of bad times' at ring-netting, but the 'beauty' of the job, Jim Campbell reckoned, was that 'ye could make it in the wan night' if market conditions were favourable. He recalled one winter week, c. 1962, when the wind blew strongly and steadily from the south-east, confining the boats to harbour. On the Friday afternoon, his and his neighbour's crew were working at a net in Shore Road car-park when the wind began to ease. He and John McConnachie decided to 'go for a wee look at it'. The rest of the Carradale crews had already resigned themselves to a blank week and hauled their nets forward on the boats.

The crews of the *Florentine* and *Bairn's Pride* assembled at the harbour about 6 pm and set off. They came on herring at the Brown Head and gathered some 400 baskets from 'a scatter o shots'. Though there were also good catches landed by the Ayrshire boats from the Ballantrae Banks, since there had been no fishing all week until that night, the market was keen and each man's 'divide' for that night's work was about £75. 'It jeest shows ye, wan night ...' Jim remarked. 'Well, see, that's what wid happen. That wid set ye up for a week or two, because ye'd maybe run intae a wee slack efter that.' [Jim Campbell, 2001]

At the Minister's Head

The following anecdote must date to c. 1880. The Minister's Head was the McLeans' fishing-station during the period when particular crews camped ashore adjacent to preferred fishing-grounds.

Davie McLean heard his father Neil say that they were three weeks at the Minister's Head and home each Saturday without earning a shilling. On the fourth consecutive Monday that they returned there, it was decided, in desperation, to try elsewhere, and they were 'up as far as the middle o Grogport Bay an took another notion an went back'. They fished £50 a man that week, Davie said, which 'wis a year's pay tae most o the folk at that time'. [David McLean, 1975]

Successful skippers

Some skippers had exceptional success. The McKay brothers, Archie, John and Denis, from Red Bay in County Antrim, were 'famous fishermen' with their pair of skiffs the *Noel* and *Annunciata*; but when John split from the partnership and had his own pair the *Angelus* and *Ascension* built (in 1904), he maintained that he took the luck with him. Archie Cook, another Campbeltown boat-owner, who had the *Polly Cook* and *Volunteer*, was 'a noted man for a while too'. Duncan McSporran, who began fishing in 1905 and retired at the age of 79, crewed with the McGeachy brothers of Dalintober in 1925, his 'best year ever'. He earned about £400. 'Everywhere we wid go we wid get herrin. Cou'na go wrang.' [Duncan McSporran, 1974]

Out on his chance

A crew might be drifting above thousands of boxes of herring and have no way of knowing unless a herring would be heard jumping and that was seldom in the West Shore summer fishing because the big herring rarely came to the surface. 'A've seen me oot on ma chance, in the place o another man sewin a net, gettin her ready for the winter, makin therty-five pound fae Monday tae Friday. That wis my divide at that, so ye may ken we put some herrin oot for that.' [Hugh MacFarlane, 1974]

'Top o the tree'

It was said to have been customary in Dalintober that when a fisherman would return penniless after another blank week, he'd throw his cap into the house and if his wife threw it back out, he was unwelcome. Conversely, one Dalintober fisherman, when returning home the worse for drink after a successful week's fishing, would call upstairs to his wife: 'Top o the tree this week, top o the tree – ye're a beautiful woman, Maggie!' [Angus Martin, author's father, 1974]

Drift-Netting
· · · · · · · · · · · · · · · · · ·

The Kintyre fishermen were drift-netting for centuries before the development of 'the trawl', or ring-net. Indeed, drift-netting persisted into the 20th century, a few old-timers preferring it to ring-netting, and some others working the methods alternately, eg drift-netting when fishing in areas where hostility existed towards the ring-net. In the 19th century, Kintyre smacks and luggers worked drift-nets from the south of Ireland to the north of Scotland and round into the North Sea.

The drift-net was essentially a passive mode of fishing. Up to a mile or more of nets would be set in suspension at evening, and nets and boat would drift together through the night. If herring were swimming where the nets drifted, then herring might be caught.

The trawl-fishermen did not always outfish their drift-netting counterparts. On rare occasions the success rate was reversed, as reported in the Fishery Board for Scotland's annual report for 1893. In autumn of that year, the trawlers worked Loch Fyne in vain for two months, but the drift-netters were getting catches – albeit light ones – by setting their nets to a depth of 35 fathoms (64 m) which the trawls could not reach.

One of the main reasons drift-netting was given up in favour of trawling was the relatively low cost of investment in boats and nets for trawling. Many fishermen thus broke clear of the economic trap of fishing as hired hands on other men's boats, became their own masters, and prospered.

The Ayrshire fishermen were much later than their Argyll counterparts in changing from drift-netting to ring-netting, which was not wholly adopted until after the First World War.

Grianan

There was a fellow who lived up Carradale Glen and he used to come across the hill to Grianan where he kept his boat hauled up. He'd come with a bucket of tar and coat the boat inside and out and then return with his few pieces of drift-nets. He would shoot them and come in in the morning and 'there wis as much tar on the herring as anything else'. [Donald McIntosh, 1974]

Skipness

There were three boats that worked at drift-nets from Skipness in the summertime and one from Claonaig, owned by a man named Johnny Cook. The small Skipness boats would be left in the burn there for the week-end, having been taken in on high water. Johnny Cook's boat was bigger and she'd be left in Tarbert and he and his brother – big strong men – would 'walk home tae Claonaig overhill'. The *Helena* was her name and she was built in Tarbert by Dugald Henderson. [Hugh MacFarlane, 1974]

To the Merchant Navy

Davie MacFarlane was in the Kyles one time and went into Auchenlochan. An old man came aboard the boat and was yarning. 'Aye, aye,' he said, 'ye're from Tarbert. Well, the Tarbertmen spoiled everywhere ever they went.' Davie didn't say much in reply. He said: 'How wis that?' – 'Well, they put all oor men off the coast at the drift-net, stabbin thir bows an cuttin thir nets, for this trawl. But they only put them home. They're all mates an skippers now.' He was a MacAllister from Kames. There was a crew of MacAllisters fishing out of there with a small boat, and a fellow Henderson too from there. 'But thon's what the man said: "They only put them home." He had a poor word o oor men. Certainly, they wir doin a lot o harm.' [David MacFarlane, 1975]

Counting herring

Drift-net herring were counted into a basket in threes, and three herring were a 'cast'. Forty-one casts counted as a hundred. That made it out at 123 for 100. Davie MacFarlane could never understand this 'long hundred' and 'used tae maintain it wis a tithe o the church' in its origins, but that was only his 'own reckonin'. Five of these 'long hundreds' constituted a 'maze' and 10 'long hundreds' were termed a 'last', which was equivalent to a cran of herring. [David MacFarlane, 1974]

'Cast, cast, Peter ...'

Henry Martin, as a schoolboy, used to rise early in the morning and go down Campbeltown Old Quay. The drift-net boats would be in and the crews counting the herring they had. The shots of herring were usually very small. They had words that they shouted to one another when counting into a basket. One time a fisherman called out: 'Cast, cast, Peter – a herrin away wi a gull in its mooth!' A gull had lifted one of the herring and the fisherman 'reversed it'. 'Peter' was Peter Hyndman, who had a small boat, the *Jean*, and boys used to shout that phrase at him. [Henry Martin, 1974]

Summer fleet

A fleet of drift-netters came to Campbeltown from Newhaven and all round the Firth of Forth, sometimes in mid-May and sometimes later. They moored at the New Quay slip and at the slip opposite the network. There were six or eight boats moored there and 'they never moved oot o that tae the furst o June'. On that day, all hands proceeded to sea and headed south to catch the first of the flood out off Sanda. They would shoot their nets there and the flood tide would take them right up the Kilbrannan Sound. That was their drifting started and they followed the herring through the summer the whole way up until they reached Skipness, 'followed the herrin lik that, driftin, driftin'. [John McWhirter, 1974]

Shooting drifts in a circle

On the west side of Stranraer Loch, herring rose and played on a Saturday morning and John McCrindle and his crew shot their drift-nets in a wee circle; but the fishery cutter 'came on them' and wouldn't permit them to do that, so they had to shoot the nets straight and got only a few baskets. Ironically, the *Queens* of Campbeltown were lying at anchor there, their crews 'sound asleep, unconscious of aal that wis around'. [Turner McCrindle, 1976]

Kippered

One of Turner McCrindle's earliest recollections of fishing was as a boy, on holiday from school, at drift-nets aboard the *Eagle* of Maidens. They shot off Pladda and hauled a few baskets. It was 'one o yon days ye hardly knew whether tae put the sail up or not', so the crew pulled home. Turner had a forward oar and was 'near kippered' in the smoke coming out of the boat's stove-pipe. [Turner McCrindle, 1976]

Paraffin down the funnel

The typical Ayrshire drift-netter of the 19th and early 20th century didn't display a light when lying to her nets, but there was always a man kept watch and if a steamer was coming close he'd pour paraffin down the stove-funnel and hope that the steamer's watch would see it flare up and keep clear. The captain of one of the Burns steamers that ran between Belfast and the Clyde was married to an Edgar woman of Dunure and knew of this practice with the paraffin, but would approach very close to the drift-net boats. He actually ran over one of them, and although none of the fishermen was drowned, one of them, named Wilson, was temporarily trapped beneath the boat and never fished again after that experience. He went into another dangerous industry, coal-mining, and years later 'had a terrible death' underground. [Mungo Munro, 1976]

Losing nets

Jake McCrindle lost half a train of 'sunk-nets' one night when the Belfast-Ardrossan ferry ran over the train and cut it. Next day, the crew went out and 'scoored aboot' looking for the nets, but failed to find them. If the train had consisted of 'surface-nets', it would have been recovered entire when hauled in the morning, because the unbroken sole-rope would have held it together. [John McCrindle, 1976]

Too many meshing

Matt Sloan remembered, as a boy, Ayr Bay alive with winter herring. The shoals – 'putting up' in red and brown and black lumps – were moving southward to spawn on Ballantrae Banks. Drift-net boats from Portavogie, Northern Ireland, were there, and he particularly remembered one – the *Boy's Pride* – because she belonged to a man named Cully who had a relative living in Maidens. One afternoon Cully shot, and, 'literally, as he shot his nets, his nets disappeared and he lost the lot'. [Matt Sloan, 1999]

A Rothesay fishing family

Of the two fishing families in Rothesay which originated on the East Coast of Scotland – the Dougalls from Eyemouth and the Hughes from Pittenweem – the Hughes family was later in arriving. Jimmy Hughes – who was widowed in 1937 – and his three sons came to the Clyde in 1940 with the *Emulate* KY 56. She was an Anstruther-built Fifie, almost 57 feet long, and was then just four years old. They left the East Coast because of wartime fishing restrictions.

There was a fishing going on in the narrow upper reaches of Loch Fyne, but they worked a lot of nets and didn't do well there. 'It wis only a day an a dinner when we got a wee puckle, maybe a fifty or a sixty baskets,' Tam Hughes recalled. Initially, they landed into Tarbert, but prices there were unsatisfactory and a local fisherman, James McMillan, persuaded them to try Ayr market. Thereafter, if they had 30 baskets and upwards, it was to Ayr they ran the herring, which consistently fetched 24s 6d a basket.

After New Year, when the herring were down between Pladda and Ailsa Craig, they did better, particularly on breezy nights when the ringers weren't able to fish. 'We used tae think it made the herrin sweem a wee bit better – a breeze stirred them up.'

It quickly became apparent, however, that the *Emulate* wasn't suitable for the Clyde, so she was sold to Aberdeen and replaced with another Fifie, a 40-footer – registered KY 106 – which was renamed *Emulate II*. They had a 'devil o a job' acquiring her, owing to the war, and she wasn't in good order, but they gradually repaired her and she served them, at both drift-netting and ring-netting, until the end of the war.

Thereafter, the family concentrated on ring-netting, with a pair of second-hand boats, the *Dewy Rose* – which they bought from Mungo Munro in Dunure – and *Pre-eminent* (ex-*Ina Bell* of Carradale). These were registered RO 5 and RO 6 respectively and together made the registration number of the first *Emulate*, KY 56. When, in 1964, the Hughes brothers got their last boat for herring fishing, the *Maid of the Mist*, she was registered RO 56 and they were back with the number they'd started with almost a quarter of a century earlier. [Tam Hughes, 2000]

Boats
· · · · · · · ·

Hugh MacFarlane, the earliest-born (1884) informant in this book, first went to sea, in the late 19th century, aboard a skiff which wasn't much over 30ft (9 m). Motor-power was still more than a decade in the future. Yet, remarkably, he lived to see the first modern motor ring-netter built (Falcon, 1922) and also the last (Alliance, 1974).

'Dreadnought'

There was an old clinker skiff in Dalintober, owned by James 'Smeegie' Smith, and she was given the sarcastic nick-name 'Dreadnought'*. He and his neighbour, Neil McKenzie – who probably had the *Elsie* at the time – were looking for herring, without success, north of Carradale. They could see and hear the rest of the fleet fishing off Arran, on the other side of the Kilbrannan Sound, and Neil was anxious to participate; but when he suggested this, Smith's reply was: 'Give us a ship and we'll cross!' There was a good breeze blowing at the time and the skiffs had their sails reefed. Smith's old boat leaked like a sieve and on a Monday morning he and his crew habitually spent three or four hours baling her out. He certainly wasn't going to risk a three-mile crossing in her! [Henry Martin, 1974]

* *After the class of Royal Navy battleship, the first of which was launched in 1906.*

Unrecognisable

There was a Campbeltown ring-netter – not to be identified, though her skipper-owner is long dead – brought across to Maidens to have her engine overhauled by Andy Marr, the Gardner specialist who was based there. Her owner was rather indolent, not least in the matter of the boat's appearance. She hadn't been well cared for and her planking was showing dark through the varnish. Certain of the Maidens fishermen – who were, as a class, meticulous in the attention they gave their boats – 'jeest cou'na look at this black plank'. She must have sorely offended their sensibilities, for they took it upon themselves to scrape her back to the bare wood and revarnish her. When the unsuspecting owner and Robbie McKellar, one of his crew, returned to Maidens to collect the boat, they were looking about the harbour in bewilderment: 'Where's the boat? She's naw there.' At a distance, they hadn't recognised their own vessel, for she was 'jeest lik a new pin'. [Archibald Paterson, 2000]

Summer Rose

The *Summer Rose* came to Dunure in the spring of 1947. She was bigger than the previous boats and when she arrived the 'expressed opinion' was that she would be unmanageable, but that prediction proved groundless. She was very basic by later standards, her equipment being simply an engine, winch and compass. A radio, however, was installed in the autumn of that year, and in the following year, when the second of the two boats, *Storm Drift II*, arrived with echo-sounder and radio aboard, an echo-sounder too was added to the *Summer Rose*'s equipment. [Iain Gemmell, 1999]

Storm Drift III

The *Storm Drift III* was ordered from Noble's yard at Girvan. She was to be the third of the 58-footers built there. The Gemmells went to Girvan to have a look at the *Aliped VIII*, which was under construction. They decided that she didn't have sufficient freeboard and asked if the *Storm Drift* could be 'a plank higher'. Alex Noble discussed the request at length with them, and it was decided that, in order to increase the height, the boat would have to be laid out a further foot. So, she became the first of the 59-footers. She was launched in 1962 and 'was out of date when she was launched'. She was the first Clyde boat to have a Decca Navigator installed and, instead of a seine-net winch, a trawl-winch – 'which wis more relevant tae our requirements' – was fitted. [Iain Gemmell, 1999]

Fairlie boats

The 17 ring-netters built from 1947 to 1967 by Fairlie Yacht Slip Ltd, had a reputation of being fine boats head-on to a sea, but 'rowly' beam-on. These traits were vividly demonstrated to Tam Hughes one night in Kilbrannan Sound.

There was a north-east wind 'howlin doon' that winter's night and the Tarbert fleet didn't put to sea; but the Carradale fleet did, and headed south as far as the Lodan. 'There wirna a lipper doon there – ye wid har'ly believe it,' Tam Hughes recalled. There were no herring there either, so they headed back up the Sound and lay off Whitefarland. Tam's neighbour, Fred Brownie, was laid up with influenza, and Raymond Gosling was in the *Silver Cloud*'s wheelhouse. He and Tam were discussing calling it a week, when somebody remarked: 'There a *winky* away, boys.' This was Jim Campbell shooting on the west side of the Rock. 'We'd better go an huv a look at that afore we run awa hame,' Tam suggested.

Out in the deep water, Tam shot against the breeze, between Archie Paterson and Alex Galbraith, who'd both shot with it. The breeze was light, but there was a motion on the sea. He rung 40 baskets of good herring, and when the *Silver Cloud* came round and 'squared', before her crew had even rigged the brailer 'she dipped aboot a dozen o herrin on tae her deck oot o the net'. One of the neighbouring crew, Douglas McIntosh, looked at Tam and shook his head: 'Dear, dear, dear ...' – 'By God, they can rowl!' Tam remarked. The *Silver Cloud* was a Fairlie boat, built in 1948 as the *Mairi Elspeth*.

After the catch was aboard and the boats were under way again, Archie Paterson in the *Harvest Queen* – another Fairlie boat – called Tam on the radio: 'What wis doin, Tam?' – 'Forty baskets.' – 'How wis the tide?' – 'Oh, the tide's goin north, right enough.' – 'Well, that's the difference it's made,' Archie replied. 'Wir neebor there's lik a wild stallion comin at ye,' Tam remarked. 'Ye're a lucky man ye're no in a Fairlie boat the night, Tam,' Archie laughed. [Tam Hughes, 2001]

Wistaria and *Watchful* – how they got their names

When, in 1949, Matt and Billy Sloan were having a boat built at Weatherhead's yard in Cockenzie, there was another boat, for Girvan, also being built there. Matt went to see the fishery officer in Ayr to register the boat, but the man was in a rather fuddled state and the discussion went badly. He wanted to know why Matt was there. Matt told him.

'What number would ye like?' he asked. 'BA 33, if possible,' Matt replied. 'Why do you want BA 33?' was the response. 'Ma grandfather [Harbison] at Dunure had a boat named the *Sunbeam* and the boat wis BA 33,' Matt said. That boat had been built by Willie Harbison in his back garden with the assistance of his two sons. But there was another reason Matt wanted that number. He was invariably the one who painted the names and numbers on the family boats and found round figures much easier to do than straight figures. The fishery officer said that he couldn't give Matt 33, so Matt asked for 36. That wasn't available either, so Matt said: 'Forget it. Tell me two or three numbers A can have.' The officer gave him a choice of three numbers, from which Matt selected 64. The fishery officer then asked for the boat's name. 'The boat's name is to be the *Trade Wind*.' – 'Oh,' said the man, '*Trade Wind*. Oh, that's funny.' – 'What's funny aboot it?' Matt queried. 'Nothin,' said the fishery officer. The boat was duly registered *Trade Wind*, BA 64.

The following week, Matt left on the Monday morning to go to the spring fishing in the Minch, and during the passage north one of his crew asked: 'Hae ye got a name for yer boat yet?' Matt affirmed that he had, adding that the boat had been registered. 'And are ye gonny tell us?' the crewman asked. 'It's no top secret or anythin lik that,' Matt replied. 'It's the *Trade Wind*.' With that, the man said he thought that was the name of the boat that was being built alongside Matt's boat for the Hislops of Girvan. 'That's impossible!' Matt exclaimed. 'We cannae have two boats named *Trade Wind* running fae adjacent ports, BA as they are.'

The first day Matt was in Mallaig, he telephoned the fishery officer in Ayr, who confirmed that the Girvan boat's name was to be *Trade Winds* and that he had thought there was 'something funny' when Matt was in registering the boat. Although the plural in the Girvan boat's name would have distinguished her, Matt felt that there was bound to be confusion and decided to change the name to *Wistaria*.

When he and his brother had been discussing names, each wrote his choice on a slip of paper. The names were put into a hat and the one that was drawn out was Matt's choice. Billy's choice had been *Wistaria*. Further, if the fishery officer had given Matt BA 36, which was the second number he had asked for, then the confusion would have been compounded, because the Girvan *Trade Winds* was registered BA 35.

In 1959, when the *Wistaria*'s neighbour-boat, the *Bairn's Pride*, was replaced by a new boat, Billy said to Matt: 'We'll no have any discussion this time as tae what ye call the boat. Jeest you name the boat. You lost yer name last time.' Matt decided that he would have *Watchful*, after one of James Alexander's herring-buying steamers*. 'A jeest liked that wee

1. A study in steely concentration – John Johnson of Glendarroch, Tarbert (1866–1937). He is at the helm of his skiff the *Sally*, heading south off Laggan. She was built at Port Bannatyne, Bute, in 1903, and five years later became the first Tarbert skiff to be fitted with an engine. Courtesy of Mrs Margaret McGougan Johnson, Lochgilphead.

2. In leather seaboots and smoking his pipe, Denis McKay of the skiff *Annunciata* of Campbeltown. Born c. 1870, he was the youngest of three Irish brothers who distinguished themselves as ring-net fishermen in the early 20th century. Courtesy of his grandson, Denis Meenan, Campbeltown.

3. The craggy features of crack Maidens ring-net skipper, Billy Sloan. He is operating the winch of the *Wistaria* as a catch of summer herring is discharged at Tarbert, Loch Fyne, c. 1966. Photograph by Niven 'Bunty' Crawford, Furnace; courtesy of his son, John Crawford, Lochgilphead.

4. In the forecastle of the *Florentine* II of Carradale. It is Christmas week, 1959, and there is a packet of Lyon's mince pies on the table. L–R Donald MacAllister of Grogport, Bill McMillan, and the McConnachie brothers Walter, John and (in bunk) James. The photograph was taken by a photographer from *The Bulletin*; courtesy of Donald MacAllister, Carradale.

5. Fishing boats in Tarbert harbour, c. 1888. The three foreground 'baldies' are visiting East Coast herring drifters – two registrations, 'LH' for Leith and 'KY' for Kirkcaldy are clearly visible – rigged with dipping lugsails. The background boats with steeply-raked masts are Loch Fyne Skiffs, which carried standing lugsails. Herring-carrying steamers can be seen anchored at left. Courtesy of Jon Hooper, Ugadale, Kintyre.

6. The foreshore at Dalintober, c. 1900. The skiff in the foreground is the *Bella* (146 CN) which belonged to the author's great-grandfather, John Martin, and was skippered by his son, Sandy. Just 7.32 m (24 ft) of keel, she was originally an open boat, but had a forecastle fitted during the 1880s when larger skiffs were introduced. Net-drying poles can be seen beyond the skiffs, and, at bottom left, water-casks and a small water-tank, removed to facilitate the annual spring-clean which the boats are undergoing. McGrory Collection.

7. William Cook's Loch Fyne Skiff, the *Enterprise*, under full sail in Campbeltown Loch, with Dalintober in the background, c. 1904. One of the long oars, called 'sweeps', are in use, and an end of the other can be seen protruding over the stern. McGrory Collection.

8. As sleek as race horses – a fleet of Ayrshire and Firth of Forth ring-netters moored at Inveraray Quay in 1938. Ironically, when herring returned in abundance to Upper Loch Fyne in that year, there was scarcely a local boat left to exploit the fishery. Photograph by Johnny Dewar, Inveraray; courtesy of John Vallis, Inveraray.

9. Diverse boat types in Dunmore East harbour, c. 1960. The ring-netter *Kittiwake* is discharging herring at the quay. The large Dutch herring-buying 'lugger', *Adriana Johanna* of Schevenigen, is moored beyond her. Photograph by Roger Shipsey, Waterford City; courtesy of Joseph Teesdale, Thomastown, Co. Kilkenny.

10. Ring-netters crowd the harbour at Whitby, Yorkshire, c. 1950. Photograph by John Tindale, Whitby. Author's collection.

11. The *Mary Munro* of Dunure shooting a ring-net off Tor Mor, Carradale, on 13 June, 1939. Jim Grieve is in the wheelhouse and John 'Pinkie' Edgar is at the soles. Photograph by Dan McDonald; courtesy of Ballast Trust.

12. Brailing a catch of herring into the hold of the *Escalonia* of Carradale off the High Rocks, Whitestone, December 1959. The crew is, 'Aleca' McDougall (hand on brailer), Angus Paterson (scooped hat), Alex 'Als' Galbraith (obscured), Argyll McMillan (soft hat) and Iain 'Ban' Campbell. This *Bulletin* photograph was taken from the *Florentine*'s wheelhouse roof, as the spar of her outrigger light, angling across the right of the picture, shows. Courtesy of James McConnachie, Carradale.

13. Tarbert skipper and boat-owner, Willie 'Gorrie' McCaffer, with a sample basket of the *Evelyn*'s herring on Tarbert Quay, c. 1967. Photograph by Niven 'Bunty' Crawford, Furnace; courtesy of John Crawford, Lochgilphead.

14. A net-barrow loaded with a ring-net for barking. L–R Danny McMillan, John Short Sr and Archibald 'Baldy' Stewart at the door of the Net Factory in Kinloch Road, Campbeltown, late 1920s. Courtesy of Neil Short, Glasgow.

15. The small stone quay at MacGougan's Turn, on the south side of East Loch Tarbert, with ring-net skiffs moored at the 'croichs', or net-hangers, c. 1885. Courtesy of Jon Hooper, Ugadale, Kintyre.

16. Net-mending aboard the *Elma* of Carradale, c. 1950. Skipper Johnny McMillan is at left; Donald Morrison is in the middle and the figure in the foreground is thought to be Hamish McKinven. Courtesy of John Galbraith, Carradale.

drifter, and A jeest liked that name, *Watchful*,' Matt explained. He felt that there was another significance to the name, because 'fishermen in general and skippers in particular had got tae be alert; they had got tae be watchful'. [Matt Sloan, 1999]

GW 19, ex-PD 498, a converted steam-drifter.

The *Quest*

The skipper of the *Quest* of Dunure, Jimmy Munro, was known to sing his own adaptation of the 'cowboy' song which contains the line: 'They're tough, mighty tough, in the West.' It was: 'They're tough, mighty tough, on the *Quest*; Big Jimmy thinks he's tougher than the rest.' [Grieve Gemmell, 2000]

Seven coats of varnish

During one spring-cleaning, the *Storm Drift* of Dunure had no fewer than seven coats of varnish applied to her deck. 'Ye could see yer face in it tae shave,' Grieve Gemmell remarked. One night they shot in Whiting Bay with the wind in and got a lot of herring in the net and could hardly hold on to it. To complicate matters, they were slipping all over the deck and the skipper, Grieve's father Sammy, was moved to comment: 'You an yer bloody vernished decks – ye're no tae put as much vernish as that oan!' [Grieve Gemmell, 2000]

Snoring

When, one summer's morning in the 1960s, the *Maid of the Mist* came into Carradale to have her stem replaced, she was beached in Port Crannag, so that local carpenters, Matthew McDougall and his son, Neil, could proceed with the work. Despite the racket the McDougalls made, hammering and boring, the Rothesay crew slept throughout the entire operation and could be heard snoring through the hull. [Neil McDougall, 2001]

Never perfect

Although the canoe- and cruiser-sterned ring-net boats were unquestionably beautiful – perhaps as beautiful as any design of fishing boat that evolved anywhere in the world – perfection was not a concept many fishermen permitted into their thinking.

Any boat coming into the Carradale fleet, new or second-hand, would be scrutinised rigorously and invariably found lacking in some detail. The late Donald McConnachie – an astute observer of human nature and witty with it – was heard to remark that if the fishermen couldn't find fault with a boat in any other way, they'd point out that the sides of the frying-pan weren't high enough! [Neil McDougall, 2000]

Last sighting

The *Jeannie II* BA 303 was built in 1947 for Girvan owners by J N Miller and Sons, St Monans. She later became the Mansons' *Jessie Alice* OB 4 of Mallaig. Subsequently, she was sold to the Firth of Forth and it was as *Storm Drift II* LH 419 that Matt Sloan last saw her. His *Watchful* was ebbed in Seahouses harbour, discharging herring, and the boat ahead was the old *Jeannie*, waiting to be unloaded. He could see, along the boat's keel-strake, the 'milky juice' of the spawny herring seeping out from the hold. 'What an awfu state that boat's bottom must've been in,' he remarked. 'What was happenin when the boat was floatin – what water was goin in?' [Matt Sloan, 2001]

Dens
•••••••

The 'den' was the fishermen's term for the forecastle, which is the decked-over forward part of a boat. The first skiffs to be thus decked, so providing accom-modation – albeit cramped – were evidently the Alpha and Beta, built in Girvan in 1882 for Edward McGeachy of Dalintober. Previously, trawl-skiffs were virtually open, and fishermen working from home slept ashore in tents or huts, or lodged in the larger smacks which might accompany the small boats to the fishing grounds. The innovation was of major significance in the lives of fish-ermen, both providing them with a degree of comfort and enabling them to extend their operational range during winter, when the occupation of tents and huts was impractical. The abandonment of open-boat fishing was signalled in an adver-tisement, in the Campbeltown Courier of 5 April 1884, of the sale, by public auction at Dalintober Quay, of the Brodie family's 'trawling skiffs' Roselea and Ardenlea, 24ft 6 in (7.47 m) long and 8ft (2.44 m) of beam, along with nets and gear and 'one wooden house and stove presently at Cour'.

First decked boat in Carradale

The first boat that came to Carradale with a forecastle was called the *Bella* and belonged to James Campbell, the grandfather of Donald McIntosh's wife, Mary Campbell. She was 'only a wee wee boat' – no more than 30ft in length – with a tiny forecastle. James Campbell couldn't get a crew for her in the wintertime. The popular opinion was that she was too big to get into the ports and the Burn at Waterfoot, one of the anchorages of the Carradale fleet when weather made the pier at Port Crannag unsafe. She drew merely 3ft of water! [Donald McIntosh, 1974]

In the skiff *Fairy Queen*

Dougie Robertson, who owned and skippered the *Fairy Queen*, apparently never removed his oilskins and seaboots when he lay down to sleep; he just lay on the locker, and the forecastle was so tiny that his feet hung outside the door into the hold. [John McWhirter, 1976]

The boy's bed

There were four men and a boy aboard the Campbeltown skiffs. Generally, the older men slept on the lockers and the younger fellows were in hammocks, while the boy slept on the 'platform', or floor. Near the middle of the hold there would be a row of sandbags piled as shifting ballast for sailing, and the joke was that the boy's feet would be resting on top of the sandbags. 'Ye know, the space wis that shoart. It wis a case o tryin tae get as much space as ye could for cerryin herrin.' [Henry Martin, 1975]

Herring in forecastle

George Newlands was in the skiff *Good Hope* in Stranraer Loch, and the forecastle door was left open one Saturday morning 'for the herring tae go in' so that extra could be taken aboard; but 'what a mess it wis an what a job it wis tae waash oot that place.' The *Good Hope*, at that time, was the only skiff in Campbeltown that was fully decked, because she had been built principally for drift-netting and had a big hatch. [George Newlands, 1975]

No way back

Jake McCrindle one winter went down to Stranraer from Maidens to join the neighbouring crew, which was working trammels there. He travelled by train, taking a small ring-net with him for use there. There were seven men sleeping in the neighbour-boat's forecastle, and his bed was in the forepeak. He went out one night to 'make water' and couldn't get back into the forecastle, so he spent the rest of the night sitting outside. 'They wouldn't do it now,' he added. [John McCrindle, 1976]

'A dinna try it'

With the advent of the modern ring-netter in the 1920s, accommodation improved immensely – table, set-in bunks and more spacious lockers (seats) became standard in forecastles – yet, in reality, there was little enough room for six men, especially when fishing away from home and confined for days or even weeks on end. It was vital, in such conditions, that crew members should, at the very least, be able to tolerate one another. That generally was the case, but there were crews riven by rivalry and resentment.

The summer's day started normally enough aboard the *Rolling Wave*. She was lying in Brodick and the young cook, Archie Paterson, had split a quantity of herring, sprinkled salt and pepper over them and laid them on a board to toast in the sun. These herring were delicious fried and the men would eat half-a-dozen each quite easily when they rose. After the meal, they went ashore to the burn with soap and towels and had a wash. Then it was a case of waiting to go back out in the evening to fish.

One of the crew, George McMillan from Torrisdale – 'a big, powerful man' – was in the habit of monopolising the small drying-rail above the 'Jack Tar' coal-stove in the forecastle, and this day was no different – his gear was hanging there toasting. Another elderly crewman, Angus Paterson, bitterly resented this trait of George's and decided to retaliate. His wife Maggie had knitted him a new pair of seaboot stockings. Angus removed them from their brown paper parcel and quite needlessly stuffed them on to the already overcrowded rail. George, who was on deck, later removed his waistcoat in the heat of the day, went below with it and hung it too on the rail.

Still later, Archie Paterson, who was nearest the scuttle, smelt singeing and hurried below, to find one of Angus's stockings, dislodged earlier by George, smouldering on top of the hot stove. When Archie took the stocking up on deck and showed it to his uncle – the foot of it was 'burnt to a cinder' – there was an almighty row.

Peace restored, the crew was assembled in the cramped forecastle, Angus on his customary seat – taking his ease and smoking a pipe – and George right forward, in the bow, seated on the coiled anchor-cable. Eventually, George started to make his way aft, but in so doing had to pass Angus. They were both big men and there wasn't much room. George's big boot came down on one of Angus's boots and the sole was wrenched off it. 'A can see it yit in ma mind's eye,' Archie Paterson recalled. 'It wis lik a big open mouth wi the nails all round.' Rubber seaboots had, by this time, replaced the traditional leather type, but the older men hated the new boots – they were afraid they would slip on the rubber soles – and had a shoemaker in Tarbert replace the rubber soles with leather. That was Angus's boot ruined – he later hammered the nails back, but the boot still leaked – and he gave George a 'right keel-haulin'. George's only response was, 'A dinna try it', and that made Angus even madder; but, as Archie Paterson remarked: 'The relationship was never good between the two of them.' [Archie Paterson, 2000]

Engines
· · · · · · · · · ·

The impact of motor-power on the fishing industry was momentous, not only enabling boats to travel further and quicker in the pursuit of fish and markets, but also, coupled with the winch, enabling the catching capacity of nets to be increased dramatically. The first engine to be fitted on the West Coast of Scotland was a 7-9 hp Kelvin, installed in Robert Robertson's Brothers of Campbeltown. By 1910, 81 boats were motor-powered on the West Coast, 40 of these Campbeltown-registered, and that trend would continue unabated, with engines of increased power coming on to the market, until, in the immediate post-war period, the engine ceased to be auxiliary to sail and oars, and these were discarded.

'Me sixty-five poun's gone'

The first engined fishing boat on the Ayrshire coast, Tommy Sloan believed, was Willie Munro's *Annie* of Dunure, which was fitted with a 7-9 hp Kelvin. He was returning home with her from Hunter's Quay, after the installation, when, just off Ardrossan, she 'ran dry' and Willie exclaimed: 'Here, me sixty-five poun's gone!' [Tommy Sloan, 1976]

A small propeller

When the engineer arrived to install the engine on the first motorised Ayrshire fishing boat, the fishermen asked him where the propeller was, and he took it out of his raincoat pocket, saying: 'I've got it with me.' [Grieve Gemmell, 1999]

'Speak quick ...'

The first engines were 'hardly makin bubbles', as Archie Paterson put it, yet, in those early days, when one crew would be hailing another at night – 'Whit's doin?' – if the other skiff was motor-powered, the order would be: 'Speak quick or they'll naw hear ye' – they'd be away by, driven on by the engine! Another yarn – also heard from Dugald 'Scavers' Mathieson – went like this. One crew was hailing another at night, and neither crew had a clue who the other was. 'Is that you?' some one called. 'Aye,' was the reply, 'is that you too?' [Archie Paterson, 2000]

Carradale

The factor to the laird of Carradale Estate, Major Austin MacKenzie, used to visit Carradale. This factor, whose name was Rhodes, had connections with the Thorneycroft engineering firm and asked a local skipper, Johnny 'Coalin' Campbell, if he would take a Thorneycroft on a year's free trial. Campbell agreed and a 7.5 hp engine – valued at £90 – was duly installed in the *Lady Carrick Buchanan**. Campbell, however, kept a share for the engine off the boat's earnings from the start and when the year was up the engine was paid. [Donald McIntosh, 1974]

**In September, 1908, at Robert Wylie's boatyard, Campbeltown.*

Tarbert

The first engined fishing boat in Tarbert was John Johnson's *Sally* (in August, 1908). She had a 7-9 hp Kelvin installed and frequently took her neighbour-boat in tow when making a passage. John Johnson's previous boat (the *Molly*) had been a 'wee clinker'. With a later 'bigger and heavier' 8-10 hp engine, a passage from Fairlie to Tarbert* in a 'good lump o a skift' was once timed at four hours. 'There wirna an err o win oot the sky.' [Hugh MacFarlane, 1974]

**Twenty-eight land miles on the straightest courses, without allowance for tide.*

Getting a tow across

The first experience Davie MacFarlane had with a motor was at Catacol, Arran. He was in a boat called the *Beauty*, belonging to Peter and Jamie Smith, 'nice decent men'. There were plenty of herring there, but they were so deep they could hardly be caught. A pair of motorised skiffs, belonging to the Blairs of Campbeltown, joined the Tarbertmen the next day. The wind eased and the Tarbertmen decided to row across to Cour, on the other side of the Sound. With that, one of the Campbeltown boats got under way, 'puffin away wi his motor, doin fine'. Her skipper, Dougie Blair, called to a Tarbert crew: 'Are ye goin across the other side, boys?' – 'Aye.' – 'Well, throw us a rope.' Then he cried to his neighbour-boat: 'Catch you that other man's' – this was the *Beauty*'s neighbour's rope. 'We sat back,' Davie recalled, 'an this ould fella – he had a whisker – "My God," he said, "we're goin, we're goin lik the *Minard*!"' This was the *Minard Castle**, the 'luggage steamer' that plied Loch Fyne. They reached the other side at Rudha Riabhach and tore the net with their first shot. [David MacFarlane, 1974]

*The first vessel – screw-driven and fast – operated by the Loch Fyne and Glasgow Steam Packet Company, which was founded in 1882. She carried both passengers and cargo.

'Tarry' and the engine

One night, when George Newlands was crewing on the *Twin Brothers*, or 'Wheetie', which was the boat's nick-name, they were 'doon in the Lodan'. George was driving the engine and having 'a hell of a job gettin her tae go – she wid go an stop, go an stop'. The skipper, Peter McMillan, whose nick-name was 'Tarry'*, was becoming impatient with the temperamental engine, and finally shouted to George: 'Ach, tae hell! Close that damnt hatch. Put up the sell!' Peter was, at heart, an old skiff fisherman and wanted only to work with the sail. [George Newlands, 1975]

*'Tarry' was a corruption of Tara, the name of a ship on which Peter McMillan served during the First World War and which was torpedoed and sunk off the Libyan coast on 5 November, 1915. Earlier in life, he owned the Loch Fyne Skiff Sweet Home, which he regularly entered in the premier skiff race at the annual Campbeltown regatta, and in 1902 won.

Scaring herring

In Lady Bay, below Milleur Buoy in Stranraer Loch, the water is shallow. Herring were jumping there, but as soon as the engine was started –

nothing! At that time, skiffs, though motorised, still carried sails and oars, and one of the crew suggested: 'Never mind startin the engine at aa – we'll putt the oars oot.' Thereafter, the crews were getting 10 and 15 and 20 baskets of herring a ring and 'made a fishin oot it,' finishing with 70 or 80 baskets in the morning. 'The engine wis no use – it wis scatterin them away clear o ye in the shoal watter.' [George Newlands, 1975]

'Pitter-patter'

When Turner McCrindle first went to ring-netting in the Kilbrannan Sound, the engines of the *Polly Cook* and *Lady Carrick Buchanan*, a Carradale pair, would be heard, 'pitter-patter', around one o' clock on a clear summer's morning. This was them leaving the West Side 'and away for the Woods for the herrin at daylight'. If crews got herring on the West Side in the evening, they hardly ever bothered trying there again in the morning, because the herring would be scared off the shore. [Turner McCrindle, 1976]

An 'infernal clang'

Turner McCrindle recalled a man going round selling diesel engines. McGown of Campbeltown, Johnson of Tarbert and Jock Grieve of Dunure all got one, but when the salesman approached Turner's father, his canny response was: 'Ye've got orders? Well, A'll see how they work before A get yin.' John McCrindle's caution was fortunate for him, because, in Turner's words, the diesel engines 'nearly ruint these three fishermen'. He remembered the 'aafu noise' the engine made when it started: 'Oh, ye thought the boat wis gonny go tae pieces. It wis more than a thud – it wis an infernal clang. We got Gardners and never regretted it.' [Turner McCrindle, 1976]

A 'hopeless engine'

Robert McGown recalled the installation of one of these luckless engines – a 'Pollock-Anderson semi-diesel', he described it – in the *Faustina*, built for him at Reekie's, St Monans, in 1927. At 42ft (12.8 m) long, with a wheelhouse, she was among the earliest canoe-sterned ring-netters built for Campbeltown; but the engine broke down outside St Monans harbour as she set off home, and she had to be towed to Campbeltown. 'That wis a start wi a new boat,' as Robert remarked. They just couldn't get the engine to run. Engineers were 'sent up fae the works', but to no avail. The 'hopeless engine' was finally discarded and replaced with a Kelvin 'Sleeve Valve', which was 'very quiet-running ... ideal for the herrin fishin at that time.' [Robert McGown, 1974]

An Atlantic

One boat on which Davie MacFarlane crewed – an elliptical-sterned East Coast type, the *Blossom* – had an Atlantic engine, which ran on paraffin. When the crew set off home from Anstruther one year, Davie started the engine and didn't stop it until the *Blossom* was through the Forth-Clyde Canal and back in Tarbert. 'Ye never heard an engine wi more noise – ye'd think it wis the crusher up at Crarae (Quarry).' [David MacFarlane, 1975]

'Goin well, that boat'

It was remarked that the *Maid of Morven*'s engine – a Gleniffer – needed an overhaul. Another Carradale ringer, Johnny Campbell's *Elizabeth Campbell*, had the same make of engine, but she was a Noble of Girvan boat, long in the bottom, and could 'walk past' the Weatherhead-built *Maid*. That was no use at all, so new pistons and liners were ordered. Johnny Campbell took the pistons and liners discarded from the *Maid's* engine and he and Donald 'Fergie' Paterson fitted them to their own engine; there was absolutely nothing wrong with the parts. One morning, some time afterwards, the two boats were going into Campbeltown and the *Elizabeth Campbell* once again streaked away past the *Maid of Morven*. Denis McIntosh, the *Maid's* owner, was standing at the wheelhouse beside his skipper, Fred Brownie. 'Goin well, that boat,' Fred remarked. 'Aye, wi my bloody pistons an liners!' was Denis's vexed reply. [Archie Paterson, 2000]

An explosion aboard the *Village Belle*

One day, in the 1960s, the *Village Belle III* of Tarbert was lying in Castlebay, Barra, with an engine – a 132 hp Kelvin – that wouldn't start. The boat's engineer, Robert Ronald – a baker to trade and 'a real clever fellow' – had tried several times without success, and half-a-dozen other fishermen had assembled inquisitively down in the engine-room. The boat's skipper, Neil Jackson, suggested trying the lit rag treatment once more, so Robert Ronald tied a cloth around a spanner, soaked it in petrol, lit it and inserted it up the air-intake, as Neil, in the wheelhouse, pressed the starter-button.

There was a terrific explosion, which brought the village children rushing out of school to see what had happened, and when the smoke cleared in the engine-room, it was discovered that the big, broad bulkhead door had blown out, several pond-boards in the hold had been broken and the hatch-boards had lifted off the hold.

Robert Ronald's scorched jersey completely disintegrated when touched and his eyebrows and eyelashes were burned off. One of the onlookers in the engine-room, a Campbeltown man, looked down his shirt-front and found that there wasn't a hair left on his chest!

The engine was finally started when Neil Jackson's brother, Willie, appeared with his engineer, Willie Johnson, and gave the *Belle* a tow with the *Village Maid* while the lit rag procedure was repeated yet again. When Robert Ronald later attended the local doctor with his injuries, he was told that he and the others in the engine-room had been lucky the bulkhead door had blown out or there could have been fatalities. [Neil Jackson, 2001]

Nets and Gear

The cost of a small 'trawl-net' – complete with ropes, cork-floats and lead-weights – in 1864 was £20 or £25. Average dimensions then would have been in the range of 100 yards (162m) long and 13 yards (12m) at the deepest point, which was the middle. Dimensions increased progressively throughout the 19th century, but the coming of motor-power and winches in the 20th century enabled fishermen to greatly deepen ring-nets and thereby enhance their catching-power where it was needed, depthwise. In 1955, a ring-net – over 200 yards (183m) long and 42 yards (38m) deep – ordered by James Manson of Mallaig, from Joseph Gundry & Co's net-factory at Campbeltown, was priced at £378 10s, 'mounted to ropes'.

The Carradale fishermen, as a community, clung to ring-netting longer than any of their Clyde counterparts. Jim Campbell's last ring-net was assembled at Bridport-Gundry's factory in Campbeltown in 1968 for his Bairn's Pride *and cost him approximately £900. The net was about 180 yards (165m) long when rigged to the ropes and could 'touch bottom at 35 – 40 fathoms' (64-73m). It was, he said, 'very effective when the herring were deep down, but very hard to work in shallow water'. That net carried about 350 three-quarter pound lead rings on its sole-rope. Jim and his father habitually 'spent many hours melting down the scrap lead to make the rings with a mould'. (Letter, 2 August 2002)*

Receipt for a 'trawl', 1874

Donald McIntosh in Carradale chanced upon a receipt for a ring-net – a 'trawl', as it was described – which was written out by the net-manufacturing firm of Walker in Kilbirnie, Ayrshire, for an old uncle of Donald's, Sandy Galbraith. The receipt was dated March, 1874, and was for the sum of £6 towards the cost of the net. [Donald McIntosh, 1975]

Sheepskin buoys

When John McWhirter was fishing with Denis McKay's crew, they were lying in Tarbert one day alongside an Ardrishaig skiff belonging to Angus Law, 'admirin the nice bows'. Angus – or 'Angie', as he got – was 'well acquant' with Denis and told him that he had some necks – the wooden stock around which the skin was bound – in his net-store and that if Denis would get a sheepskin or two he'd make him a set of buoys. The Ardrishaig men were 'grand hands' at making not only ring-net buoys but also the smaller buoys for drift-nets. By that time, the Campbeltown fishermen had changed to factory-made canvas buoys. Angie was as good as his word, and, at the end of the year, gave a set of buoys to McKay's crew, who poured a mixture of Archangel tar and linseed oil into them and then coated them on the outside. The skins would get so tight and hard that, 'God, ye wir aye thinkin tae hear them burstin in the sun'. [John McWhirter, 1976]

Damage

Turner McCrindle never lost an entire net in all his years at fishing, but he did lose a bag and shoulders at Towmont End, on the north side of Great Cumbrae. This was with the *Margarita* and *Senorita*. The *Margarita* shot there in a gale and 'went up on a wee point', and that's where the damage was done. They got 40 baskets of herring in a ring after that and then went into Balloch Bay and lay. 'Oh, it wis a wile night, an we come oot roon by Millport an ye could hardly see Millport for spindrift'. They put into Rothesay and sold the catch there. [Turner McCrindle, 1976]

Assistance

The last time the Firth of Forth ringers *Aurora* and *Summer Rose* were in Carradale, it was to land a cotton net torn from end to end off the Phone Box at Pirnmill, Arran. The crews hauled it on to Carradale Quay and began mending. When the Carradale boats came in that morning, some of the local men said that they'd assist with the work after dinner. They were as good as their word, and, by joining the torn edges of the net here and there, to give a larger number of hands a start, the repair was finished that day and the net hauled back aboard the boat in readiness for the night's fishing. The Pittenweem men, who had prepared themselves for days of mending, 'cou'na believe it'; but, as John McConnachie observed, fishermen in those days were eager to help one another. [John McConnachie, 2001]

'Auchies'

During the final 'brief summer' of ring-netting, in 1977, when two Carradale pairs – *Golden Sheaf* (James Tait Rennie) and *Silver Fern* (Argyll McMillan) and *Silver Lining* (John McKinlay) and *Shemaron* (Sandy Galbraith) – were operating from Tarbert, there were boats from Avoch (pronounced 'Auch') there too. These 'Auchies', from the Moray Firth, were herring-trawling, but they had once favoured the ring-net, and older hands aboard the *Adventurer* and *Vision* took the young crew-members aboard one of the Carradale ringers to show them the net and to explain how it was operated. [John Galbraith, 2001]

A good haizin

When Fred Brownie was skippering Denis McIntosh's *Maid of Morven*, he shot at the Bennan on the south end of Arran during the winter spawny herring fishing there and nearly destroyed the net. The net had been 80 score of meshes deep and had to be cut down to 60 score and have a good deal of new netting put into it as well; all in all, it was an extensive repair operation that was performed on Campbeltown Quay. Fortunately, it was a good day for the task, with a dry easterly wind blowing steadily. When the job was finished, Fred remarked to Denis, by way of consoling him: 'Ach, well, she got a good haizin anyway, Denis.' – 'Aye,' Denis replied, 'a damned expensive one!' A 'haizin' was a 'drying', and cotton nets were always the better of a drying, but Denis reckoned, no doubt, that there were cheaper ways of airing a net. [Archibald Paterson, 2000]

Nothing should change

Fishing expertise depended, to some extent, Archie Paterson believed, on 'who ye're trained wi'. His own father, Robert, like many fishermen of that generation, was a firm traditionalist, and when it came to ring-nets his idea was that a net had 60-yard wings, 60-yard shoulders and a 60-yard bag and nothing should change.

Down at the Cruban, where the Carradale fleet frequently operated in summer, Archie saw Ayrshire crews getting perhaps 250 baskets of herring a haul, while Archie was getting only 50. 'Ye blamed yersel,' Archie said, 'but it wisna us at all – it wis the gear, and at last A couldna stand it any longer.' He watched 'Bunty' McCrindle of Maidens working one night with the *Silver Fern* and *Silver Lining* and approached him later with the question: 'What kinna net hae ye got, because we're naw catchin herrin.' – 'Just go tae the factory – they'll give ye the plan,' Bunty told him. 'He never kept a bit from us,' Archie said.

So, without discussing his intention with his father, Archie went to the net-factory in Campbeltown and ordered a net identical to Bunty's, which was designed with longer and wider-meshed wings – at 85 yards and 14 rows of meshes to the yard – and narrow netting that was lighter in the twine and even narrower in the mesh – at 42 rows-to-the-yard – to eliminate the meshings of herring that put the net out of shape and reduced its effectiveness. It was, in Archie's estimation, 'a sweeter net every way', but when he returned home with the plan his father was not at all pleased. 'Ye'll never get a damnt herrin wi that net – they'll all be through these wide wings before ye get them!' was the older man's verdict. Archie, however, was vindicated in the end, because that net marked a turning point in the *Harvest Queen*'s fortunes: 'We started then catchin herrin.' The next net Archie ordered was made to his own spec-ifications and was much deeper. [Archie Paterson, 2000]

The Kyles and Loch Striven

The Kyles of Bute are the narrow sounds that separate the north end of the island of Bute, and Cowal on mainland Argyll; Loch Striven penetrates northwards at the eastern end. These were dark stretches of water, narrow and oppressed on either side by hills. The fishermen operated there periodically, when herring were to be found. John McWhirter's stories, below, all refer to c. 1906.

A leisurely fishing

The Kyles were 'filled fuul o herrin' during the first fishing that John McWhirter remembered there, but it was a leisurely fishing. The fishermen would get under way in the morning after breakfast, sailing or rowing from bay to bay. Here and there they'd see other crews ringing and would hang on in case called alongside to assist, then they too would get a boatload. He saw the fishing over at three or four o' clock in the afternoon, the herring-steamers loaded. Some crews that failed to sell to a steamer would have to run to Rothesay.

There were five or six steamers there, and after they had left for Fairlie there was nothing to do but return to an anchor. A crew might occasionally miss out on a fishing if they tore the net, but there was never a day but 'ye'd hear a man roarin for assistance'. In the Kyles, 'the water's near as deep intae the shore as it is in the middle', and there were places the steamers could put their sides alongside the rock and remain afloat.

'Ye tipped wi the oars an wee breezes wi the sail intae every bay, havin a look, an it wis packed wi boats.' Herring could be located by 'putting up' (p 15). It was a sheltered fishing ground; there would have to be 'a good breeze o win afore ye'd feel it'. On calm nights, the sound of the herring playing 'wid deifen ye ... an ye never touched them tae the next deh'.

The crews were supplied with provisions by small boats from Tighnabruaich and Kames. They'd come alongside with bread and butter, mainly, from the shops, and the fishermen could order loaves for the next day and try to be back there to collect them.

The McKays, with whom John McWhirter crewed, would also set drift-nets between the Bootack – a point of land – and an adjacent island, made fast at either end to the shore. They'd be left there until morning and would often yield 50 and 60 baskets.

That Kyles fishing lasted for three years and in the fourth year the herring were through in Loch Striven. That fishery too lasted about three years. They'd try to be first out on a Monday to get up to the head of the loch quickly, because there would be herring in the shallows there; but after Monday, there would be no more herring there until the following Monday. Thereafter, 'ye wir here an there through the loch'. During the week-end, when there were no boats working and the loch was quiet, the shoals would find their way back to the head of the loch. [John McWhirter, 1974, 1975]

Where the Ayrshiremen made their money

There was a big fishery in the Kyles long before Donald McIntosh started
the fishing, but it died away and there were only small herring there.
During the First World War, however, the Dunuremen 'made most o
thir money' there, fishing small herring. 'That's hoot the Ayrshirmen
made thir money on. That's hoot started the Ayrshir fleet. We cou'na
be bothered killin them, the herrin wis that wee. They wir gettin a pound
a basket for them. It wis for freshin an that, because there wir nothin else
in't.' [Donald McIntosh, 1974]

Herring in bags

'Jeely Jock' McCrindle was the only man Davie MacFarlane ever saw
with a deck cargo of bagged herring. This was in Loch Striven and the
Klondykers were there, but all pretty well filled. He had a 'dose o bags
aboard' and when his boat wouldn't take any more herring in the hold,
he had his crew fill 20 or 30 bags on the deck. [David MacFarlane, 1975]

Turner McCrindle recalled the occasion. The McCrindles went into
Loch Striven on their first night with the 'wee' *Margarita* BA 117 (built
1927). At the head of the loch both she and her neighbour-boat were
filled to the hatches. As the catch settled in the hold, the stacked bags
were emptied, one after another, into the hold, thus topping up its
contents. They went into Rothesay, expecting a Klondyker to arrive
there that day, but she was two days late, by which time the herring were
'a little bit gone'. [Turner McCrindle, 1976]

Drift-nets a nuisance

When the East Coast drift-netters came through to work in Loch Striven
after the First World War, they were 'an awful nuisance'. The two sets
of fishermen just couldn't work together, and the ringers needed a light
forward all the time to look for drift-net buoys. Having shot a ring-net,
a drift-net buoy might then rise in the middle of the net. Some ringers
would stab the buoys so that the gear would sink away, but Donald
McIntosh wouldn't allow that and never saw it done, though he saw the
ripped buoys. If he ran foul of a drift-net, he generally hauled the buoy
aboard, cut it off and hung it on the boat's forestay, whence it would be
removed in port by its owner. [Donald McIntosh, 1974, 1975]

Davie MacFarlane's skipper – probably Sandy 'Fadje' MacFarlane, a
cousin – likewise 'winna allow a bow tae be stabbed'. If they had a netful

of herring and the tide was carrying them down on a drift-net, they'd be frightened one of the buoys would tear the bag of the net. 'Catch it; cut it; cut the lanyard an keep the bow,' his skipper would insist. 'That'll go doon, no do any herm, an we'll hing the man's bow on the riggin in Rossa (Rothesay) an the man'll come along an claim it.' And that's invariably what would happen. The owner would recognise his own buoy and he had only a new lanyard to attach to it. [David MacFarlane, 1975]

An apparition

The Campbeltown fleet was at anchor in the Kyles one dark night. Aboard one of the boats, an old fellow rose from his bunk to empty his bowels. As was customary, he hung over the stern, holding on to a rope, to do the business. One of his shipmates, having been disturbed, also rose, and had just stepped sleepily on to the deck when, to his terror, the old fellow, clad only in white combinations, hauled himself up on the rope, appearing to rise like an apparition out of the sea. [Angus Martin, author's father, 1974]

Ballantrae Banks
●●●●●●●●●●●●●●●●●●●●●●●

The Ayrshire coast was for centuries the centre of a winter herring-fishery which was prosecuted on the spawning grounds of the Ballantrae Banks. The Kintyre fishermen, like the native fishermen, initially used set nets – commonly and erroneously called 'trammels' – on the Banks. These were drift-nets, cut in strips three fathoms (5.49 m) deep and anchored overnight with stones. Many fishermen, however, had misgivings about the destruction of spawning herring, and of the spawn itself, which occurred on the Banks. In 1887, ring-nets were introduced there by the Argyll fishermen, despite local opposition.

Lodging ashore

The Tarbert skiff-fishermen always left for the Ballantrae Banks on 20 February, sometimes arriving before the herring and sometimes after. When 10 March would come, the fishermen would be making for home. The open-boat fishermen of the earlier generation would take *kists* of stores with them – butter, sugar, cheese, hard biscuits – and lodge ashore in Girvan. The landlady 'got the workin o all the stores while they wir there'. These were supplemented by loaves and fish. [Hugh MacFarlane, 1974]

A second trip

John McWhirter only once in his life had two trips to the Ballantrae Banks in the same season. He was crewing with Archie McKay in the *Noel*, and returned to Campbeltown on 25 or 26 March, by which time there was 'nawthing tae be seen'; but word came that there were herring on the Banks again. The *Noel*'s neighbour, the *Annunciata*, was by then laid up having a strake added, so the McKays got the *Twin Brothers* on loan and went back across. They had two nights' fishing before the weather worsened and they were confined to harbour for four or five days. When Monday came, the weather was fine and they decided to 'go away doon an see if there wir anythin left'. They weren't long out till the herring were 'playin in aal directions', but the fish were spent and there was no market for them. Nevertheless, they decided to take some aboard and, while so engaged, a Dunure Nabby appeared. The Campbeltown crews told her crew to get a grip of the net if they wanted herring. The Dunure skipper took his boat in stern-first. She was square-sterned and his heel or rudder caught the net and burst it before he had removed 20 or 30 baskets. He left and went for Girvan and the Campbeltown boats returned home, with 12 or 13 baskets aboard. Pat McKay was 'boy' on the other boat and he and John were told that they could sell the herring themselves. They got 2s per basket and kept the proceeds. [John McWhirter, 1976]

Trammels

Davie MacFarlane fished with a cousin, Sandy 'Fadjie' McFarlane, who was 'married on a Girvan woman' and was fond of going there in the wintertime. They worked at trammels – three fleets of nets, seven 'pieces' to a fleet – which could be bought cheaply and, if barked at all, were barked only once, to tighten the knots. They were 'practically white' and 'fished better' than barked nets. When the fishery was ended, these nets were never mended, as a rule, but cut from the ropes and replaced with new netting next season. Davie MacFarlane would spend up to 14 weeks at Girvan, 'sleepin jeest on the bare boards … no mattresses an mats an all the gear they have now'. [David MacFarlane, 1975]

Inconsiderate

'Fishermen,' Davie MacFarlane remarked, 'are inclined tae be very inconsiderate o wan another.' He had occasion to 'check' a Girvan man who was fishing with them on the Ballantrae Banks. They were lifting their 'spannie-nets', or trammels, and there was another fisherman's net foul of theirs. 'Now,' Davie said, 'the rule is, ye cut yer own furst an then, if he's still over ye later on, ye cut him.' The Girvan man, however, wasn't in favour of that and got a grip of the other man's nets to cut them. 'Now, stop you that,' Davie ordered. 'That man's got tae live the same as you an me. Don't destroy anybody's gear.' [David MacFarlane, 1974]

At drift-nets

One night, Turner McCrindle's father John and his Uncle James were lying at drift-nets on the Banks 'and all at once a spot o herrin rose an played at the head o thir boat'. They lit a torch and waved it, and the ring-net boats, which had been ranging over the Banks, came in and got a big fishing on that spot. Herring on the Banks are apt to congregate on certain areas of ground, Turner said, and he once saw a 'three-mile whiteness' in the sea, which he attributed to the reflection of spawn on the bottom. [Turner McCrindle, 1976]

Sharing

When a trammel-fisherman saw the ringers coming and getting 'big rings', he wouldn't bother hauling his trammels but would go alongside a ringer and 'ten chances tae wan, he'd get the fill o his boat'. [John McWhirter, 1975]

Mungo Munro's father told him that the Tarbert ring-net fishermen were getting so many herring one night that they couldn't take them all aboard and shouted Ayrshire drift-netters alongside. A crowd of Ayrshire boats got round a particular net, but the Tarbert skipper was in a hurry to get away to market and he shoved a sweep (oar) down through the sling and burst it, letting all the herring go free. Another Tarbertman, by the name of Johnson, who was already loaded with herring, shouted to the disappointed Ayrshiremen: 'Never mind, boys – come on an A'll get ye a puckle!' He shot and the Ayrshire boats that were waiting were filled. At that time, they didn't have ring-nets. [Mungo Munro, 1976]

De Wet

Christian de Wet was a noted General in the Second Boer War (1899-1902), during which period the following incident occurred.

John Weir Sr got his nick-name, 'de Wet', one year on the Ballantrae Banks when a restriction on ring-netting was in force there and some Ballantrae fishermen put to sea to ascertain the Tarbert skiff's registration number, in order to report the breach to the authorities. John Weir took the big jib and spread it around the bow to conceal the number, and, brandishing the boathook, so intimidated the local fishermen that 'they wouldn't come near him'. An elderly crewman, Duncan 'Moora' McAlpine, remarked to John: 'Ye're a pure de Wet!' [John Weir, 1976]

Black lumps and gannets

About the time Andy McCrindle first went to sea, in the *Golden Sheaf*, c. 1941, the Ballantrae Banks were reopened to ring-netting after a brief closure. He was with his uncle, 'Wee Tam' McCrindle, neighbouring Dick Andrew in the *Maireared*. 'We went doon on tae Ballantrae Banks in the efternoon an ye never saw anythin like it wi herrin jeest rollin aboot in black lumps an the gannets gan doon in thir thousands.' The *Golden Sheaf* shot first and netted one herring! Then the *Maireared* had a go and caught two or three. A third ring, by the *Golden Sheaf*, filled both boats. The crews hadn't much sleep that week between 'herrin an torn nets'. Still, they were usually in Girvan 'in time for the second hoose o the pictures most nights; we had enough herrin tae dae us'. That winter culminated in big fishings on the Banks and many English buyers arrived in Girvan to bid on the spawny herring. [Andy McCrindle, 2001]

Ireland
· · · · · · · · · ·

The Donegal fishery, on the north-west of Ireland, first attracted the attention of Clyde fishermen in the latter half of the 18th century and was opened up to ring-netting in 1904, a pioneering venture popularly credited to Hugh McLean of the skiffs Good Hope *and* Good Will. *The fishery continued to attract ring-netters – principally from Campbeltown – periodically, and with mixed success, until the late 1920s.*

Drift-netting

Archibald 'Baldy' Stewart was cook on the *Good Hope* as a boy and was at the drift-nets in her. Her owner, Hughie McLean, fished as far south as Killybegs in the summer of 1902 or 1903; he'd been going to the drift-nets at Donegal for years before. 'Baldy' first went to the ring-net there in the *Elsie*, built at Robert Wylie's boatyard in Campbeltown and belonging to Donald 'Denny' McLellan. They were working further north, at Kincasslagh. Robert Robertson – the 'Hoodie' – was also there that year with the *Brothers*. [Archibald Stewart, 1974]

There and back

John McWhirter recalled a trip to Burtonport with the McKays. They left Campbeltown in a thunder and lightning storm. The wind came from the north-east and the first landmark they got was Portrush, on the north coast of Ireland. None of them had been in there before and they got 'a devil o a fright', because the Atlantic was piling straight into the harbour and they could see nothing but white foam until they got in a bit and found 'a corner tae turn intae'. The steamer that ran between Ardrossan and Portrush, the *Hazel*, was lying there and when the fishermen saw the size of her mooring-ropes they decided it was 'a tight place'. Anyway, they lay a day there and when the weather 'came fine' on the Sunday, got away through the Sound of Innistrahull, sailed by Innisboffin and then into Burtonport. 'Oh, man, we did it in a day an a half. That wis great!'

It was a 'terrible bad winter' that year. There had been eight pairs of Campbeltown ringers down. Five pairs went home. The remaining three pairs lay in Burtonport until a good day came. They had a 'nice run' to Portrush and spent a night there, but soon after they left the next morning, a gale came away and they had to take in every reef on the sail and run south from Rathlin Island along the coast until they reached Cushendun. They spent almost a week moored there. The wind was southerly and on the Sunday blew a whole gale. The fishermen saw two vessels in trouble offshore. One of them lost her sails and was blown all the way to Carradale Bay. The other was driven ashore on MacRingan's Point, at the mouth of Campbeltown Loch. Several days after the gale, the skiffs got a suitable day and ran home with a fair breeze. It was the last day of February when they made Campbeltown Loch at break of day, and off the Maidens' Planting the McGeachies and Brodies were taking herring aboard. [John McWhirter, 1974]

Natives appeased

Initially, the native fishermen were alarmed by the visiting ring-netters. 'They thought we wir gonny take away the whole bay o herrin when they seen us catchin the herrin. An they wir gonny chase us oot, till we filled thir boats, an then they wid've gied us Heaven if they had it tae give.' [John McWhirter, 1974]

Losing a net to herring

When the McKays first went to Donegal, the sea was red with massed herring. Seeing the abundance, the McKays 'went two pair' with old Archie Cook's boats. The first shot Cook had, the herring 'waalked aweh wi the whole net', and big Dunky Lang lamented bitterly: 'Ye come aal the wey fae Campbelton tae Donegal tae see that!' [John McWhirter, 1975]

Donkeys

The Campbeltown fishermen spent Christmas and New Year on an island with ten donkeys on it, five old ones and five young ones. The men passed many a day riding on the small donkeys, but had no success with the warier elders. 'As soon as ye'd get on, they'd give a heave an off ye went.' The animals appeared to be wild and unattended, their hooves turned up with lack of dressing. [John McWhirter, 1974]

The Black Hole

Where the boats lay was known as the Black Hole, and the three herring-steamers that attended the fishery – the *Talisman*, *Louise* and *Nightingale* – were also able to moor alongside the rock-face, there being no quay of any description there. The fishermen passed time by fishing *cuddins* – small saithe – with bent pins. The native fish were strong-flavoured 'ocean herring' and so large that they'd be halved before cooking and only the tail portion eaten. On Saturdays, the fishermen would go up to Burtonport and purchase a chunk of mutton – unweighed – from a spring-cart, and that, at a cost of only 2s 6d or 3s, would feed a crew for two or three days. Beef was unobtainable. [John McWhirter, 1974]

Atlantic swells

That first trip, the boats managed out only thrice. The crews would walk to the crown of a hill to watch the tremendous breakers running into the bay. There was an offshore island, Aran Mor, which natives had warned the fishermen against rounding. The McKay pair and Duncan O'Hara's pair, working in a foursome, ignored that advice and, almost fully-loaded with herring, 'risked it round'.

'We got a nice wee breeze the whole wey, but, oh, ye'd rise on wan swell, aweh up, an ye seen yer neebor aweh doon God knows how far. Ye riz a wile height on the sea, an that wid run in an hit the island, the rocks on the island, an the spray wid be flyin. So that did us. We never ventured it agane. Neether did anybody else ... When we went up tae Burtonport [and] the natives heard we come roon Aran Mor, they gied us a wile doin. The very priest gied us a doin for venturin on such a thing wi boats loaded wi herrin. He says: "Of course, ye're not natives – ye don't know the thing."' [John McWhirter, 1974, 1975]

A rescue at Sheephaven

The *Polly Cook* and *Enterprise* were returning home from Donegal for New Year, c. 1905, when a gale came away. They got into Sheephaven Bay and let go their anchors on a sandy bottom to windward of a reef; and 'a good job too', as Bob Morans remarked, because the anchors held. He remembered passing sand-filled ballast-bags on to the deck. These were 'slipped down the chains tae get the weight off the anchors'. Alec Cook on the *Enterprise* – a son of Willie Cook – somehow produced a maroon, which he 'sent up'. His distress signal was answered from the shore by the Coastguards at Dunfannaghie, and a lifeboat – her oars double-manned – came out and took the crews ashore, the men suffering a 'terrible waashin' on the way in. The skiffs were later taken into Port na Blan and moored there 'tae swing it out till the weather got better'. The two crews caught a train to Derry and travelled from there to Greenock by steamer, thence by sea to Campbeltown. It was summer before they returned to fetch the boats. They fished the Sound of Tory, their catches fetching £5 a cran. It was 'some money then ... We got a couple o *touches* an then we came home. Well, that wis my furst experience at the fishin. That's a good while ago'. [Robert Morans, 1974]

A warning

The Blairs frequented Sheephaven, in Downings Bay, where 'the natives wis very bitter against the ring-net'. They were lying in harbour one night when some Scottish coopers, who were based there, came to the boats with word of possible trouble: 'For God's seck, men, clear out. They wouldn't think twice on rollin a barrel o salt on to yer forecastle.' The Blairs heeded the warning and shifted to Ards River. [Dugald Blair, 1974]

'That man sure can mow'

Davie MacFarlane was never himself at Donegal, but a brother, Geordie, who crewed with the Jacksons, went one year when two or three Tarbert pairs tried the fishery. They were based at Kincasslagh, but there was, according to Davie, a local 'law' confining the fishery to 'a certain radius' within which the herring had to come before they could be fished. The herring never did come in, and the fishermen had nothing to do but 'wander aboot the crofts there', finally returning home with only 'a dose o royal ferns' to show for their sojourn. 'That wis what they got oot o Ireland.'

While thus idling ashore, Geordie MacFarlane and Angus Law chanced upon a man, sitting smoking as he rested from hay-cutting. The MacFarlanes had a croft at Tarbert and Geordie was a 'dab hand' with a scythe. 'Gie us a shot o yer scythe,' he said. When he started cutting, the Irishman turned to Angus Law and remarked: 'By Jaysus, that man sure can mow.' He'd refill his clay-pipe and repeat, in admiration: 'By Jaysus, he can mow, that fella.' As Davie remarked: 'That wis suitin the Irishman fine!' [David MacFarlane, 1975]

Dunmore East

Dunmore East, on the south coast of Ireland, was the base of a ring-net fishery for several years in succession. Campbeltown fishermen first went there in 1956 to skipper and crew locally-owned boats, and three pairs of Ayrshire ringers – Silver Fern *and* Elizmor, Arctic Moon *and* Arctic Star, *and* Silver Lining *and* Integrity *– were able to fish there by the expedient of the boats' being re-registered in Dublin.*

Andy McCrindle of the *Silver Fern* – which became D 148 – explained that the business was merely a 'paper transaction'. 'We nominally sold fifty-one per cent tae the fish-salesman doon there, H J Nolan,' he said. Thus legitimised to engage in the fishery, they set off south in October of 1959 and remained at Dunmore East until February of the following year.

In their first week, the *Silver Fern, Elizmor, Arctic Moon* and *Arctic Star* – all of Maidens and formed into a foursome – 'got held up with bad weather'. Andy then had to return home to attend to business connected with the transfer of the boat's registration. He was home only a day when his younger brother Robert telephoned him with the message: 'Ye'll huv tae get Andy Marr the engineer tae come an huv a look at this engine.' – 'Whit's wrong?' Andy enquired uneasily. 'Nothin,' his brother replied, 'we're in wi the foo o the four boats!' That success was repeated three times that week. The *Silver Lining* and Wattie Shields's *Integrity* of Girvan joined the fishery later.

The herring were being found just half-an-hour from Dunmore East, in a bay named Baginbun, east of the Hook. The boats were always left for the week-end up-river in Waterford, because Dunmore East wasn't a safe harbour if the wind backed southerly or south-easterly. A 'steam' of an hour-and-a-half took the boats to Waterford, where they were moored alongside pontoons.

Relations with the Dunmore East and Wexford fishermen were excellent – the ringers had 'absolutely nae bother' with them – but 'the crowd from Passage East' – mid-way up the river – were 'very much against the Clyde men'. They themselves fished herring with ring-nets and also salmon with drift-nets.

Andy recalled these two years as 'The best A ever had at the fishin', and with the proceeds of his first winter there he was able to buy his first car, a Wolseley 1500. The following year, however, a big fleet of foreign trawlers – Spaniards and Russians among them – appeared on the fishing grounds. 'They jeest cleaned it oot, absolutely cleaned it oot. We went away home for a week-end. We come back on the Monday. There wirnae a herrin tae be seen. The place wis jeest barren.' [Andy McCrindle, 2001]

First contingent

Jake Wareham was with the first contingent of Campbeltown fishermen that went to Dunmore East, in 1956, to crew the *Kittiwake* and *Kestrel*, which had been bought into Ireland and re-registered*. These boats were skippered by 'Baldy' Stewart and Jock Wareham respectively, and the other Campbeltonians, aside from the skippers and Jake himself, were James 'Fog' Robertson, Duncan Black and Walter Brown. The crews were completed by three local fishermen in each boat. Jake, indeed, met his future wife, Peggy Lane, in Dunmore East that year, and they married in Campbeltown in 1958. Peggy, who belonged to Cork, was a children's nurse with a wealthy family on holiday in Dunmore East. Coincidentally, the family yacht, which was based there, was named the *Kittiwake* – also the name of the boat on which Jake was crewing! Jake returned to Dunmore East in 1959, as part of an increased contingent of Campbeltown fishermen. [John and Peggy Wareham, 2002]

The Kestrel *was sold to Ireland on 25 August, 1955, and the* Kittiwake *on 28 February, 1956.*

East Coast
•••••••••••••

The first venture through the Forth-Clyde Canal, to the herring fishing grounds of the Firth of Forth, was in 1929, and in the following year no fewer than 72 Clyde ring-netters were at work there. As happened on every other fishing ground to which the ring-net was introduced, the method was bitterly opposed by native drift-net fishermen. In the immediate post-war period, the centre of the ring-netters' operations on the East Coast shifted to Whitby on the Yorkshire coast.

'In wir own country'

Charlie McKinven, later harbourmaster at Campbeltown, was fishing in the Firth of Forth when a 'hell of a row' broke out one day between the Clyde ring-net and the Forth drift-net fishermen. Charlie was something of a diplomat and was prepared to go among the opposition and argue the case for ring-netting. While this debate was going on, old Jamie 'Mirlinns' Durnin, who was in the forecastle of one of the ringers, heard the noise and opened the scuttle. 'Wait tae we get ye's in wir own country!' he was shouting. 'Where's that?' somebody shouted back. 'Scotland,' Jamie replied. 'Wait tae we get ye in Scotland.'* Charlie shouted to him: 'Be quiet, Mr Durnin, and get below.' [John McIntyre, 1974]

* *Since Davie MacFarlane on p 112 – ' … if ever A'll get back tae Scotland again' – also referred, in Fife, to his native West Coast as 'Scotland', some attempt at explanation is required. Bob Smith (letter, 12 Jan 2002) wonders if Jamie Durnin knew the saying, 'Farewell Scotland, I'm headin for Fife', and points out that Fife is known as 'The Kingdom'. It is impossible to know now.*

Guns at the ready

One night, in the Forth, in the winter of 1930, the *Nulli Secundus* and *Nil Desperandum* had a good ring of herring – about 100 cran – dried up and were about to take the catch aboard when an East Coast steam-drifter came towards them making to pass between the boats and split the net. Archie 'Scone' Black had a twelve-bore shotgun and Eddie McKay had a point two-two, and the two of them were standing on deck with the guns loaded as the drifter bore down on them. 'Scone' let go with the first barrel, and as soon as the drifter's crew heard the shot, the boat wheeled away. [John McIntyre, 1974]

St Monans

Donald McIntosh of Carradale went to the Firth of Forth before Christmas of 1929, when the Clyde fishery was very slack. They operated first near Granton, then shifted to St Monans and Anstruther. The St Monans drifters he described as 'natural bad'. They didn't want to see the ring-net boats there at all. 'They wid come up an they wid go right through yer net, steam right through. Or maybe yer two boats wir tied together, takin the herrin aboard. They'd come up in between the two boats. Aye, they wir wile an bad. An the worst o it wis, they wir all preachers. But the men in Pittenweem wir different altogether. Pittenweem wis the only harbour we'd go intae.' [Donald McIntosh, 1974]

Anywhere the 'Hoodie' (Robert Robertson) went, he made a point of going among the local fishermen to test their attitude to ring-netting. The worst place the Campbeltown ringers went was the East Coast. They were put out of St Monans harbour and denied water and bread. The harbourmaster there 'stood up' for them and was abused by the local drift-net fishermen as a consequence. In the end, the ring-netters made their headquarters in Newhaven, where a fleet of local ring-netters operated. [John McIntyre, 1974]

The only opposition that Robert McGown ever experienced as a ring-net fisherman was in St Monans. He was 'turned out the harbour'. His pair had been up the Firth, fishing around the Bridge, and had several crans of herring, but there was nothing doing after that. The St Monans and Pittenweem drifters came to Loch Striven to fish at that time and 'they spoke so much aboot this winter herring that came in along there, we took a turn down to see if there wir anything doin that night, but there wis nothing, so we went into St Monans in the mornin'. He was acquaint with the port, having been there in 1927, when his *Faustina* was being built by Walter Reekie. She was the first ring-net boat that Reekie built for the West Coast and Robert had advised him on the deck lay-out, etc.

When the McGowns went into St Monans, the local fishermen 'got up in arms'. They warned the fish-salesman that if he sold the McGowns' herring he would never sell another herring for them, and the boat-builder – who also supplied oil – was warned that if he fuelled the ringers, his place would be burnt down. It was, Robert said, 'the only place ever A wis turned out in me life'. They were welcomed in Pittenweem and fished from there all that winter of 1930. [Robert McGown, 1974]

Documented corroboration of oral history is seldom possible, but in the case of the above story, a report from the East Fife Observer *of 13 February, 1930, provides just such corroboration:*

' ... *On Monday morning ... two ring-net boats, the* Faustina *(Skipper John McGowan) and the* Mary Campbell *(Skipper Peter McGowan) arrived at St Monance. The* Faustina *had eight crans of herrings, but when they attempted to get them sold they were told that the local salesmen would not handle ring-netted herring.*

'The local fishermen gathered in force at the harbour when they heard of the arrival of the West Coast boats.

'While there was no demonstration of open hostility, it was made clear to the crews of the Faustina *and* Mary Campbell *that their presence in St Monance was not desirable. They were asked to leave the port, but they had not enough oil to put out into the firth.*

'Fresh supplies of paraffin were accordingly sent for, but when the lorry arrived to supply the paraffin the oil merchant was told that if he supplied any paraffin to the ring-net fishermen he would get no more local trade. Accordingly with what little paraffin they had aboard, the two vessels left St Monance and made for Pittenweem. There they were courteously received, and their herrings sold at 70s per cran.'

Jim Tarvit, Anstruther (letter, 15 November, 2001) remarks further: 'By 1932/33, ring-netters were allowed to use Anstruther harbour, although some skippers were still against ring-netting. However, by 1935/36 a number of Cellardyke* fishermen were crewing Girvan and Dunure boats and continued to do so until 1945/46. Indeed, during the War at least 30-40 Cellardyke men were on board Ayrshire ringers such as the May II, Alipeds, Avail. *The main reason for this was financial (1935-39) and the lack of boats here during the War (only three boats from Anstruther were not on Admiralty service) along* *with the lack of crewmen in Ayrshire. A lot of lasting friendships were made as a result of this intermingling.'*

There were also men from Eyemouth, St Monans and Buckie who crewed on Ayrshire boats during the War, and in the early 1920s at least three Buckie families – MacKenzies, Forbes and Coulls – settled in Girvan and produced ring-net skippers and boat-owners. Such, indeed, was the high esteem in which the East Coast men were held in the Ayrshire ring-net communities, that one native Girvan skipper was reputed to have boasted: 'Give me a new boat and a crew of East Coast men and I'll run Tommy Sloan off the sea.' He got his new boat, if not his East Coast crew, but he certainly didn't dent Tommy Sloan's reputation. (Jim Tarvit, letter, 27 Nov 2001)

*The generality of Anstruther fishermen either originated in or lived in Cellardyke.

An angry woman

The crew of the *Blossom* had a badly-torn net and went into Anstruther to mend it. They couldn't find any unoccupied ground that was convenient, and ended up taking the net to a park, distant among villas. They were passing the net over the park railings when two women came out from one of the houses. The older woman was visibly upset. 'An awfu net that,' she would say. 'Awfu work. A dinna ken when ye'll mend that net.' – 'Ach,' the Tarbertmen reassured her, as they continued passing the net over the railings, 'we'll mend it.' Then the younger woman said: 'It's an awfu lang net.' – 'Aye,' one of the Tarbertmen replied, 'she's a lang net.' – 'Is that a ring-net?' the young one queried. Without thinking, Davie MacFarlane said: 'Aye.'

Then she started. 'Awa hame tae the West. Ye're takin the bite oot the bairnie's mooth.' She gave Davie the 'greatest muckin-oot ever'. At last the old woman interceded: 'Ach, dinna tak any heed o her. She doesna belang here. She belangs tae Johnshaven*. She's mairried on my son an he's skipper o the *Plough*.' [Robert Meldrum] Gardner was his name, and he passed and went into the house and didn't bother with the Tarbertmen. Davie, at last, got 'crabbit' with the young woman and said to her: 'Look here, ma good woman, we're here nine weeks an A never put salt on ma kail, an if ever A'll get back tae Scotland again, A don't give a damn if the May Island'll flott in an block Anstruther harbour.'

That finished her. 'Aye,' Davie remarked, 'they wir against it. Of course, likely they had reason, ye see. The [ringers wid] be stabbin men's bows. It wis the big drifter wis the worst o the lot – he wid try tae run some o oor boats doon.' Thereafter, Davie watched how Gardner fished at Yarmouth and he proved to be a good fisherman. The crew stayed in the park all day, mending, and when they went back to the boat for dinner, Davie remained. He was lame in one leg and the harbour was too far for him from there. 'A'll stick it tae night,' he said. 'An not a damn sowl gied me a cup o tea up among them villas. A wid've got a cup o tea from a Turk, never mind from Scotch people.' [David MacFarlane, 1975]

*Portgordon, in fact.

A long stint

Jimmy McCreath of Girvan went through to the Firth of Forth on 9 January one year and remained there – 'on the boat aa the time' – until 21 April, though his wife twice travelled to Edinburgh to see him. He found travelling home by train at week-ends too exhausting, explaining: 'Mibbe ye wir workin all week an gettin very little sleep, if any. So we used tae make wir sleep the week-end, jist.' [James McCreath, 1976]

A 'daft notion'

The last Ayrshire ringers to use the Forth-Clyde Canal were probably the *Silver Fern* and *Arctic Moon* of Maidens in the mid-1950s. Their skippers, Andy McCrindle and Matt 'Gush' Sloan, took a 'daft notion' to try the East Coast and ended up in St Andrews Bay, where North East drifters were prosecuting abundant small herring.

'They wir mixed wi sprats an we had herring bags in,' Andy McCrindle recounted, 'an we dried up a big ring o this sma stuff off St Andrews an before ye could say Jack Robinson, there wir aboot fifty cran left in the net. They aw went oot through the sling, they wir that sma. We wir left wi the wee herrin that widnae go through the mesh. We landed them in Anstruther.'

They remained scarcely a fortnight there, and, on the first week-end, Andy returned home by train to spend his wedding anniversary – 27 March – with his wife, Marjory. He was accompanied by Matt Sloan's brother 'Harbie' (Thomas Harbison) Sloan, and the two men had Saturday night in Maidens, then back through to Anstruther on the Sunday.

While the boats were returning home through the canal, on one of the 'long stretches' the water was inexplicably drained and the crews were delayed until the waterway could be refilled. 'We wir left wi wir

rudders aboot twa fit oot the watter – we couldn't go anywhere!'
Furthermore, the boats' propellers were 'ruined' by striking shopping-
trolleys, old bicycles and other rubbish dumped in the canal. [Andy
McCrindle, 2001]

Dutchmen at Hartlepool

Tam Hughes, who belonged to a Pittenweem fishing family which settled
in Rothesay (p 80), fished the Yorkshire coast with drift-nets before the
West Coast ring-netters went there. He was cook on an uncle's Fifie, the
Fortunatus, based at Hartlepool. One week-end, a carnival was held in the
town and the harbour was 'jam-packed full' of big Dutch boats whose
crews had come in to sample the festivities. These boats – which carried
up to 30 men, some of whom fished and some of whom cured the catches
– generally worked about 40 miles offshore.

While Tam was cooking dinner, a Dutch boy of about his own age –
from Scheveningen – came aboard and began chatting to him in good
English. During the course of the conversation, he invited Tam aboard
his boat to look her over; but first Tam had to go ashore and buy stores,
and the Dutch boy accompanied him and helped him carry the laden
herring-basket back to the *Fortunatus*.

The skipper of the Dutch vessel – who was also the boy's father – had
a private cabin aft, but the crew slept in a communal compartment which
Tam described as 'a great big dance-hall of a place'. Around the sides of
the compartment straw was piled and that straw, when scattered on the
platform, was the men's bedding. In the middle of the platform stood a
big tub of cured herring, to which the crew-members could help themselves. Raw herring, however, did not appeal to Tam's taste and he
declined to sample the fish. The Dutch boy afterwards accompanied
Tam ashore to the carnival. Also with them was a local boy whom Tam
had befriended. His name was Arthur Horsley and he worked aboard
an uncle's inshore trawler, the *Trusty*.

One feature of the Dutch fleet which intrigued Tam was the great
numbers of young boys incorporated in their crews – five, six and seven
of them in every crew, their ages ranging from eight to 12 years' old.
They all seemed to have mouth-organs and 'aw ye could hear wis mooth-
organs'. His Dutch friend explained who the boys were and why they
spent their summers with the fishing-fleet, working all the way from
Shetland to Yarmouth until the time came to return to their schooling.
Most were orphans and the rest were 'delinquents', and their experience
in the fishing fleet 'broke them in' for service in the Dutch Navy and

Mercantile Marine.

Tam's Dutch friend wrote to him 'till the Germans invaded Holland, and that wis the last I heard fae him'. [Tam Hughes, 2001]

First Ayrshire ringers at Whitby

In 1945, the *Veronica*, *Margarita* and *Storm Drift* got permits to go to Seahouses to fish. They spent a few weeks there and then moved south to Whitby. Matt Sloan wasn't 'demobbed' until 1 January, 1946, and fished the Yorkshire coast later that year, but the Sloans preferred to land in North Shields and – especially – Bridlington, 'a case o trying yer chance tae get an extra bob or two'. They'd put a link-call through to the main fish-merchant in Bridlington 'an the lorries were sittin there on the quay ready'. Catches would be consigned to Hull or Grimsby and sold there. He believed that Sammy Gemmell might have landed herring in Grimsby once in 1945. The McCrindles certainly landed there towards the end of the decade. [Matt Sloan, 2000]

First Campbeltown pair at Whitby

As the *Enterprise* and *Bluebird* were steaming up Kilbrannan Sound, they saw a Carradale pair, the *Irma* and *Amy Harris*, ahead of them and ran close by the *Irma*. 'What did ye get there?' Sandy McKinlay shouted. 'Oh, sixty baskets,' the *Irma*'s skipper, Jamie Campbell, called back. 'Oh, well, we're gan tae Whitby,' Sandy announced. 'Well,' said Jamie, 'it'll be an adventure for ye.'

The two boats got through the Forth-Clyde Canal and were heading down the Firth of Forth when the *Bluebird*'s engine broke down. 'Even the bloody engine's naw waantin tae go!', the engineer Jock Durnin remarked to his brother and skipper, Charlie. Having had the engine repaired at Leith, the pair carried on and reached Seahouses on the Northumberland coast. They tried two or three rings there, but were tearing the nets, so they carried on to Whitby. There were no boats to be seen off the Yorkshire coast, which puzzled the Campbeltown crews, but Alex Black in the *Enterprise* 'came across them in the watter' and the shot yielded 150 cran of herring.

They took the catch into Whitby, only to be told that the port was closed; but they were allowed 60 cran – the quota – and the surplus went into the 'kitty', to be 'stokered through the fleet' at the week-end. That year – 1946 – was a failure. There were too many herring for the market and the boats were only out a couple of nights a week. Duncan

Campbell's divide for six weeks at Whitby was £5. 'The next year,' he said, 'when we went doon – oh my goodness, we cou'na gie them enough herrin.' [Duncan Campbell, 2000]

Sabbath-observance

The Campbeltown crews, when going home for a week-end, would leave Whitby on the Thursday night and return on the Sunday. Week-end fishing was prohibited there and the East Coast men were very strict in their Sabbath-observance; but, as Francis McWhirter recalled, when it came twelve o' clock on the Sunday night, the first boats out the harbour were the 'Easties'. They wouldn't touch their nets until midnight had passed, but, leaving harbour, they'd be hauling the nets aft as quickly as they could. The Campbeltown men would take their nets aft on the Sunday evening, when they arrived. [Francis McWhirter, 1999]

Abundance

In August, 1948, Iain Gemmell had his first trip to Whitby with the *Summer Rose*. The herring were in abundance. On the echo-sounder, 'complete black-outs for mile after mile' were not uncommon, and in the darkness 'there wis nothin but white sheets of herrin tae be seen on the surface'. The fishermen's biggest fear was that they'd ring too many and lose their nets. There was a bell-buoy off Whitby and 'if ye could hear the bell in the harbour, there wis too much wind tae put tae sea'.

Whitby was a thriving holiday resort and the fishermen were 'plagued' with visitors watching them discharging herring and mending gear, and asking to see through the boats; but entertainment was plentiful in the form of pubs, clubs and shows. On one occasion there was a dance that the young cooks were particularly keen to attend, so they formed an alliance and – unusually – attended a meeting called to discuss the lowering of the quota. They moved the suspension of that night's fishery and outvoted the furious skippers – the fleet stayed in port.

Provisioning the boats wasn't a problem, but English bread was 'the worst feature' – the local loaves 'could hardly be eaten'. The cook on an Anstruther drifter solved this problem by giving the 'Co-op' bakers in Whitby a recipe for Scotch bread and demonstrating how it was made.

Iain was four years in succession at Whitby, but the abundance of that first year was never repeated. In the second year, Dutch and Norwegian pair-trawlers arrived on the fishing grounds and 'swept everythin up before them'. Year by year the fishery declined until there was nothing worth going for. [Iain Gemmell, 1999]

Landing at Grimsby

The *Nobles* and the *Glen Carradale* had been fishing well enough around Pladda, but decided to try Whitby. The fishing had been slack there, but, by good fortune, on the night they arrived, as they were steaming down along the coast, they could see the lights of a busy fleet – the fishing had begun.

Early on the Friday night, with the quota per boat merely 20 crans, they rung a netful of herring. 'We're naw gonny let these go – A think we'll go tae Grimsby wi them,' Fred Rennie, on the Carradale boat, announced. 'How the hell will we get tae Grimsby? We haevna a chart,' somebody countered. 'If we follow the coast,' Fred said. 'I wis there aa durin the Waar'.

So they started brailing the catch into the boats 'as hard as they could', and, as they were doing so, a pair of Leith-registered ringers, the *June Rose* and *Rose Valley*, came alongside and cautioned them: 'It's a twenty-cran quota.' Back again they came: 'Ye've got mair as twinty cran in these boats.' – 'We're gan tae Grimsby wi them,' somebody shouted, which prompted an angry outburst from the Fisherrow crews, who'd been waiting to be called in to take their quota from the supposed surplus. The *Nobles* and *Glen Carradale* reached Grimsby, only to find an Ayrshire crew there ahead of them! [David McNaughton, 1999]

That Ayrshire boat was probably the *Investor* BA 58 of Maidens, and Angus McCrindle was aboard her with his brother Willie. He recollected that it was a Saturday morning – in 1948 or '49 – and they were in with about 90 cran. They were rather taken aback, however, to be told by the dock-labourers that if the herring weren't discharged by a certain time that morning – 11 o' clock perhaps – then they 'could keep them'. There was an important football match on that day – a local derby – which the labourers had every intention of attending! As it happened, the catch was discharged in good time. The crew of the *Investor* spent the week-end in Scarborough and met up on Monday with the neighbour-boat, the *Margarita*, which had lain in Whitby over the week-end. [Angus McCrindle, 2000]

A hundred miles off

In 1946, the *Margarita** and *Monsoon* left Tarbert and went to the Isle of Man. There was nothing doing there, so they returned to Tarbert, then went through the Caledonian Canal and finished up in Wick. They landed a shot of herring from Sinclair Bay, but the fishery there was effectively over, so they left Wick for Whitby, breaking their passage south with a night in Montrose. When they left there on the Sunday morning, Malcolm Johnson in the *Margarita* laid out a course for Whitby which was said to have put the pair a hundred miles off the Firth of Forth! This eccentricity, as it was judged by the average fisherman, whose inclination was to hold to the coast, was attributed to Malcolm's possession of a foreign master's ticket!

Robert Ross was already on the Whitby fishing grounds, aboard Angus 'Molly' Johnson's skiff the *Psyche*, and on the Monday morning reported the far-travelled pair's arrival to his shipmates. 'There the *Monsoon* there,' he remarked, seeing her 'black, durty exhaust'. 'The *Monsoon*'s in Wick,' somebody countered. 'She might be in Wick,' Robert insisted, 'but that's her, the *Monsoon*.' Robert's mother opined that 'all she got oot the Whitby fishin wis durty clothes'. [Robert Ross, 2001]

*TT 141, previously Margarita *BA 56. The later* Margarita *was registered BA 325.*

John McConnachie of Carradale also ended up in Whitby via Wick that year. He was a 16-year-old aboard 'Dunks' McDougall's *Lily Oak*, which was neighbouring the *Silver Crest*, skippered by George Ritchie. They fished 90 cran of spawny herring off Lybster, but they were likewise 'too late o goin' and departed for Whitby, stopping off at Peterhead for a night. Both the Carradale and the Tarbert pair, the *Monsoon* and *Margarita*, had put a spare ring-net ashore at Wick. The Tarbert men took the wrong net, which they shot off Whitby in expectation of a big fishing; they instead got 'a wile mashin'. The nets were later exchanged. [John McConnachie, 2001]

Telling tales

While one of the Carradale ring-netters was at Whitby, her young cook was suspected of writing home with scurrilous accounts of the week-end night life enjoyed by her crew. 'A think that buggar's writin home,' someone said, when the crew was assembled in the forecastle. 'He might be tellin tales aboot us.' To settle the matter, the letter was opened and read. Sure enough, it contained the information that two of the crew

were drinking heavily and a third consorting with women. The woman-
iser was unconcerned – 'A'm no carin aboot goin wi weemen – A've got
that name anyway,' he reasoned – but the other two were furious, and
one of them, who was religious, advised the boy: 'A've a good mind tae
kick yer arse! Is that the furst o them bloody letters?' 'Aye,' said the boy,
who was then ordered to write, as his punishment, 150 lines – 'I must
not tell tales on my shipmates' – and display them next to the forecastle
clock. [Jim Campbell and John McConnachie, 2001]

Isle of Man

*Though Kintyre and Loch Fyne drift-net fishermen were operating in Manx
waters before 1852, the ring-net was not taken there until the mid-1930s.
Thereafter, the Isle of Man became a popular summer herring-fishery, not least
on account of the shore attractions, such ports as Peel and Douglas being also
thriving holiday resorts.*

*In the summer of 1932, Betty Fleming, a 20-year-old Scottish student at
Oxford University, visited Peel for a week in a yacht and accompanied the crew
of the* Chrysolite *of Fisherrow to drift-netting. In her memoir of that week, she
writes of ring-netting: 'They can't use this net off the Isle of Man as the Manxmen
(who are extremely old-fashioned themselves and still work with open boats and
dipping lugs) boycott any fish brought to their markets caught by the ring-net.'*

Beginnings

Duncan McSporran first went to the Isle of Man in 1935 with the *Nulli
Secundus* and *Nil Desperandum,* and he thought 'that wis the furst
Campbeltown pair that went doon tae the ring-net there', though
Campbeltown boats had been there drift-netting before his time. They
happened to arrive in 'the week o the moon', and didn't do well, but they
'stuck it' and made an adequate wage by running their herring to
Annalong, Kilkeel and Ardglass in Ireland, wherever they reckoned
they'd get the best market. Latterly, he said, there were fishings all round
the island and the fishermen got on to the spawning banks to the south
and took big fishings from there. 'The big Irish boats came along wi their
mid-water trawl, got big fishins. That feenished it.' He reckoned that
the Isle of Man herring were the 'nearest-tasted' to the Loch Fyne
herring. [Duncan McSporran, 1974]

Neil Short was along on that same trip, crewing on his father's *Nulli Secundus*, which was neighbouring the *Nil Desperandum* (skipper, Willie McIntyre). Additionally, there were four other Campbeltown pairs – the *King Bird* ('Baldy' Stewart) and *King Fisher* (Jock McIntyre); *Kestrel* (Dan 'Cooma' Black) and *Kittiwake* (John Wareham); *Falcon* (Duncan Graham) and *Frigate Bird* (Bob Morans) and *Nobles* (James McKay) and *Silver Grey* (Andrew Brown) – plus the Sloans and McCrindles of Maidens.

There was a 'brash of ringing' among the boats, but the herring were 'light', or small, and the Ayrshiremen and crews of the *Falcon*, *Frigate Bird*, *Nobles* and *Silver Grey* got 'fed up' and cleared out, leaving three pairs, whose crews hoped, despite the fullness of the moon, that the herring would come on to the grounds again with darkening. Happily, a concentration of herring did appear, off Bradda Head, and the crews' patience was rewarded.

It was Neil Short's understanding that the suitability of the Manx grounds for ring-netting was first realised by Girvan crews who were working drift-nets there and saw that when the herring moved closer inshore around Bradda Head and Port Erin – out of the 'motion' that often bedevilled ring-netting in the open Irish Sea – the operation would be more manageable. [Neil Short, 2001]

TT Races

Matt Sloan's first visit to the Isle of Man was in about 1932, but though fishing then, as a boy on the family ringer *Veronica*, he was on the island only to spectate at the famous Manx motorcycle races. He had gone – to the autumn races – with a butcher's son from Kirkoswald, a farmer and the Maidens mechanic and Gardner engine specialist, Andy Marr, who was competing in the races. Matt used to 'hang about' Andy Marr's garage, which was across the road from the Sloan house at that time. Andy travelled not only to the Manx TT (Tourist Trophy) races, but also to the Ulster races, in which he competed one year as a member of the Scottish team. The first time Matt saw him riding was in 'sand races' on the beach at the south side of Ayr harbour.

During his stay in Douglas that year, Matt went through to Peel and saw the *Unitas* of Girvan in harbour there; but her owner, Alec 'Rin Tin Tin' McCrindle, was at drift-netting and Matt reckoned that there were no Ayrshire ring-netters at the Isle of Man until 1933 or '34. The *Unitas* had been bought from one of the Munros in Dunure. She was a traditional Nabby type and the Munros, by their own efforts, had replaced her original raked stern with a rounded one. [Matt Sloan, 2000]

Opening up the Douglas Bank

The *Boy Danny* and *Golden Dawn* are credited with having opened up the Douglas Bank to ring-netting. The story goes that the *Boy Danny*'s skipper, 'Baldy' Stewart, suggested to his neighbour John Conley: 'Ach, come on we'll go roon an spen the week-end in Douglas instead o in Peel wi the boats.' As Duncan Campbell recalls: 'An, God, did they naw see the whale in Douglas Bay, an Baldy an the *Golden Dawn* wis the furst tae get the herrin oot there on the Douglas Bank.' Other boats started to leave the west side of the island, which had until then been the customary fishing ground. [Duncan Campbell, 2000]

Against that, Turner McCrindle of Maidens maintained: 'The Girvan men were at the Isle o Man long before us, but they wir fishing off Port Erin. They never went round tae the Douglas Bank. We went tae Port Erin, too, but we landed on the Douglas Bank wan night, ye see, an started that fishin. As far as A know, we wir the furst boats tae shoot a ring-net on Douglas Bank.' [1976]

Turner's brother, Angus, named the three boats that took that fishing off the Douglas Bank as the *Arctic Moon* (skipper, Matt 'Gush' Sloan), *Elizmor* (Eddie McEwan) and *Margarita* (Jimmy Andrew). The *Investor* (Willie 'Pin' McCrindle) – the fourth boat in the company – had gone to Portpatrick with herring. Angus was crewing on her at the time. 'We had the RTs (radio transmitters) in by that time,' he recalled, '[and] we got the news they wir comin wi a big fishin tae Portpatrick, so there wis nae point in us leavin.' Angus spent his school summer holidays, during the period 1935-37, at the Isle of Man ring-net fishery. In 1938 he left school and went to the fishing. [Angus McCrindle, 2000]

Acres of herring

'A've seen us steamin through acres o herring roon on that Douglas Bank,' Andy McCrindle recalled, 'an ye'd ring on them an ye widnae get a basket oot them, whether they wir fleein. They must've shifted quick when ye shot the net. An other times ye'd shoot an ye'd get too many.' [Andy McCrindle, 2001]

Dogfish and sharks

The big spurdog Squalus acanthias *was a serious nuisance at the Manx fishery, especially on the Douglas Bank.*

If there were herring meshing in a net, the dogfish 'caught the piece an they caught the herrin an they jeest tugged at it an took the piece oot. Ye had always tae knit a wee piece o net in where every hole wis'. The Douglas Bank fishery was a spawning fishery, flourishing in late August and September, but one year the Sloans returned to the Isle of Man in October. Dogfish and bad weather, however, ended that late venture. 'We used tae think,' Matt remarked, 'if we were in the North* at Hallowe'en, we wir fairly early for the winter fishin there.' [Matt Sloan, 2000]

*The Minch

Andy McCrindle recalled that Jimmy Sloan in the *Virginia* had a net ruined by dogs. 'He wis mendin that net for a month after that. They jeest took lumps oot the net. If there wir a herrin mashed in the net, they jeest took the herrin an the bit o net it wis in an aw.' When the deck lights would be switched on, once the soles of the net were aboard, 'ye'd see aa these wee green eyes at the back o the net – this wis them pokin thir heids oot the water.' [Andy McCrindle, 2001]

Angus McCrindle spoke of the packs of sheer-dogs which frequented Douglas Bank. 'Sheer-dog' is Scots for the spurless shark more commonly known as the tope Eugaleus galeus.

'Wi the moon shining on the water,' he recalled, 'ye could see thir eyes sparklin – that's the density they wir. An ye could smell them; ye could actually smell them when ye wir steamin, an whenever ye smelt them ye kent ye wirna far away fae herrin.' Almost every year, at the end of September, when the Douglas Bank fishery ended, and before the McCrindles set off for the Minch herring fishery, they had to put a new set of cotton wings into the ring-net to replace the wings that the sheer-dogs had damaged repeatedly. He often saw the after wing of a ring-net 'half-way up the wheelhoose, wrigglin wi dugs – mair or less yin in every mash – an the wings wir absolutely torn tae pieces'. He knew of French trawlermen going aboard ring-netters in Peel to remove entangled sharks for eating. The Frenchmen would *redd* – or clear – the nets in the process.

This would be when the ringers had run for port in a breeze of wind and before the opportunity arose to clear the nets; perhaps the catch had to be discharged first. [Angus McCrindle, 2000]

James Macdonald referred to these sharks as *buck-dogs* and attested to the damage they caused on the Douglas Bank. They would destroy the nets while herring were being brailed – they 'took lumps out of the bag' – and the fishermen would hit them with *skiddoags* to try to drive them away. Older fishermen spoke of these sharks as having been a nuisance at the herring fishing at Buncrana, Ireland. The fishermen would watch 'red feeding' from the cliffs and fish among it in the afternoon, but as soon as the buck-dogs arrived 'in droves' in the evening, fishing would cease to save the nets from destruction. [James Macdonald, 1998]

An unexpected netful

Andy McCrindle of Maidens first became aware of the fishery in 1936, when, as a boy of 12 years attending Girvan High School, he'd watch, at 'playtime', the Maidens and Girvan boats going away for the Isle of Man on a Monday.

One Monday evening, more than two decades later, his *Silver Fern* got held up in Portpatrick and was late in leaving for the Douglas Bank. His neighbours – the *Silver Lining*, *Seafarer* and *May Queen* – had set off a couple of hours earlier. While Andy was passing Port Erin, he happened to switch on the echo-sounder and the herring were seen to be 'top tae bottom – ye couldnae have fallen doon through them'.

The neighbour-boats were already on the Douglas Bank – Andy was listening to skippers speaking on their radios there, reporting 'nothing doing' – so he put a 'very secretive call' through to his partners and 'hung aboot till they came roon, aboot an oor-an-a-half later'. The four boats were filled, though the herring were 'mixed' and of poorer quality than those from Douglas Bank. The bulk of herring landed, however, was sold for fish-meal and 'Chappies' (pet-food) so quality was hardly a major concern. [Andy McCrindle, 2001]

'Last kick on a Saturday mornin'

One Saturday morning, about three or four o' clock, the whole fleet was preparing to clear out. Andy McCrindle in the *Silver Fern* could hear Matt and Billy Sloan, of the *Watchful* and *Wistaria*, talking on the radio. Billy was 'away ootside', while Matt was inshore, north of Maughold Head.

'Matt wis aye runnin aboot, in an oot this bit, but Billy widnae come near him – he wis for home.'

Andy and his neighbour, Eddie McEwan in the *Elizmor*, ran in towards where Matt was searching and they came on a spot of herring. 'Last kick on a Saturday mornin, we got two hunner an fifty cran in a ring an away doon tae Peel. We got them aw oot for curing,' Andy recalled. It was well on in the afternoon before the catch was discharged and, the tide suiting for the Isle of Whithorn, the boats were moored there and the crews piled into a hired bus to take them home for the week-end.

'Of coorse, wi it bein a Saturday night, the boys had tae stop off in Newton Stewart for a pint, because the pubs wid be shut bi the time they got home. Eleven o' clock at night we got back tae the Maidens. It wis worth it, [but] we wirnae usually as lucky as that!' [Andy McCrindle, 2001]

'Nae blissed potatoes'

Malcolm 'Googie' McGougan had no liking for Isle of Man week-ends, because the general custom was that, after discharging the catch in Pccl and putting aboard stores for the following week, the crews would make do with a quick 'fry' – gigot chops or the like – the sooner to catch a bus to Douglas, where such star entertainers as Joe Loss and Ivy Benson appeared in the dance-halls. At that time, Malcolm was crewing on the *Boy Danny* and his regular complaint would be: 'Nae blissed potatoes on a blissed Seterday – every blissed Seterday's the same.' As Duncan Campbell commented: 'A dinner wis nae use tae him withoot potatoes!' [Duncan Campbell, 2000]

A nightmare

The old *Mairi Bhan* of Carradale was returning home from the Isle of Man with Pat McKay of Campbeltown at the wheel. Malcolm 'Kruger' McMillan – another Campbeltonian – was asleep in his bunk, while Alec McDougall was reading in his. When Alec had had enough of reading, he threw the book out of his bunk and it hit the floor with a bang. Malcolm, meanwhile, had been dreaming that the boat was about to strike a rock, and when he heard the bang he leapt out of his bunk, still half-asleep, and dashed to the side of the wheelhouse, where he began frantically operating the hand-pump. 'What in the hell are ye doin, man?' Pat McKay enquired, leaning out the wheelhouse window. 'We're sinkin! We're sinkin!' cried Kruger, still gripped by his dream of disaster. [Neil McDougall, 2000]

The policeman who never was

One warm day in July 1946, the *Nobles* of Campbeltown was steaming back across the Irish Sea to the Isle of Man fishing grounds, having landed a catch of herring at Ardglass, Ireland, that morning. Davie McNaughton was alone in the wheelhouse when he saw an English policeman, complete with helmet, emerge from the forecastle and purposefully walk aft, looking in at Davie as he passed the wheelhouse. Davie shook himself in disbelief and reached for the throttle.

Having heard the engine suddenly slow down, the skipper Duncan McSporran appeared on deck and asked Davie what was wrong. Having heard his story, Duncan told him to get to his bunk and himself took the wheel. To this day, when Davie thinks back on his exhaustion-induced hallucination, he breaks into a cold sweat, wondering what might have happened had he left the wheelhouse and, in his drowsy state, followed the policeman, whose face he still remembers vividly. [David McNaughton, 2002]

Deep sleep

Sleep deprivation was a common experience among fishermen. In the summer of 1957, Hugh Edgar, as a 17-year-old aboard his father's *Hercules*, was fishing at the Isle of Man. One week, they had the fill of the boats every night and had 'very little time in bed'. The *Hercules* returned to Dunure on the Saturday of that week for the wedding of Hugh's cousin, Greta Gibson, to Tom Shields. Hugh, who was teetotal at the time, went to bed after the celebrations and slept for 16 hours. He would have slept longer, but for his mother, who decided to wake him, fearing there was 'somethin wrang'. 'Jeest physical exhaustion,' he explained. [Hugh Edgar, 2000]

As a 16-year-old, Davie McNaughton slept even longer. He lay down at five-thirty one Saturday evening, after a hectic week, telling his mother that he'd rise in time to have a bath and meet Duncan Campbell to go to the second house at 'the pictures'. He woke, bewildered, to the sound of church bells ringing at six o' clock on Sunday evening! [David McNaughton, 2002]

Near Things
· · · · · · · · · · · · · · · · ·

Compared with their counterparts on the East Coast of Scotland and in the Shetlands, the Clyde fishing communities were never ravaged by sudden and massive loss of life. This was no doubt attributable to the relatively sheltered lochs and kyles in which they generally worked, but disasters there were. The loss, with all hands, of the Victor *of Campbeltown in 1909 and of the* Mhairi *of Carradale in 1911, for examples, stunned the Kintyre fishing communities to a degree not again experienced until the* Antares *of Carradale was snagged and sunk by a submarine off Arran in November 1990, with the loss of her four-man crew. The following accounts are of 'near things', collective and individual.*

'A dustin'

One night Jake McCrindle of Maidens shot drift-nets off the Cleets of Arran. The neighbour-boat was there too with drift-nets. It was blowing half-a-gale and the crew hauled the nets stern-on. The rudder was always removed before drift-nets were shot, but, having hauled the nets, when the time came to ship the rudder back on and get under way, the bottom rudder-iron wouldn't go over the pintle. The neighbouring crew had already hauled their nets and were 'away for Pladda'. There were no engines in the boats at this time. A paraffin torch was lit, which the neighbouring crew fortunately saw. They returned and took the disabled boat in tow. In the 'quiet watter' at the Isle of Ross, the crew managed at last to ship the rudder.

'Fae that intae Campbeltown, what a dustin we got,' Jake recalled. 'Oh, it wis a gale o win, close-reefed sail.' The pig-iron ballast in the sternsheets was 'forever slidin – it wis a wonder some o it didnae go oot through the side of the boat'. As they were going up Campbeltown Loch in big showers and thunder and lightning, they met the Campbeltown lifeboat running down the loch on her way across Kilbrannan Sound to a ship ashore at the Brown Head*. When the Campbeltown crews got in that day, they said they wouldn't have believed that 'these two wee boats went up Campbeltown Loch that mornin'. They had all been lying along the shore, in 'any place they could get intae the rocks', unwilling to risk the passage home. 'Seats, lockers an everythin else' lay wrecked in the middle of the forecastle. [John McCrindle, 1976]

Possibly the Bessie Arnold *of Whitehaven, wrecked on 28 December, 1908, at Sliddery, which is actually south of the Brown Head, Arran.*

In the *Harvest Queen*

The *Harvest Queen* of Campbeltown was caught in a storm at the Coves of Arran, c. 1909. She had a ring of herring, which her crew estimated at 30 boxes. On that assumption, the neighbour-boat *May Queen* was sent away; but there were 120 boxes in the net. With the catch finally stowed, the *Harvest Queen* also headed away. She was just clearing Imachar Point when the storm struck her. Reef after reef was taken in until none remained; the net was hauled on to the weather shoulder and the anchor-chain piled on top of it; then the herring had to be emptied out of the lee side, because 'she wis dippin her lee quarter below the water ... well, that wis her gonny founder'. The run from the Coves to Grogport Bay took all of seven hours, 'jeest pumpin an improvisin, daein everythin possible tae keep her afloat'.

'We wir aa nearly drowned,' Davie McLean recounted. 'Never had such an experience in ma life. If the win had tae veer anythin at all that we cou'na clear Imachar, we'd've had tae put the boat ashore. If by any freak o nature the win had suddenly changed, the boat wid've upset wi the weight we had up on her shoulder.'

At Grogport, the crew found a steamer which took the herring they had managed to save, but every man was soaked to the skin, the fore-castle wrecked and the fire out. The following day, however, was lovely, and the *Harvest Queen*'s crew returned alone to the Arran shore, where they came on John McIntyre's *Frigate Bird* and *Brothers* with a netful of herring. They were taken alongside the net and got their share out of it. 'So that wis a bit o luck,' Davie concluded, 'an oor cloes wir sorta half-dried.' [David McLean, 1974, 1975]

A south-easter

One Friday night, the *Fame*, heading south, came across plenty of herring off the Iron Wharf at Skipness. Her neighbour having gone into Tarbert, the net had to be shot and hauled without assistance. There was a gale of wind, which 'put the whole net on the top o the watter', but 50 baskets were secured. Lights were seen in Loch Ranza and, when the *Fame* went over, there were two or three herring-steamers being loaded, so she was brought alongside one of them and the catch discharged.

The *Lady Edith* and *Lady Charlotte* – the biggest of all the skiffs – had been moored in the Doogan (*Dubhaigean*), at the back of Loch Ranza Castle, their crews intending to go home to Campbeltown by steamer in the morning. Robert Robertson's *Falcon* and *Frigate Bird* (the first of a generation of modern, fully-decked boats) had earlier passed by the *Fame*, running for Tarbert. Yet the *Fame*'s skipper, Dunky Martin – 'a kinna stubborn man' – took her down Kilbrannan Sound that night.

From Isla Ross south, there was 'a mountain o sea – I never seen it as high in the Kilbrannan Soon – an somebody passed the remark: "There's something at the back o that."' There was. The *Fame* wasn't 'right moored up' when the wind came away in full fury. The Weigh-House at the head of Campbeltown Quay was completely obscured by spindrift blowing from the inner harbour. Henry Martin considered that the risk had been unacceptable – the *Fame*'s crew was a father and four sons – and demanded of the 'Ould Fella': 'Wid ye lea tae go tae the Kyles now?' He was vexed he'd spoken, however, because 'all hands got at' his father, and when they all walked through the door at Gayfield Place, Caroline Martin 'near passed out'. Having recovered, she gave her husband another 'doin'.

The following summer, a Dalintober McKinlay, who crewed on William Robertson's steamers, was home on holiday and standing with a group of men at the Weigh-House. Someone passed a remark about 'the wile winter it wis', whereupon McKinlay began to tell a story about 'the maist watter ever he got in his life wis fae the Holy Isle tae Pladda wi a sou-easter'. – 'An when wis that?' someone asked. Having settled on a date, McKinlay was informed that there was a fishing boat came down Kilbrannan Sound that night. He didn't believe it. [Henry Martin, 1974]

A near-drowning

John McWhirter was in the Kyles of Bute the year of the first big fishing there. They shot with a couple of reefs on the sail. There was a 'strange man' aboard – a newcomer to the crew – who 'flung the eye o the bridle in the wrong place'. John couldn't see the rope in the dark and was waiting until the net was well out so that he could grab it and make it fast to the sweepline for the towing of the net. He did see it and stepped forward to catch it, but he put his foot into a bight of rope between the back and sole and it trapped him below the hips and carried him overboard. To compound the disaster, the *winky* blew out, so the neighbouring crew missed that end. The latter end had run overboard, because John was in no position to secure it, so that was the net adrift in darkness.

John felt the back-rope and worked his way along it until he came to a concentration of corks. He gathered a bunch and got his arms through that. The last thing he remembered before he became unconscious was seeing the flashing buoy at Ardlamont. Meantime, the skiff had tacked back, discovered the buoys of the net and ran down along the back-rope until John was sighted near the end; but of that he remembered nothing. When he came to consciousness he was in the forecastle of a small herring-steamer, the *Jura*. He remembered being put back aboard the skiff and lying in a hammock, stripped of his wet clothing and covered with other men's coats. The skiff headed home and got a 'tooslin, a proper doin', tacking against southerly wind the whole way from the Cock of Arran to Campbeltown. That was a Thursday night. He was back at the fishing on the following Monday. [John McWhirter, 1974]

The *Manx Lily*

The Isle of Man ring-netter, Manx Lily, was wrecked at Torrisdale on 7 February, 1948. The story, as reported in the Campbeltown Courier *of 14 February, had the vessel 'lying peacefully at anchor on the lea (sic) side of Dippen Point, and the next minute dashed helplessly against the rocks' as the gale veered from the north-west into the south. There were 70 mph squalls and torrential rain that night, and the crew scrambled ashore to safety using a rope, which had been secured on the rocks, to guide them. The skipper of the* Manx Lily *was an ex-Royal Navy Petty Officer, 44-year-old Frank Gallagher from Peel. Two of his crew were also from Peel, while the remainder were Campbeltown fishermen. Of the incident, Gallagher later remarked: 'While I was in the Navy I had much worse experiences than this.'*

The crew of the *Manx Rose* remembered the *Lily*'s destruction rather differently. The fishing was 'erratic' that night and they went into Torrisdale and dropped anchor along with three or four other pairs. The *Manx Lily* followed and was simply tied alongside the *Rose*, instead of lying to her own anchor. Now and again the *Lily* would take a roll and pull on the *Rose*, and this began to increase in frequency. Finally, one of the *Rose*'s Campbeltown contingent, Willie McKenzie, could tolerate it no longer and remarked: 'There naw a Campbeltown man or a Carradale man or any other man wid put up wi the lik o this. He wid go up and make them men put oot their ain anchor or else go away tae herbour.' This outburst was directed at the *Rose*'s skipper, who did then go on deck and shout across to the *Lily*'s crew to let go their own anchor. The crew paid no heed, so the skipper came back below and turned in. One of the *Rose*'s crew, Henry Martin, couldn't sleep, fearing that something would happen, and it did. There was a sudden crack 'lik a shot oot a gun'. 'That's it now!' Henry shouted.

Willie McKenzie leapt from his bunk and went on deck. The forward rope had burst, and before he was able to dash aft to the only rope that was now holding the two boats, that rope also parted. He called for lumps of coal and Henry began passing coal up to him. He pelted the *Manx Lily*'s deck with the coal and shouted, but none of her crew appeared on deck, and the boat drove ashore on Dippen Rocks, on the south side of the burn. The wind was 'back' and 'came away a tightner'. The unfortunate *Lily* lay with her side against the rocks and the crew 'walked' ashore. Then the boat got a battering on the rocks and became a total wreck. A Carradale skipper, Johnny McMillan, bought the wreck and salvaged what he could from her. Henry Martin's judgement on the incident was: 'Pure neglect.' [Henry Martin, 1975]

The *Golden Dawn*

The *Golden Dawn* was neighbouring the *Boy Danny* at the Isle of Man fishery in 1954. They'd been working between Ramsey and Douglas. The *Golden Dawn* was running herring to Portpatrick one morning when the wind fell away and a bank of mist engulfed her. All hands were on deck. The foghorn on the Mull of Galloway could be heard. The boy shouted that breakfast was ready, so the skipper John Conley left the wheelhouse to go below, saying: 'A think we're a good wey in. Away wan o ye's an take the wheel.' By good fortune, in the light of what was about to happen, big Dennis McKay took charge.

Davie 'Towser' Robertson and Francis McWhirter remained on watch forward. The rest of the crew weren't long below when Francis and Towser suddenly saw 'this black lump in front o us'. They shouted, with one voice: 'Hard astern!' Normally, to take the gear out of 'ahead' and into 'astern', the boat had to be slowed right down, but Dennis McKay, who was powerfully-built, was able to instantaneously wrench the gearwheel into the 'astern' position, and, with a mighty shuddering, which threw the breakfast off the forecastle table and dislodged the mainmast from its crotch, the *Golden Dawn*'s way was checked, though, with the weight of the herring aboard and her momentum, she continued 'sailin right in'. Said Francis: 'We could see the blackness o the face comin.'

She'd been heading right into the Mull of Galloway and was so close to destruction that Francis and 'Towser' felt drips from the cliff land on their heads. The men below came up on deck at once and the entire crew looked about in horror. To both port and starboard there was 'a reef right oot the watter', but the *Golden Dawn*, though badly scored along one side, was still afloat.

'That,' said Francis, 'wis the biggest fright ever I got in ma life. A thought we wir finished. A thought we wir gonny run intae the face an be smashed tae pieces an naebody wid ever know whoot had happened tae us. It went through me mind, if we had'ae hit that face she wid've jeest gone down lik a stone, because actually there wis plenty water below … If anybody else had tae go intae that boat's wheelhouse, we wirna here the day, because he hadna got time tae slow her doon.'

They continued to Portpatrick and eventually emerged from the mist-bank. It was reckoned that the tide had taken them off course and that the foghorn had deceived them into thinking they were further off than they actually were. [Francis McWhirter, 1999]

Tide in Pabbay Sound

The most frightening experience of Jim Campbell's life happened in the Minch in the 1960s, and after it was over he went below still trembling. He felt under his bunk and brought out the half-bottle of whisky kept there for emergencies. He had never touched drink, but as he looked at the bottle he said to himself: *Will A take it or will A naw?* He rejected the temptation and instead took the bottle on deck and gave the whisky to those of his crew who would drink it gladly. 'That's the nearest A ever wis tae takin drink.'

He and his neighbour John McConnachie were in Pabbay Sound with a fleet of ringers. The herring were abundant, 'jumpin oot the watter lik troot (trout)'. They went out the Sound as far from the fleet as they could go, and Jim shot. 'A lot o it wis doon tae inexperience,' he admitted. 'There wir too many herrin in the net. We wirna acquaint wi such a huge amount o herrin.' With the wisdom of hindsight, they should have rid the net of the bulk of its contents, but they commenced brailing from both boats, and one of his crew, young Billy Martindale, actually swung himself on the brailer-wire across the swollen bag of herring to reach the deck of the *Florentine* to assist John McConnachie and John MacAllister with the boating of the herring.

Unconcerned, they brailed and brailed and had about 700 baskets out the net when a Campbeltown skipper, Jim Meenan, came in from leeward with the *Stella Maris* and shouted: 'Ye better, Jim, get oot o there as quick as ye can. Ye've got a quarter o an hour an ye'll be in among the rocks.' The crews tried to liberate the catch, but couldn't, so Jim told his neighbour to 'clear out', and then let go his anchor. But before John

McConnachie could take his leave with the *Florentine*, the *Bairn's Pride* swung into the raging tide and, in less than half-a-minute, net and herring had been swept away, and if the men hadn't jumped clear of the net, they would have gone with it. The anchor, too, was lost – as it spun out with the force of the tide, no one was able to effectively secure the cable. 'The net just went flying ,' Jim Campbell recalled. 'I got hold of Tait Rennie's oilskin and pulled him off the net, as he would have been away also – Tait was trying to save the net.'

The net was virtually new – 'bought in August and gone by November,' as Jim put it – but, as luck would have it, the crew of an Irish pair-trawler, the *Green Pastures*, later picked up the net, out in the Atlantic, and reported its recovery on the radio. The *Bairn's Pride*'s crew was 'in great trim' with this news, but it transpired that the net wasn't complete, though enough of it remained to make up a small ring-net for use on the Ballantrae Banks. [Jim Campbell, 2001]

Provisions
....

Until the latter half of the twentieth century, food provisions on fishing-boats were basic, even sparse, and the mainstay of the fishermen's diet was fish.

Barter

When Hector McKinven of Dalintober was ashore in Arran with a chip-basket of herring – perhaps 40 or 50 fish – to barter and his companion would say, 'An where will we go, Hector, dae ye think?', Hector's answer would be, 'A thackit cottage for yer life.' He would never approach boarding-houses or any dwellings on that scale. 'They might an they might naw,' was his reasoning, but, at a thatched cottage, 'Ye'll get eggs, ye'll get scones an ye'll even get a prunt o butter* sometims.' [John Campbell, 1980]

A moulded pat, imprinted with a decorative motif.

Herring

The Tarbert skiffs had no designated cook, boy or man. The fellow who was 'doon furst' would put on the kettle and make the toast while another of the crew gutted and cleaned herring, which would then be handed down to the man in the den for cooking. 'That,' said Davie MacFarlane, 'wis the feedin. We wir awful fond o herrin, boiled herrin, but whenever we wid come home, we winna eat herrin if we wir eatin them all week. A'm no exaggeratin – A used tae eat sixty a week. That's all ye wid get tae eat.' [David MacFarlane, 1975]

Kippers

When George Newlands was fishing at the Isle of Man, he and Robert McKinven, 'Young Captain' (Duncan Wilkinson Jr) and Robert McGown, went into Douglas one afternoon. It was the Glasgow Fair fortnight and there were thousands of visitors there. The fishermen went into a small cafe and were shown the menu, which included kippers. 'God, we wir eatin kippers an herrin aa week, an it wis kippers we had!' [George Newlands, 1975]

Ham and Eggs

When George Newlands was cook aboard the *Waterbird* of Campbeltown with Sandy Cameron, Hughie McLean, Charlie Durnin, Jamie Brown and Charlie Cameron from Peninver – most of them old men at that time – he went ashore in Loch Ranza and sold a chip-basketful of herring. With the proceeds, he bought a dozen eggs and a pound of bacon and returned to the boat. 'They chased me!' he recalled. 'Ye should've heard ould Sandy Cameron: "Who ever seen ham an eggs aboord a boat!" My God, A dinna know hoot tae dae, an A haena mind hoot A did wi them, whether A cooked them or hoot.' [George Newlands, 1975]

Mince

When Archie Paterson was a boy, cooking on the *Rolling Wave* of Carradale, the boat was lying in Rothesay one day. His cousin, Robert Paterson, who was skipper, asked him to go up for 2lb of steak-minced. 'Be sure that it's steak-minced ye get – don't take anythin else,' Rob insisted. Archie, however, being young and shy, just asked for mince, and the butcher took it out of the window, seeing 'a great chance to get rid of it'. The meat was rather bad, but Archie's uncle, Angus Paterson, was in the forecastle when Archie returned with it. 'Let me see,' said Angus, taking the mince from him. He put it into a pot, browned it, stewed it and then emptied a bottle of Worcester sauce into it. Rob 'liked to talk about food' and was greatly taken with the meal. 'It must have some spice in it – it's a great flavour,' he enthused. Archie himself didn't touch the mince, but, he said, 'A can see Angus yit, givin me the wee wink.' [Archie Paterson, 2000]

An unwanted gift

The *Lily* of Campbeltown neighboured the *Fionnaghal* of Tarbert during the Second World War, and the Campbeltown crew was given six 'dookers' (guillemots) and a 'scart' (shag or cormorant) one day by Donald McDougall, skipper of the *Fionnaghal*. The Tarbertmen had been over on the Kerry Shore shooting seabirds on the Sunday and had seen signs of herring. When the *Lily* came to join her neighbour on the Monday, her crew wasn't expecting to be out that night owing to the 'smoker o win' encountered on the passage from Campbeltown, but they went across with the *Fionnaghal* to the Kerry side and fished 600 baskets of herring. Next day, Donald asked Dan McNaughton on the *Lily* if he and the crew had enjoyed the dookers. 'Aye, they wir fine, fine, Donal,' Dan replied.

Two or three nights later, the *Lily* had 130 baskets of herring aboard and was lying in Tarbert waiting for the sales to begin. Donald came aboard and wanted to look at the herring. Somebody offered to lift off the hold hatches, but, 'Naw, naw, naw,' he said, 'A'll go through the fore-peak'. The first thing he put his hand on was the bunch of dookers still hanging there. 'Aye, aye, Dan, an they wir great, Dan,' said Donald sarcastically, adding: 'That's the last bloody dookers ye'll get fae us!' Unlike the Tarbert men (whose collective nick-name is 'Dookers') most Campbeltown fishermen had no stomach for seafowl. Dan McNaughton had told his son Davie and another crewman, Willie Galbraith, to dump the birds over the side at the first opportunity, but they hadn't got around to it. [David McNaughton, 1999]

'Tap's' hard tack

Ship-biscuits consisted basically of flour and water and were made to last, but Willie 'Tap' Smith had lard in his recipe. A native of Irvine, he had a bakehouse and butcher's shop on Tarbert harbourfront, and whenever fishermen would go to him to order biscuits, they would specify: 'Now, we're naw waantin them that we canna eat them. Ye'll put some lard in them.' Hugh MacFarlane remembered their being 'lik shortbread. Ye know, they wir hard an still ye could munch them up. Butter – oh, it wid be a quarter o an inch thick, the butter. I winna look at breid as long as them biscuits wis there'.

The MacFarlanes were lying in Girvan, preparing to go ashore, one day. A man named Ingram, who happened to be a baker in Girvan, came aboard. He was given a bowl of tea and Tap's biscuits with butter and cheese. Ingram was eating thoughtfully, then turned to one of Hugh's brothers and said: 'Where are ye gettin the biscuits?' – 'Them biscuits wis made in Tarbert,' the brother replied. 'Tarbert?' – 'A man the name o Smith.' – 'Well,' said Ingram, 'A've never ett hard biscuits lik that. Will ye gie me wan tae take it tae the bakehoose?' – 'There lard in them,' Hugh volunteered. 'We told the baker tae put lard in them afore we went away.' Ingram went away with three or four biscuits as samples. [Hugh MacFarlane, 1974]

Swedish fishermen

When Swedish fishermen (from the island of Öckerö) came to the Clyde to seine-net for hake in the 1920s, they became familiar with the sea-biscuits, or 'crackers', that Joe Black was baking in Campbeltown, and went to his shop in Saddell Street 'tae get him tae make a dose tae take away wi them'. [Henry Martin, 1975]

Banana sandwiches

This anecdote must date to the earliest years of the 20th century, before engines were installed on fishing boats and presumably when bananas were something of a rarity.

Crawford Morans was in town with his father, Bob, when they met old John Wareham, who invited Bob – a past shipmate – into the Commercial Inn for a 'wee blether'. Bob had just one drink and Crawford didn't take anything. He was only 17 or 18 years old at this time – about 1950 – and was at the fishing himself. The two older men began reminiscing about the skiff era and John asked Bob: 'Can you remember what we had tae eat on the way over tae Ireland?' – 'No,' Bob replied, 'A canna.' – 'Well, it wis banana pieces,' John said. 'Aye, ye're right,' Bob agreed. 'But the wan thing A can remember – there wir nae wind that day an we had blisters lik half-croons on oor hans wi rowin. A remember that.' The 'pieces' were made for the trip by the skipper's wife. [R Crawford Morans, 2000]

The last match

James Conley of Carradale was aboard a skiff working long lines (a spring occupation certain crews annually adopted when herring-fishing was slack) between Ru Stafnish and Ailsa Craig. A gale of northerly wind came away, and a blizzard with it, and the crew ran to the Craig for shelter. They were a week anchored there before the wind took off, by which time there remained only one blue-moulded loaf 'an they'd tae cut the sides off it an make it spin oot'. There was only one match left aboard the boat, with which to relight the fire if it went out: 'Me fether had it in his poaket an he wis frightened it wid get damp an he used tae rub it in his hair tae keep it dry. If it dinna light, it wis fatal.' [Bob Conley, 1975]

Water and Whisky

Prior to the advent, in the 1920s, of the modern generation of ring-netters, fitted with capacious tanks, water was a limited commodity, generally held in wooden casks, which required to be refilled wherever a source – be it spring or tap – existed. Cooking utensils, crockery and cutlery were all washed in sea-water and the boat's supply of fresh water was definitely not for use in maintaining personal hygiene, no matter how modest the requirements.

Attitudes to alcohol in the 19th and early 20th centuries were certainly more polarised than now: fishermen tended either to drink much or not drink at all. A large part of the population abstained from strong drink on religious or other moral grounds, so drunkenness and its attendant vices could elicit reactions of horror and disgust. Public affrays involving fishermen not infrequently resulted in court appearances.

A lengthy editorial in the Campbeltown Courier *of 29 September, 1883, contains the following observations: 'It is saddening to think of the waste – the reckless squandering – that goes on amongst a certain class of the fishing population when they happen to get a share of what they call good luck. Riotous living, revelling and debauchery hold sway as long as the money lasts, and all too soon the big pile is swallowed up, leaving the simple, thriftless souls to squalor and want once more. Our readers would hardly credit us if we told them in how brief a space a twenty pound or thirty pound "divide" is dissipated in this way. The possession of money to these men simply means the power and opportunity of ministering to the lowest desires of their nature.'*

Watering places used by Tarbert fishermen

Away from home, the fishermen would check any burn they intended using water from to see if it was clean, especially if there were farms or other habitations near it. In their 'own quarters', however, they knew where the wells were and would always keep them clean. There was one in Camus an Tobair – the Bay of the Well its translation – north of Skipness and another south of Skipness, at Creag Aornaigh. That one was a big pool in the rock – 'ye wid sweem in it' – and the water was 'as cool as ice … a spring comin oot the solid rock'. At Creag Aornaigh, water-casks could be filled at any time because a skiff would float there even at 'deid low watter'; but many wells along the Kintyre shore were inaccessible from the sea because the shore was shallow and fishermen couldn't get in with their boats. At Claonaig, further south, water could be filled from the burn; at Uamh nan Calman – the Doves' Cave, 'aye full o doos, the wild pigeons' – on the north side of Crossaig Bay, there was a well, which was also used by the people in the house there; and there was a well at the Minister's. [Hugh MacFarlane, 1976]

Watering places used by Campbeltown fishermen

The running hill-water filled at Laggan kept better than the static water from Saint Mary's Loch, south of the Minister's Head at Grogport, which heated. At Cour Head, an anchor would be dropped astern and the skiff run in close to the shore. A boy would clamber on to the rocks over an oar and fasten a rope, then go and fill water. Mostly the McLeans went ashore for water at the Minister's Port, north of the Minister's Head, and would even take a 'bad net' ashore there and mend it. South of Carradale, when the tide was ebbed, 'beautiful spring water' could be filled at Stroolag, which name is from Gaelic *An Sruthlag*, 'The Little Stream'. [David McLean, 1976, 1979]

'Never mind, boys, there's plenty water here!'

This Tarbert nonsense-tale is based on a play around the Gaelic word coileach, *'cock'. The Cock is a boulder on the north end of Arran.*

When boats were open, a brazier was carried for the boiling of water and fish and for heat. It was called a *coileach* from the red comb of the fire. There was a boat out fishing on a calm night and the sail was lying forward. The brazier somehow fell over and set the sail alight. The crew were stamping on the sail to put out the fire, but couldn't. 'Where is there water?', they all asked with one voice. 'At the Coileach – there's a well there,' they answered as one. The Coileach was the Cock of Arran and they started rowing there, one man stamping on the sail and another standing on the bow with a bucket in his hand, ready to land at the Cock and get water out of the well. They rowed and rowed till the sweat was flying about them and reached the Cock. As the boat's forefoot struck the shore, the man on the bow fell head-over-heels into the sea and when he surfaced he shouted: *Coma leibh 'illean, tha gu leòir de dh'uisg an seo!* 'Never mind, boys, there's plenty water here!' [George Campbell Hay, 1979]

All equal

A Campbeltown lugger was at the mackerel fishing off the south coast of Ireland one season in the late 19th century and her crew fished well enough. To a man, however, they were over-fond of drink and had many a drinking session. Going home at the trip's end, and half-sober by then, they were assembled on deck trying to make sense of a notebook one of them had been keeping to record loans.

'Now, jeest a meenit – you got ...'

'Aye, aye, that's right.'

'Well, A've it doon here then. That's your name there, ye see.'

'Yes, yes, that's right enough; aye, ye're right enough.'

'Well, I canna mind o gettin that,' another man would say.

'Oh, ye did,' the book-keeper would insist, 'for there it's there – A haev it in print.'

The book-keeper, of course, might have been as drunk as any of them when he was entering the figures.

'Now this haes got tae be settled before we go home.'

'Well, A can't remember gettin that, now. An tae be fair ...'

At this, one of the crew, Duncan 'Foffar' McLellan, interrupted.

'Let *me* see thir book.'

'Here.'

He looked at it.

'Aye, aye, aye – there you.'

'Aye, A see where A am there, aye. An where are you?'

'Well,' the fellow to whom the question was addressed said, 'A don't know.'

Foffar's patience was by now exhausted.

'Well, here,' he said, throwing the notebook overboard, 'we're all equal now!' [John Campbell, 1980]

Leezie Campbell's

There were two public houses which Dalintober fishermen frequented in High Street. The crew of the *Fame* divided the week's earnings in the one kept by Leezie Campbell. When a crew went in to divide, some one always 'stood a round'. After the money had been shared, some of the men would wait and continue drinking. One week, the skipper-owner Duncan Martin was on holiday and his young son Henry had to 'lift the boat's money'. He went to Leezie's with the money and one of the crew said to him: 'Henry, ask her for a half – say ye waant a half.' Henry went to Leezie and said: 'Gie me a half.' She didn't look at him, but returned with a bottle of lemonade and a glass and put them down in front of him. She was very strict, and if a man came into the pub smelling of drink she would say to him: 'Away oot o here – ye've plenty.' [Henry Martin, 1976]

Thrapple

John McWhirter remembered fishermen wearing tweed waistcoats with inside pockets. They would put their half-pint of whisky in one of these pockets when they were coming aboard the boat. 'Ye winna dae athoot yer dram in them days,' John remarked. In the morning, before or after breakfast, when work was finished, the drinkers would have a 'wee tot' and then go to sleep. They would waken at 11 or 12 o' clock and, when at Carradale, would go into the wharf and walk up to the hotel for whisky. 'Ye'd have the dinner ready – nobody wid come', John recalled. 'Ye'd have the tea ready nearly in time for gan tae the fishin afore they wid come.'

A prominent Carradale citizen came aboard the boat once and was given a 'good yin' in a bowl. He looked at it a while, then remarked: 'A wish me thrapple wis three mile long.' This was so that he would feel the whisky running all that distance down his throat. [John McWhirter, 1974]

A Ne'erday disappointment

Davie McLean and his crew were discharging herring in Ayr one New Year's morning. They were waiting for boxes to come and Davie went across the street and rapped at a door and asked the woman who answered if he could have a glass of water. 'Och, my goodness,' she said, 'ye're naw wantin water on a New Year's mornin.' Said Davie: 'That's all A want.' She was 'nearly takin a convulsion because I dared tae refuse whisky', he recalled. When the herring had been discharged, one of the crew asked: 'A wonder where A could get ma moarnin?' This was the morning dram. 'Away over there tae that house an rap at the dorr an ask for a glass o water an ye'll get a glass o whisky,' Davie advised. The man did that, and, when the woman answered the door, wished her 'A good New Year.' He got a glass of water and she never mentioned whisky! 'She must've thought they wir all teetotallers as well as me,' Davie explained. [David McLean, 1975]

'Is ma bottle broken?'

Tommy Sloan's uncle, Andy Girvan, looked after Ailsa Craig for Lord Ailsa and ran a boat to and from the island, carrying visitors and blocks of quarried granite which were sent to Mauchline to become curling-stones. Andy was with a party of visitors at the castle 'half-roads' up the Craig. He had whisky inside him and still more whisky in a bottle which he'd secreted in the inside pocket of his jacket. While he was at the castle, he took a dizzy turn and plummeted to the bottom. The appalled visitors thought that Andy must be dead, and one of them ran for a doctor who happened to have come across on the boat and who was having a cup of tea in the tearooms. The doctor immediately ran to where Andy was lying, examined him and remarked, 'Oh, he's all right', at which Andy looked up into the doctor's face and said: 'Is ma bottle broken?' [Tommy Sloan, 1976]

'Ten shillins for a pun o mince!'

There was a 'wee pair', the *Catherine* and the *Peggy*, ring-netting from Tarbert during the Second World War. One summer, they had a good week, getting fish every night and some nights at the herring-steamers two and three times with catches. Every morning the crews were going up to the Commercial – now the Islay Frigate – 'for a dram on the strength o the fishin the night before'. When Saturday came, they went to the hotel to divide the week's money, and, having halved the proceeds, the crews parted. The *Peggy*'s crowd went into a side-room to settle. The week's account for drink came to no less than £40, but not a word was said about that. Then one fellow, going through the expenses, noticed a staggering detail. 'Ten shillins for a pun o mince! Ye could buy a sheep for that!' he bellowed. 'There wis bloody near a war,' as Robert Ross remarked. [Robert Ross, 2000]

Tobacco Habits

·····················

The chewing and smoking of tobacco were almost universal habits among fishermen before health considerations altered attitudes. Yet, some present-day skippers, in particular, chain-smoke cigarettes to pass the solitary hours in their wheelhouses.

Chewing

When fishermen were working and unable to fill the pipe – such as when hauling the net – some of them would have about an inch of tobacco in their mouths, 'chowin an spittin all the time'. Some 'cerried it on ashore'; some 'wid dae nawthing else but chew'. Of the dozen or more men standing at 'the Corner' in Tarbert, the half of them – 'landlubbers too' – might be chewing. 'They wid put in the big chow o tobacco, and, boys-o-boys, ye wir up tae yer ankles in spittles at the corner.' Colin Bruce 'wid chow fadoms o tobacco in the week – there wir a *rotach** o tobacco-juice runnin doon his jersey, an he winna put the pipe in his mooth. Very funny'. Latterly, a brand named 'Lady's Twist' was the preferred chewing-tobacco. One old fellow, 'Cocky' Smith, who chewed till he was 80 years old, would roll up the twist 'in a knot away as big as half a golf ball, an chow at that the whole day, sittin at the Breist'. [Hugh MacFarlane, 1976]

Probably, in this sense, meaning 'thickness'.

'Young' John McKay was 'the man forrid on the boat' – the chief watcher on the bow – and when he was about to go forward at night he would cut six or seven inches of tobacco off the roll and that lasted him all night. The roll – of thin 'Lady's Twist' – was kept in a locker in the forecastle and anybody who wanted a chew just had to 'nip a bit off'. Some men actually slept with a lump of tobacco in their mouth. 'Shoogeldy' (Donald Thomson) and the Blair twins (Archie and Dougie) 'chowed a loat tae'. [John McWhirter, 1974]

The chewing-tobacco was about the thickness of a finger and in some Dalintober skiffs a quarter-pound of it came with the provisions, along with a half-pound of thick black for smoking and a bag of clay pipes. Mostly, tobacco would be chewed only when smoking was impractical. Angus Martin's uncle, Willie Martin, neither smoked nor drank but would chew about three ounces of tobacco every week. 'He wid lie doon in his bed wi the tobacco in his mooth an he'd chow it away up at the side o his teeth, and wis sookin away at it noo an agane. He wid go tae sleep wi it still in his mooth. A wee bit in my mooth wid lea' me seeck. His teeth wis broon.' [Angus Martin, 1974]

Stealing tobacco

The tobacco that came with the stores would be divided equally among the crew, and if there was someone who didn't smoke, then that was his 'ain fault' – the tobacco was there for him – but he might take it anyway to give to someone else. Some of the crew used to keep the tobacco in their lockers, and boys would steal a bit now and again and get a clay-pipe and have a 'wee smoke'. [Angus Martin, 1974]

Filling the skipper's pipe

The helmsman had to have his hands free, so somebody would fill his pipe for him if he smoked. If it was a breezy night, that man would go down into the den to fill and light the pipe and then go aft and give it to him. Hugh MacFarlane knew a fellow, John MacFarlane, who started smoking in that way. He was a big man, well over six feet, and he 'used tae fill the skipper's pipe tae him; well, he started himsel, as heavy as the rest o them'. That's the way John Weir Sr, too, started smoking. 'He'd fill Johnny Eachunn's pipe tae him, the fella that wis steerin the boat; take her doon an light her. At long last Johnny had the pipe an the tobacco. They wirna smokin afore it. That's how they started, the two that A know o masel.' [Hugh MacFarlane, 1976]

Throwing the pipe away

Jake McCrindle was in the Kilbrannan Sound one morning when word came that there were herring got on the Ayrshire side. He threw his pipe over the side, chewed an ounce of tobacco between there and Girvan and finished with tobacco for two or three years. Previously, he'd been smoking and chewing his way through eight ounces of tobacco each week. When tape-recorded in 1976, he was still smoking, but only two ounces of 'Erinmore' weekly, a restraint that had more to do with the price of tobacco than any other consideration. [John McCrindle, 1976]

Personalities

· · · · · · · · · · · · · · · · · · ·

Alec McMillan

Henry Martin and his friends were all 'the fright o oor life for some o the ould worthies'. One such was Alec McMillan in Dalintober. He had a 'wheen o boats', including a pair of ring-net skiffs, the *Dart* and the *Arrow*, and a smack, which lay on Dalintober beach below Sandbank House, her stem close to the sea-wall. She was called the *Sir Charles* [*Napier*] and there were half-a-dozen planks missing down in the bilges on each side of her so that 'the watter got leave tae come in an ebb oot'. When Alec would see boys playing around the hulk, he'd come out with a rope and threaten to leave welts on their arses that they 'wanna be fit tae sit', his white whisker waggling all the time he was shouting. Yet, if a boy would stand looking in the door of Alec's net-store, he would 'speak away'. In later life, Henry realised that the man was afraid some boy would fall into the smack 'an maybe go oot through the holes'. [Henry Martin, 1974]

'Captain'

'Captain' was the nick-name of an old skipper, Duncan Wilkinson, who, in retirement, used to amaze others with his knowledge of boats' names and numbers. If there was a company assembled, invariably the conversation would turn to boats, and somebody would ask: 'Hoot number had that boat?' Captain would know. He would 'go away back … boats ye could hardly mind on, an tell ye thir name an thir number an who they belanged tae … even boats belongin tae otherwheres'. His oft-repeated challenge was: 'If ye tell me thir name, A'll tell ye thir number.' [Henry Martin, 1977]

'Smeegie'

'Smeegie' was James Smith, an old Dalintober fisherman who was at drift-nets one summer in the days of sail. His boat was coming up Campbeltown Loch with full sail and a jib on her and collided with an anchored steam-yacht, the *Sea Horse**. If Smeegie would 'get a drink in him on a Seterday', all the boys had to do was shout '*Sea Horse* ahead!' and they would be chased. [Henry Martin, 1974]

*Owned by Major Austin MacKenzie, proprietor of Carradale Estate from 1899 to 1938.

Andy McKinlay

A Royal Navy destroyer came in through the Blin Soon – between Davaar Island and the mainland – and 'beeried itsel' in the shallows, a remarkable navigational blunder. The following night, her crew was 'manned wi shovels an wis diggin the san away fae her tae get her tae float'. There was a pair of Dalintober skiffs 'dodgin doon through the Lodan' when another Royal Navy ship appeared and hove to when the lights of Campbeltown opened out. A Morse lamp began flashing aboard the Naval ship, and one of the fishermen remarked: 'There a Navyman oot there. He's waantin a pilot, flashin a light.' One of the skiffs went across to the ship and Andy McKinlay called out: 'Dae ye want a pilot?' Her crew declined to answer – probably, as Henry Martin remarked, they wouldn't have known what Andy was saying – whereupon Andy 'opened fire on them' with the following observation: 'Ye's know as much about navigation as a cow knows about an eclipse!' [Henry Martin, 1974]

'Lachie Dougie'

'Lachie Dougie' was one Lachlan MacDougall, a Tarbert fisherman who flourished in the late 19th and early 20th century. His natural eccentricity was compounded by an imperfect command of the English language.

In Glasgow

He'd never been in Glasgow. A younger fisherman came to him one day: 'Lachie, A'll take ye to Glasgow and A'll show ye Glasgow.' – 'Right,' said Lachie, 'we'll go.' Away they went and reached Glasgow. One evening they were walking along a road and the younger fisherman pointed to a factory and said: 'Lachie, dae ye see yon hoose?' – 'Aye,' said Lachie. 'That,' said his companion, 'is where they sandpaper the elephants doon intae greyhoonds.'

His cat

He was sitting in the house with his wife one evening and the cat was sitting in the hearth with its ears cocked. Said Lachie to his wife: 'The cat's sitting at the fire all standing.'

His spectacles

One night at the fishing Lachie was hauling the sole-rope and fell over the side into the net. His oilskins swelled up with air and the crew managed to pull him back aboard, minus his spectacles. Back in Tarbert, he was telling everyone he met about the accident, saying: 'A fell over the side an A lost ma specs an A nearly lost ma corpse as well.'

A summoning

He was standing at the door of his house in Back Street one morning, in his shirt-sleeves and braces, when a child came running to him and breathlessly delivered a message: 'Lachie, there's somebody at the quay wanting to see you!' – 'Wait,' said Lachie, 'till A go in an rise.'

Polite usher

When he'd be ushering a visitor into his house and wanted to say, 'You go first', his manner of expression was invariably: 'Whether would ye rether or walk before.' [George Campbell Hay, 1979]

Davie MacFarlane

Davie MacFarlane, whose stories appear in this book, was another Tarbert character.

John McConnachie remembered engaging Davie in conversation on Tarbert Quay one morning while waiting for a lorry to arrive and transport the *Florentine*'s catch. 'It's a wile job we canna get a market for the herrin,' John complained. The older man looked at him and replied: 'There'd need tae be a chocolate roe in the herrin before the youngsters wid eat it.' [John McConnachie, 2001]

Niven MacVicar

There was a 'namely man' in Loch Gair at one time, Niven MacVicar; he was the 'heid yin' there. He had one of the big 'Howthers' (smacks). There was a fellow in Tarbert, Jimmy Murray, 'a big braw man' who belonged up Loch Fyneside but who married and settled in Tarbert, and he was with MacVicar in his youth. He recalled lifting the drifts at Barra Head one morning in the summertime – no herring. There was a breeze of north wind and MacVicar set every sail and shot his nets at Ardglass, Ireland, that night. He had a 'great run' and he was a 'great fisherman'. [David MacFarlane, 1975]

Jock Meenan

One night, in the early 1950s, Jock Meenan in the *Stella Maris* and his neighbour Pat McKay in the *Regina Maris* were working their way south along the Kintyre shore from the Black Bay. They had seen lights and found four or five other pairs hunting through the Lodan. About half-an-hour before daylight, the two boats were brought alongside each another. 'A don'know,' Jock Meenan speculated, 'but I think there herrin up in that Black Bey.' – 'Well, we're a bit late now,' Pat McKay replied. 'Ach, A don'know,' Jock persisted. 'There naw much doin here. A think we'll take a wee run up.' – 'Well,' said Pat, 'everhoot ye think. If ye think it's worth oor while …'

Some of the other pairs were already heading into Campbeltown and there were those in the Meenan-McKay crews who were 'quite amazed' by the decision to steam north again. 'We wir har'ly in the Black Bey,' Francis McWhirter recalled, 'jeest the *scad* o day wis in the sky, an we jeest slowed right doon. Gosh, the herrin wis startin tae play right off.' They 'birled round' and shot away the net – 400 baskets of herring. When they got into Campbeltown with the catch, the other boats were all tied up. The landing was unexpected, so they had to wait for fish-lorries to arrive. [Francis McWhirter, 1999]

On another occasion, during the War, Jock Meenan's *Gratitude* and Dan Conley's *Frigate Bird* were on the Ballantrae Banks. Other pairs had taken big fishings and were already away loaded for Ayr and Girvan. Meenan and Conley had just about 200 baskets for their night's work and were still 'tricklin around' as day came on. Then they got a big shot, and, having taken the herring aboard, were lying discussing what to do. 'Whoot aboot gan tae Campbeltown?' Jock suggested. Dan was dubious, worrying about being prevented, by bad weather, from getting back across to the Ayrshire side and so missing the next night's fishing. 'Well, Dan,' said Jock, 'if you think goin up intae Ayr or Girvan we're gonny get oot here the night agane, A think ye're up a gum-tree, because there too many herrin away aheid o us.' – 'Aw, well, Jock, you're the man; you're the man, Jock; if you think …'

They went to Campbeltown, and, after a delay while lorries arrived, got the herring out at the wartime control price of 24/6d a basket. While the *Gratitude*'s crew was hosing down the decks, Dan Conley came aboard. 'Well,' he said, 'A think we'd better away, Jock.' – 'Aw, Dan,' Jock argued, 'A think we've done very well. A don't think we'll bother now. A think we'll give the boys a night off.' This was Friday and the week's fishing had been satisfactory, but Dan was desperate to get back across to the Banks. He finally relented, however, and the boats remained where they were, and just as well, because a gale came away that night and the Campbeltown boats on the other side had to lie in Ayr and Girvan and didn't get home that week-end. [Francis McWhirter, 2000]

Bob Morans

When the Hughes family decided, in 1940, to move from Pittenweem to Rothesay, their whole tradition was in drift-netting. Of ring-netting, which prevailed entirely by then on the Clyde, they knew a little, but were essentially, as Tam Hughes admitted, 'green'. Tam's real education in the method began when he shipped a Campbeltown fisherman, Bob Morans, aboard the *Pre-eminent*. Bob had started fishing on Loch Fyne skiffs, in the final years of sail and oar, had crewed with the legendary 'Hoodie' – Robert Robertson – and skippered boats, though he had never owned a boat. He spent about a year on the *Pre-eminent*, advising Tam Hughes from the deck, often on small technical matters. 'A learnt more aff o Bob Morans than A learnt aff anybody,' Tam said. [Tam Hughes, 2001]

A Carradale skipper

This skipper was 'well got' in Tarbert. He was a good fisherman, but 'envious'. Although he had 820 baskets of herring, if another fellow had 825 baskets, he 'wisna pleased'. Davie MacFarlane, who knew him well, would reason: 'What the damn are ye worried aboot? As long as ye're gettin a good share, what's the odds whether ye're top o the league or no?' [David MacFarlane, 1975]

The Sloans

Tommy Sloan, father of Matt and Billy, was born in 1892 in Maidens. He worked on a farm at Turnberry for a year after leaving school, then joined the crew of the *Eagle*. He later bought, from Dunure, the near-new *Kelvin*, built by John Thomson in Ardrossan. At first his father and uncles formed a partnership at ring-netting, but later the Sloans neigh-boured the McCrindle brothers, a long-lasting and highly successful partnership. 'We wrocht hard,' Tommy Sloan recalled. 'We made a little, certainly; but A've seen us at the sea when none o the rest o the boats wis out. Often. Lyin at thir anchor. Yes. We took a lot oot o oorsels when we wir young. Workin single boats many a night, ye know, at the herrin. Sometimes we wid go tae the herrin when the boats wirna on the go at all; they wouldnae come out in the moarnin. An we'd get herrin; we'd be in Ayr wi them the next day – they wunnered where we goat them. Of'en an of'en, the same pair o boats, Turner (McCrindle) an us. That's what they used tae say: "These Sloan boys wid get them in a ploughed field."' [Tommy Sloan, 1976]

The Sloan crews always went on holiday in the second fortnight in June, when the boats would be taken home to Maidens and tied up. Around 1970, on the Thursday morning, just before they went on holiday, they were in the mouth of the Clyde and got herring – the only herring caught – at Heystack Bay. The *Wistaria* went to Ayr market and the *Watchful* went to Tarbert. When they returned to the mouth of the Clyde later that day, the whole fleet was there. It was a 'beautiful evening' and the two boats were lying tied together.

Matt's son-in-law, the Rev Sandy McDonald, was 'out for a night at the fishin just tae see it done' and the crews were grumbling supersti-tiously: 'That's the last thing we want aboard – a minister.' As the two crews yarned 'in the darkenin', Matt went into the *Watchful*'s wheelhouse and switched on the echo-sounder to show his son-in-law how it worked. Minutes later, he looked out the wheelhouse window and said to his brother Billy: 'Have ye got yer meter oan?' – 'No.' – 'Jeest gie her a wee kick out wir road the now, will ye?' Matt said. Then he shot round the spot of herring he had seen on the meter and, as Hugh McPhee put it, 'we got exactly the fill o the two boats, an there wasn't another herrin got that night.'

On another occasion, up Loch Striven, Billy shot a new tarry net one afternoon simply to wet it in readiness for fishing, because a new net was inclined not to sink well first time shot. Quite by chance, the net surrounded 600 baskets of herring! [Hugh McPhee, 2000]

To the question, 'What are the qualities that make a top-class skipper?', Jim Campbell and John McConnachie of Carradale – retired skippers, and for many years partners at ring-netting – offered the following attrib-utes: keenness; patience; willingness to listen to others, particularly older hands, but combined with the ability to 'take yer own diagnosis out it'; finally, intelligence.

As examples of keenness, Jim Campbell offered two anecdotes concerning the Sloans. He had visited, in Maidens, several weeks earlier, Matt Sloan – one of his fishing 'heroes' – and Matt had related how he and his brother had been fishing at the Isle of Man, one autumn in the late 1960s, and doing well there. Towards the end of the week, however, the wind shifted into the south-west, threatening to disrupt operations, so Billy suggested returning to the Clyde and spending a couple of nights there. They did that and, searching through the Lodan, came on spawny herring and shot. With one ring, they secured 350 baskets. 'Now that's keenness,' Jim remarked. 'After bein in the Isle o Man – maybe they wir doon there for a week-an-a-half – most folk wid waant tae go straight home, but naw them.'

His other example was told to him by Andy Alexander, one of Matt Sloan's crew on the *Watchful*. The Sloan pair was in Loch Striven with a fleet of other ringers, which had '*reenged* it up an doon' without success. The fleet cleared out, leaving the Sloans, who spent some three hours going round and round the sides of the loch on a winter's night. Just when the crews had tired of the seeming pointlessness of the exercise, Billy shot and rung 200 baskets. 'Ye need the patience along wi the keenness,' Jim remarked, adding with a laugh: 'Whether the herrin are there or naw, ye've got tae believe that they're there.' [Jim Campbell, 2001]

Boys
······

The vast majority of fishermen went to the job as soon as they left school, receiving, in the earliest years of their training, a quarter- or half-share of the divided profits and graduating to a full share once they were judged fit to do a man's work, which included the more specialised skills such as net-mending and splicing. As with all traditional industries, sons generally followed fathers and grandfathers into the job, though a few fathers insisted that a son serve his time as a tradesman before going to sea, in order to have remunerative employment should the fishing fail disastrously, as it periodically did.

Things lost

One afternoon in Tarbert, Alec Brown, Davie McNaughton and

Duncan Campbell were sitting together on the deck of the *Lochfyne*, peeling potatoes for the evening meal. Alec was 'boy' on the *Lochfyne*, while Davie took week about as boy on the *Lily* with Willie 'Cully' Galbraith; Duncan 'Kemmel' was on the *Enterprise*. After Alec had dumped his peelings over the side, he realised to his horror that the knife belonging to his skipper, Archie McKillop, had also gone overboard. This was no ordinary knife, having earlier belonged to another Campbeltown skipper, Dan 'Cooma' Black, whose widow had given it to Archie as a memento. When Archie heard of the loss of the knife, he was philosophical. 'Alec,' he said, 'as lang as ye never lost yersel in the water.' The response was, perhaps, hardly surprising, because Archie McKillop was one of the quietest and most civil of men and got on well with boys. [David McNaughton, 2000]

One afternoon, during the Second World War, the *Lochfyne* and *Lily* of Campbeltown were at anchor together off Skipness, each awaiting the return of her neighbour-boat. Davie McNaughton, who was fifteen or sixteen at the time, wasn't long out of his bunk and when he went aboard the *Lochfyne* he began telling her crew about some article that had been lost aboard the *Lily* and then found. 'A bate,' said Henry Martin, one of the *Lochfyne*'s crew, 'ye found it in the last place ye looked.' – 'Aye,' replied Davie, who was still half-asleep, 'that's right – how did ye know?' – 'That's for you tae find oot,' was the enigmatic answer from the older fisherman. Later, of course, Davie realised that he'd been thoroughly tricked! [David McNaughton, 2000]

A stowaway

On the pier at Maidens one day, when Turner McCrindle was a boy, he felt a strong urge to go to sea and was encouraged by a young lady, a Miss Wotherspoon. His father's boat the *Eagle* was out at drift-nets at the time, but the *Sea Flower* was lying at the pier and Miss Wotherspoon said to him: 'A'll tell ye what tae dae. You get away down in that cabin, in before the mast, an come out at the sea.' That's what he did; the *Sea Flower* set sail and Turner emerged from hiding half-an-hour later. But the crew went alongside his father's boat with him. 'A got a good whackin for that,' he said. 'A remember that aa me days.' Miss Wotherspoon, meantime, had informed Turner's mother that he had slipped off to sea and his mother was 'in a state'. [Turner McCrindle, 1976]

At drift-nets

Jake McCrindle recalled being out with his father and an uncle in a small drift-net boat off the Cleets of Arran, and they put him aboard another boat that was going home to Maidens. That boat left the south end of Arran about 4 o' clock in the morning in a dead calm. The crew had to row all the way back to Maidens and didn't arrive until afternoon. On the evening of that same day, Jake went out with his grandfather to drift-nets in a small line-boat which the old man generally worked alone. It was a 'perfect calm night' and so clear that Jake could see the nets from end to end by the *blethers* (pig-bladder buoys) floating on the surface. 'And the herrin played on the top o oor nets that night an we never got a fry. We never got a fry. They played all night long. I wis only a boy then.' [John McCrindle, 1976]

First sight of a ring-net

Davie McLean remembered the first time he ever saw a ring-net in the water. He was about 10 years old and it was something of great interest to him, 'lookin at this thing in the water wi the corks and the black bladders'. He said to his father: 'Hoot's that in the water out there?' – 'Oh,' his father replied, 'that's a net. That's what we put out tae catch the herrin.' [David McLean, 1974]

A bathe in Saddell Bay

When 'Baldy' Stewart was a boy, cooking aboard a skiff, ring-net crews used to go 'intae the rocks' for a wash and to refill the water-flask. One day, at Saddell, old Dugald Robertson was swimming in the bay and took Baldy out on his back and let him go a little way from the shore. 'Jeez,' Baldy exclaimed, 'A canna swim yit! A'm bloody frightened! Jeez, A've been over seeventy year at sea an A canna swim yit. Naw. Can't go a bloody stroke. A got that much o a fright.' [Archibald Stewart, 1974]

Dangling

When Hugh Edgar of Dunure, as a boy of about 10 years, was going out nights to ring-netting on the Munros' *Incentive*, one of the crew had a habit of catching him and hanging him over the side by the feet as the two boats were coming together. This was just a carry-on to the older man, but Hugh had no liking for the sport. 'Every time, when the boats come thegither, when A seen him A ran awa.' [Hugh Edgar, 2000]

A 'touch' in Bight Lucky

When Hugh MacFarlane was a schoolboy in Tarbert, he went out to the fishing for a night one Friday. The year was 1896, and the month October, when the herring shoals left Loch Fyne. The boats – the *Britannia* and *Goldfinder* – were in Bight Lucky, south of Battle Isle. Hugh remarked to the boy on the boat: 'There a herrin efter jumpin.' – 'Did ye hear it?' the boy asked. 'A heard it,' Hugh replied. 'A wis hearin it *bizzin* (fizzing) oot there.' – 'Where?' – 'There,' Hugh said, indicating the spot.

The boy walked aft and told his father that a herring jumped. The two crews went inshore, almost to the rocks, and threw out the end-buoy. They shot – 'a wee ring' – and they couldn't haul the net against the weight of herring in it. There was a man with a 23-foot oar 'at the cork on each side', and these men were talking to each other in Gaelic. The crews, having 'no bottom net at all', filled both boats 'oot the watter'; and after the boats had been loaded, the corks were let go and the remaining herring – 'thousans an thousans o baskets, the whole circle o the net' – were rolled over the rope. One of the herring-steamers was leaving Loch Fyne empty and going for the Clyde, and the catch was purchased by Dunky Carmichael, the buyer aboard her. 'Thon's what he gied the men, eether half-a-croon or three shillins a basket, an every herrin wis lik that – lik a machrel', Hugh recalled, still annoyed, nearly 80 years later, at how little the fishermen received for their herring. Hugh himself 'got a pound oot the *touch*'. [Hugh MacFarlane, 1974]

Precocious line-baiting

When Henry Martin returned home from school one afternoon, he found his father just after starting baiting small lines. There was nothing unusual in that, but what happened next was unusual. When his father rose and 'went tae take a rasher', Henry sat down and began himself baiting the trough of lines. His mother was 'horror-struck', because there was a way of baiting the hooks and a way of laying them on the scoop of the trough so that the line ran clear when shot. A good baiter always left the very point of the hook bare, and if the hooks were placed the wrong way several could catch together and go out in a tangled lump. When his father returned from his meal, Henry's mother exclaimed, 'Look at that – look hoot he's doin!', but his father only said to 'lea him alane'. 'Lang before A left the school, there wir yins comin tae get me tae bait, but in my opinion, even then, it waasna worth it for aal ye wid get.' [Henry Martin, 1976]

In a Greenie

Angus Martin's father John had a small double-ended line-skiff of the type known as a 'Greencastle Skiff' or 'Greenie'. She was called the *Kate*, and when his father would go away to the fishing, Angus would go up into the net-loft for the *Kate*'s mast and sail. The sail was very seldom used in these boats, which, being shallow-draughted, were useless going into the wind. Angus and his schoolboy friends, however, 'dinna know better aboot it'. On one occasion he and his crew tried to beat up Campbeltown Loch, but she wouldn't stay. 'A'll bloody soon make her stey,' Angus said, and grounded her on the gravel spit of the Doirlinn. With oars, the boys shoved her bow out and she went away on the other tack, towards the Maidens' Planting. Older men would 'get on to' Angus about his trips on the *Kate*, and one of them finally informed his father, 'an that wis hit feenished. She wis fine for runnin oot, but, ach, she winna come up the loch an ye used tae go back tae where ye started an ye wir jeest gan back an farrid in the same place … We used tae go oot tae the han'lin' (handline) wi her, away oot off the Island, an then we'd pull back in'. [Angus Martin, 1976]

'Brought up wi an oar in yer hand'

Angus Martin's son, Angus – known also as Innes – likewise, as a boy, found the lure of boats irresistible; but the line-skiffs of his father's time had, by the late 1920s and early '30s, disappeared, and Angus and his friends targeted the Dalintober fishermen's 'punts', which were used for ferrying nets and crews to and from the skiffs at their offshore moorings. These 'punts' were about 16ft (4.88 m) long, square-sterned and heavily clinker-built. They could be conventionally rowed or else sculled over the stern, which was Angus's preferred technique. Some boat-owners, such as James 'Crusoe' Robertson, were unperturbed by these infringements, but John McKinlay – the 'Blue Fella' – would appear on Dalintober Quay bawling at the boys: 'Come in – A'll droon ye's all!'

This threat wasn't taken lightly, and the boys would bring the punt into the steps at the quay, jump over the side and make their escape up the beach. On one occasion, when John ordered Angus and his two-man crew ashore, the youngest of the boys, Hamish Craig, just sat on the steps and when the 'Blue Fella' arrived to take possession of his punt, he simply clapped Hamish on the head and advised him: 'Go home, ma boy.' This unexpected response rather peeved Angus and the other boy, who were 'soakin wet wi jumpin over the side'.

Angus's expertise with oars later paid off, however. During the War, he trained at Lowestoft in the Naval Engineering School there, and when in 1944 he returned to take his Chief Engineer's ticket, an engineering instructer at the School, Matthew Speed, approached him and said: 'You're comin wi us.' Matthew, a Campbeltown man, who, like Angus, had been a fisherman before the War, was forming a crew to participate in a rowing competition on a lake near Lowestoft. The three other crewmen – Matthew was coxswain – were Ayrshire fishermen who had also trained as Naval engineers. The fishermen won the race, beating, among others, a crew of Royal Marines, and received £50 worth of War Bonds as a prize. As Angus commented: 'Ye wir brought up wi an oar in yer hand.' [Angus Martin Jr, 2001]

A basking shark

Angus had been going out to the herring-fishing from about the age of 10. When fishing was in progress, he'd be told to sit behind the sail on the skiff's starboard side, where he could watch in safety. One of his most vivid memories was, as a boy of about 10, being out on his uncle Neil Martin's skiff the *Renown*. The fleet was 'channel-fishing' in the middle of Kilbrannan Sound that summer and the *Renown* was lying waiting for evening to come and *burning* to start in the water. A huge basking shark – or *sail-fish* – nosed up to the rudder. Angus could see the 'suckers'* attached to its back and its size fascinated him. 'It looked lik a submarine,' he recalled. [Angus Martin Jr, 2001]

*Eel-like lampreys, which feed on sharks' tissue.

A restless apprentice

When Henry Martin left school, about 1905, he went to work in Campbeltown Shipyard, 'drivin the steam-hammer in the blacksmiths' shop', but on Mondays in the summertime he used to 'drap everythin an run oot' to watch, through a gap in the fence, the fishing fleet heading out to sea under full sail. One day, while he was thus preoccupied, one of his workmates shouted to him: 'Away ye go an go tae the fishin, for that's where ye'll feenish!' Some time afterwards, when work in the yard became slack, he did go to the fishing, on his father's skiff the *Fame*, but he was plagued with seasickness, as he would be for many years afterwards, so he went back to the shipyard to serve his time as a blacksmith. In his second year back, the work-force at the yard was paid off in the summer and put on to half-time in the winter, so he decided: 'Seeck or naw seeck, A'm away tae the fishin, an A got back wi the Ould Fella agane.' [Henry Martin, 1974]

First divides

John Conley's first job was in the Post Office at Carradale. His wage was 5s a week and he 'stuck it' for about a year-and-a-half. After he left there, he was 'knockin aboot for a wee while', then he 'studied an said, Well A think A'll go tae the fishin'. So, in about 1901, at the age of 15, he was shipped as cook on the skiff *Puritan*. She had belonged originally to Campbeltown, but was bought into Carradale by Sandy Galbraith. John was on a half-share and his first wage at the fishing was £4 10s for the week. [John Conley, 1974]

George Newlands of Campbeltown had an even greater first divide. He'd been working in an ironmonger's shop – for six shillings a week – after he left school, but was restless there, having a notion to go to the fishing. He was at the shop-front one day when an old skipper, whom he knew to speak to, came along. 'Would ye like tae go tae the fishin?' he asked. 'Aye,' George replied, 'A'd jump at it.' – 'Well, we want a cook,' the man said. 'Come down on Monday.' At the end of George's first week at the fishing, he was handed £27, being the half of a man's share. This, in 1917, was a vast sum of money, and when George went home with it his mother nearly fainted. [George Newlands, 1975]

A fall-out

When Duncan Campbell left school in 1940, at the early age of 13 – exempted owing to the War – he became a message-boy with a grocer in Campbeltown. One day, in the summer of 1942, while he was out delivering groceries, one of the bicycle tyres was punctured and he was late returning from his round. He and the shopkeeper consequently fell out and Duncan told the man: 'There's the bicycle an there's the basket – waalk wi it!'

Shortly after this rancorous leave-taking, Duncan met a crewman on the *Frigate Bird*, Sam Galbraith, and asked him if he could go out to the fishing that night. When Duncan appeared at the boat that evening, the boat's boy at once asked him if he would do the cooking. He agreed, and cooked and fished all week aboard the *Frigate Bird*.

Come Saturday, the cook asked Duncan if he would wash out the forecastle. When old Dan Conley came aboard later and saw the result of Duncan's efforts, he remarked, 'That's the first time I've seen this fore-castle clean for years', and handed Duncan a note. Duncan assumed it to be a pound, but it was a five-pound note. When the cook came aboard, still later, he too was delighted with Duncan's work and gave him another five-pound note.

Duncan was emptying dirty water over the boat's side, when the skipper of the *Enterprise*, Willie 'Toon' MacDonald, saw him and asked what he was doing. 'A wis waashin oot, Willie,' Duncan replied. 'Well, come ower here, son,' Toon said to him. He now had the forecastle of the *Enterprise* to wash out! The first thing he saw, when he went below, was a wireless-set lying under the boat's stove. 'See that there,' said Toon, 'don't bother aboot that.' But Duncan decided otherwise. When he picked up the set, there was water running out of it, but he worked on it and then had the accumulator recharged … 'and it went!'

When Willie MacDonald returned, he was impressed with the appear-ance of the forecastle and asked Duncan what he was doing on Monday. 'A wis gonny ask Mr Conley if A could go oot wi him on Monday,' Duncan replied. 'Yer shirt!' was Toon's reply, and that was Duncan shipped as cook aboard the *Enterprise*, where he was to remain for some 14 years. Duncan received yet another £5, but when Toon discovered the wireless to be working again, his comment was: 'Ould Alec Black'll naw be pleased wi that wireless gan – he hoped tae get a new yin.' Duncan went straight home to his Granny and gave her the £15. He had been earning 15s a week as a message-boy. [Duncan Campbell, 2000]

Condensed milk

Harry McIver's summer holidays, as a boy, were spent at Carradale. During the Second World War, sweets – along with much else – became rarities owing to rationing. The tins of condensed milk found aboard fishing boats, for milking and sweetening the men's tea, were a big attrac-tion. One day, in 1943, Harry and three or four of his local pals slipped aboard one of the boats lying in Carradale Burn, went down into the forecastle and plundered the supply of condensed milk. An opened can was 'sooked dry' and another intact can was opened and likewise drained. They hadn't, however, been stealthy enough, because the boat's owner spotted them from his house and came aboard and closed the forecastle hatch over them. They were left in darkness for what seemed like an hour, and, when finally released, were one by one booted over the side and given a 'stern warning'. When Harry got home, soaked, another 'doing' awaited him, this time from his mother. The raid was never repeated. He later got to know ring-net boats a bit better when he began going out occasionally on Willie Galbraith's *Cluaran*. His mother's cousin Angus MacDonald was cook aboard her. Harry's one regret was that he never got to Ayr to land herring; it was always the neighbour-boat's turn to run the catch. [Harry McIver, Campbeltown, 2000]

Seaview

Grieve Gemmell was raised, until the age of 13, in a row of houses named Seaview, by the shore at Dunure. The sea would sometimes wash round the corner of the house and he remembered throwing buckets of water over the windows to wash off the 'sea-lice' (sand-fleas). The Gemmells' house was at one end of the row and comprised a living-room, another smaller room and a tiny kitchen. His old Aunt Mary lived in the opposite side of the common entry, and when she died his parents rented that house too. The loft, or attic, was used as a store for nets and other fishing gear, which had to be hauled through the house to the front door, and he remembered that the dried-up *scalder* – stinging jellyfish – tentacles still stung when a net was brought out of the loft months later. The toilet was outside and dry, and the bucket would be emptied into the sea at ebb water. Water had to be carried to the house, but the supply was 'nae distance fae oor door' and the pipe whence it issued is still there, though stopped. He was able to recall everyone who lived in the row and 'every stick o furniture that wis in the hoose'. After the row was abandoned in 1938, the rooms were used as fishermen's stores, but since then the building has been renovated and extended. Grieve, however, remembers it as it was in his boyhood. 'A can jeest see it the noo, as if it wis still there.' [Grieve Gemmell, 2000]

A small suit of oilskins

Grieve was going out to the fishing in his grandfather's *Mary Sturgeon* before he even started school. He remembered having no oilskins for the fishing, but, when he was four years old, his grandfather John Gemmell made him 'a wee suit o ileskins' from canvas, which was later coated and recoated with varnish to waterproof it. With his 'wee bits' (boots) on, the rig was complete. [Grieve Gemmell, 2001]

A tattie-digger

Grieve was eight years old when his father's first *Storm Drift* 'came home' to Dunure from the yard of Weatherhead, Cockenzie, in 1933. He was walking down to the harbour with Hughie Anderson's daughter Agnes, when, at the Turn of the Pump – a well which supplied the fishermen with water for net-barking – Agnes exclaimed: 'Oh, there's Tommy Sloan's boat in the harbour.' – 'No it's no – it's ma Daddy's new boat,' Grieve replied. The *Storm Drift*'s crew was taking iron bars aboard for ballast. 'A ran doon,' Grieve recalled, 'went abaird the boat, stracht intae the wheelhoose, an A think A wis in bloody tears. It wis yin o these tattie-diggers* for a wheel.' Even at that early age, the design of the steering-wheel displeased him. [Grieve Gemmell, 2001]

Named for its resemblance to a potato-harvesting machine. It had the usual eight spokes, but these protruded from the centre without any intervening radial structuring.

First recollection

Iain Gemmell's first recollection of anything connected with fishing is dateable to 1938, when he'd be about four years old. There was still no electricity in Dunure at that time, and he and his mother were in the kitchen lighting an Aladdin lamp when his uncle came in with tragic news. The Dunure boats had been returning home in a gale of wind. The crew of the *Dewy Rose* were all on deck, pumping most of the time. Two of them, Mungo Munro and John 'Domino' Munro, were lying on the aftermost bit of net when the boat took a lump of water which swept net and men overboard. A strong swimmer on the boat tied the anchor-rope around his waist and went to the men's rescue. He heard 'Domino', who was also a strong swimmer, shouting: 'Get Mungo, Hughie – A'll be all right!' Hughie duly got hold of Mungo and that was the last anyone heard or saw of 'Domino'. [Iain Gemmell, 1999]

A broken foot-rule

When Matt Sloan's younger brother Billy was born, he proved to be a rather 'fractious' baby, so, to take some pressure off his mother, Matt was sent from Maidens to his Harbison grandparents in Dunure (where Matt had actually been born). He must have been about three years old when he was with his grandfather, William Harbison, and his two uncles Willie and Jimmy Harbison. They were working about a boat and one of his uncles left a foot-rule lying. Matt was attracted to this instrument and managed to break it, whereupon one of the Harbison brothers protested to his father, 'Are ye no gonny check him?'; but the older man, to Matt's relief, took his part and reasoned: 'An who put it doon there? If ye hadnae put it doon there, he widnae have got it.' [Matt Sloan, 2002]

Finding the right boat

When 'Iver' McKinven was a boy in the 1940s he dreaded being sent down Campbeltown Quay with cigarettes and suchlike for his father, because all the boats looked the same to him – varnished mostly – and some days there would be more than a hundred of them in the harbour. His father James* told him to look for the boat's number on the stern if he couldn't see it for'ard, and that number always stuck in his memory: CN 97, the *Falcon*, skipper-owner Duncan Graham. [Duncan McIver McKinven, 1994]

*James McKinven, who was born in 1906, was the oldest fisherman in Campbeltown when he died in 2001. He went to sea at the age of 15 with 'Big Switchum' (John McKay) on the Maris Stella.

Helping at Barfad

In common with a few other Tarbert fishing families (p 107), the Jacksons had a stake in the land as well as the sea. Neil Jackson's maternal grand-father, Neil Kennedy, was a farmer in Barfad, on the north side of East Loch Tarbert. Indeed, Neil was named after him and has Kennedy as a middle-name. As a boy, he'd spend weeks at a time on the farm, usually during school holidays, helping with harvesting and herding, but there was one task he hated and that was lifting rocks ahead of the plough, because the sensation of dried earth on his hands was unbearable to him. One day, at about the age of 14, he was assisting his uncle Sam Kennedy who was ploughing, and Sam couldn't understand why Neil kept going to the burn to wash his hands. 'Where are ye goin?' he'd ask. The land, therefore, didn't agree with Neil, who went to sea when he left school; but his brother Tommy worked on Barfad until the ground was sold for afforestation in the 1970s, and, at an unusually advanced age, briefly became a fisherman. [Neil Jackson, 2001]

Superstition
· · · · · · · · · · · · · · · ·

Superstition is a vast subject, with roots that vanish into remote history. Difficult to define concisely, it might best be described as a self-protective discipline. Fishing has always been a chancy and a dangerous job, so fishermen became concerned with luck – good and bad – and evolved a complex system of observances, some common to all communities and others peculiar to certain communities or even to individuals. Desiring, at all costs, to avoid bad luck, they religiously avoided the people and things that were connected with bad luck. Fishermen, on the whole, are less superstitious than formerly, but some maintain old beliefs.

The Cuckoo

It was a widely-held belief that to fail to hear the cuckoo in a particular year meant that you wouldn't hear it the next year because you'd be dead! To hear a cuckoo before having eaten was considered very unlucky, and some men would sleep with a biscuit beneath their pillows so that they could eat immediately upon waking.

Archie Paterson was crewing on a Tarbert skiff that was lying off Cour. He was sitting in the boat's den 'trimmin the pipe' – cleaning it – to have a smoke before his breakfast. A cuckoo started calling from a tree in the middle of Cour Bay and Archie listened to it and then exclaimed: 'Ya buggar, if A had the gun A'd go up an A wid chip the bloody heid aff ye!' His shipmates were smiling at 'this ould joker' and didn't know what to make of the outburst. Archie, who 'used tae go away in the sailin ships', was a native of Carradale, but settled latterly in Tarbert. [Hugh MacFarlane, 1976]

John McConnachie of Carradale remembered saying to his father, Walter, one day at Woodside: 'There the cuckoo.' But his father decided not to hear the bird and replied: 'A canna hear her.' He went into the house, ate something and then came back out to listen. [John McConnachie, 2001]

One summer, when Denis MacIntosh was at the Canna fishing, the island was 'full of cuckoos an corncrakes' which were making a terrific racket. It was a 'no-use fishin', the crews getting only a cran or two of herring for their labours. Archie Kerr of Tarbert, who, according to Denis, was as like Emperor Haile Selassie as 'two herrin', and a cross man forby, denounced the cuckoo as 'a damn gortach bird!' *Gortach* is Gaelic for 'famine' or 'want' and Archie had decided that the cuckoos were to blame for the slack fishing. [Denis MacIntosh, 1978]

An Ominous Pigeon

The pigeon has never figured among those birds considered unlucky; indeed, Neil Jackson used to take homers from certain lock-keepers on the Crinan Canal and release them off Barra. When, however, the *Village Belle* of Tarbert was in the Minch one year, her skipper Dougie 'Dooker' Smith had anxieties peculiar to himself concerning the bird. When one was about to alight on the boat, Dougie stuck his head out the wheelhouse in a panic, shouting: 'Don't let that bloody bird land on this daik 'cause he's got a message! Don't let him land on this bloody daik!' [Neil Jackson, 2001]

Rats

Rats were no more welcome aboard fishing boats than anywhere else, but in addition to that, 'rat' was a taboo word aboard boats, 'long-tail' being the permissible alternative.

George Newlands was in a skiff, the *Waterbird*, neighbouring the *Regent Bird*. They always lay at the north side of Campbeltown Quay. A small drifter arrived one day and tied up at the quay. She was 'loaded' with rats and some of the rodents jumped ship and took up quarters on the *Waterbird* and several other local boats. The *Waterbird*'s crew brought aboard the boat a little dog named 'Jucka' that ran about the quay. He was a great ratter and killed 15 or 20 of them, but one remained aboard the *Waterbird* and was seen to jump out the scuttle and run along the gunnel, with the dog after it. It ended up in the water, and the old skipper of the boat remarked – somewhat cryptically, it must be admitted – 'A dinna laik tae see that tae themorra'. That night the *Waterbird* was run down and sunk in Machrie Bay by the *Maggie McNab*. [George Newlands, 1975]

Salmon

'Salmon' was another taboo word and there was a time when the fish itself, when caught with herring, would be flung overboard by some crews. It was spoken of as a 'billy'.

The whole Campbeltown fleet went up to Carradale Bay one night about the end of August and lay at anchor. Salmon started jumping and one pair of crews got under way and shot, securing a big haul. One crew went to Ayr with salmon and the other went to Campbeltown. The Campbeltown Police, however, were 'on the job', and the boat's skipper got 'the tick-tack' of this. Suddenly apprehensive, he took a punt in tow and went out to Davaar Island, ferried the salmon ashore and covered them with a sail, which by that time – engines were installed – was seldom used. What he hadn't allowed for, however, was that the sail had the boat's registration number on it. The Police, acting on a report, went out to the island and seized all the fish and the sail. 'They dinna claim the sell – it wisna theirs!' [Angus Martin, 1974]

Deirdre

Women – and particularly red-haired women – were considered unlucky on or near fishing boats, though it has to be said that wherever ring-net fishermen were, they were generally willing to flout the convention in the case of young female holidaymakers.

In the following examples, however, the girl in question was Deirdre Sloan, fourth daughter of the *Watchful's* skipper, Matt. During her first night at ring-netting, in 1969, a submarine, HMS *Onyx*, practically destroyed the *Watchful's* net. Matt shot off Ardrossan and he and his brother Billy in the *Wistaria* were towing the net to 'meet the boats', when Andy Alexander, standing forward, called to Matt: 'Here's yer wee cabin cruiser comin.' It wasn't, however, the pleasure craft they thought they'd been monitoring on radar, but the periscope of a submarine, the phosphorescent wash of which Andy had seen in the 'semi-darkness'. When Matt switched on the searchlight and directed it on to the object, he realised at once what was approaching. 'Had it been a minute later,' Matt recollected, 'we'd probably have been meetin the two boats an he wid've sunk both boats.' As it happened, the net alone was damaged.

Several months later, the Sloan pair was late in leaving Ayr one evening and by the time they got up between Sannox and Scalpsie the bulk of the fleet was already ringing. They took the eastern edge of the fleet and Matt saw a 'deep stroke' on the echo-meter, turned and shot. After the herring had been taken aboard, Bert Andrew in the *Pathfinder* called the *Wistaria*: 'Ye surely got a good ring there.' – 'We got aboot a couple o hunner,' Billy replied. 'A thought ye got a lot more than that,' Bert replied; but Billy was 'talking in crans' and not in baskets, so the estimate required to be multiplied by four.

Two trips to sea by Deirdre Sloan; two entirely different results. 'So take yer pick.' [Matt Sloan, 2000]

A lucky boy

When James Wareham of Campbeltown was 13 years old he was put aboard the skiff *Polly Cook*, which belonged to his mother's uncle, Archie Cook*. Archie – a big man with huge hands – was ageing and losing his sight and James's duty was to sit with him at the tiller and act as his eyes.

In James's first month with the boat, each man's weekly 'divide' was between £12 and £15, big money in 1913; but James wasn't receiving his half-share, because his father John was insistent that since he had received half-a-crown a week when he started fishing, that's what his son too should receive. Archie Cook was so annoyed by this attitude that he visited James's mother to apologise. Margaret Wareham was just as annoyed – she could have been doing with the money – and decided that James should leave the boat.

He was offered a job in a shop at 5s a week, news of which reached the wife of one of the *Polly Cook*'s crewmen. She told her husband and he was so angry that he collected the rest of the crew and then approached John Wareham with the ultimatum – if James left the boat, then the crew would also leave. It was his firm belief that James was bringing the boat luck and that if he went, the luck would go with him. 'It's no use if the boy's not there,' he insisted. John Wareham was forced to relent, so James stayed *and* he got his half-share. [James Wareham, 1974]

*James Wareham's mother, Margaret, was a daughter of Edward Morrans, fisherman, and Mary Cook.

No turning back

It was a widely-held belief in fishing communities that if one left the house to go to sea and forgot something – no matter how trifling – one must never turn back for it. Matt Sloan was not himself superstitious, but his mother, Agnes Harbison, was. 'A've known us,' he recalled, 'often an often on a Monday gettin tae the gate o the house an discoverin we'd left somethin behind. She wid be at the door watchin us and we daren't go back in that gate. She wid go an get whatever it was, but it was bad luck for us tae go back in that gate.' [Matt Sloan, 2000]

Thirteens

The Girvan brothers, Jock and Jimmy McCreath, who neighboured each other at ring-netting, between the wars had each a boat the registration numbers of which added up to 13. Jock had the *Southern Sun*, which was BA 175, and Jimmy had the *May*, BA 193. This coincidence – if such it was – was a talking-point in Girvan, but the conjunction of thirteens was short-lived, because not long after the *May* arrived, Jock replaced the *Southern Sun* with the *A J J & T*, which was BA 73. [Matt Sloan, 2000]

Friday 13th

Two Campbeltown boat-owning brothers, Jimmy and John Macdonald, had opposite reactions to the idea of putting to sea on Friday 13 March, 1998. Jimmy adhered to the superstition concerning that day and didn't go out fishing, while John did and was none the worse for it. [James Macdonald, 1998]

With the sun

The belief that, when leaving harbour, a boat must be turned clockwise, or 'with the sun', quite possibly preserves a pre-Christian religious observance.

James Macdonald of Campbeltown maintained the superstition faithfully to the last. Peter Laing, who crewed with him in the *Crimson Arrow* in the early 1970s, noticed that if James was unable to manoeuvre his boat with the sun when leaving harbour, he'd circle her thrice sunwise in Campbeltown Loch to cancel out the bad luck. [Peter Laing, 2002]

Deformity

Contact with human deformity brought on bad luck.

Colin 'Jazz' Campbell, who skippered Murdoch Weir's *Shenandoah*, lived in Glebe Street, Campbeltown, but would never walk along that street on his way to the boat, preferring to use less frequented lanes in case he would meet a particular lame shoemaker. Occasionally he did meet the man in the Well Close, and his reaction was to press two shillings on a child with the instruction: 'Away doon tae the *Shenandoah* an tell them A'm no gan oot the night.' [Duncan Campbell, 2000]

Old boots

Shoes feature extensively in superstitions worldwide. In certain parts of Scotland, a shoe thrown after a fisherman going to sea was considered lucky, but the following belief appears to be rather more obscure.

Donald Blair of Tarbert, who now teaches English in Ullapool, had a singular experience of the custom when, in the winter of 1982, he first went to the fishing, aboard Robert Ross's *Sunbeam*. One morning, after the first tow, when the trawl was lifted off Brodick, an old boot was spotted amid the catch. Robert salvaged the boot and threw it on to the wheelhouse roof, saying that it would bring good luck, a conviction of which Donald expressed himself sceptical.

Not long into the second tow, the trawl came fast. 'That'll be the boot,' Donald remarked with unconcealed cynicism; but Robert cautioned him not to be too hasty in his judgement. The snag, however, was a bad one and John 'Tar' McDougall in the *Nancy Glen* was radioed to come and assist. With the concerted efforts of the two boats, the net was finally winched to the surface and was seen to contain a practice torpedo, which, when returned to the Royal Navy, fetched a substantial salvage reward, adding about £150 to each crewman's wage. For long afterwards, when Donald would meet Robert socially and was expressing himself dogmatically on some subject, Robert would advise him: 'Remember the boot, Donald.' [Donald Blair, 2001]

Buying a fair wind

Hugh McLean of Campbeltown, in the *Good Hope*, was on a passage home from Ireland and became utterly becalmed. 'Good Lord, give me a ha'pennyworth of wind,' he intoned as he spun the coin over the stern. A breeze of wind arose, as though by magic, and blew fair all the way back. [Angus Martin Jr, 1997]

A charm against sickness

One day in 1964, the *Regina Maris* of Campbeltown was coming out of Ayr in a north-westerly gale, having discharged a catch of herring. Ralph, a West Indian student who was visiting Campbeltown and spent a week aboard the boat, hopped into Andy 'Spotchy' McSporran's bunk. Ralph was jingling something in one of his hands and Spotchy said to him: 'Hoot's that ye've got?' Ralph showed him a handful of coins and explained: 'This'll keep me from being sick.' Less than a minute later, he vomited over Spotchy's mattress and was ordered out of the bunk in no uncertain terms. As Peter Laing, who was cooking aboard the boat, reasoned: 'A think if ye're goin tae be seeck aboard a boat, ye'll be seeck.' [Peter Laing, 2002]

Ministers

Ministers and priests were considered unlucky aboard fishing boats and even the words would not be spoken. Some fishermen even hated meeting a clergyman ashore.

Archie 'Molly' Johnson of Tarbert wouldn't go to the fishing if he met the minister on his way to the boat. 'Ye'd need tae tie him an tow him aboard,' Robert Ross remarked. [1998] Yet Matt Sloan's son-in-law, the Rev Sandy McDonald, was at sea on the *Watchful* one night when a memorable catch was secured at the mouth of the Clyde (p 148).

The owner of the *Enterprise* of Campbeltown, Archie Cook, approached his skipper, Willie 'Toon' MacDonald, one day to say that he was going out to the fishing that night, adding that he would be taking a friend, all of which was fine by Toon; but when the friend stepped aboard that evening wearing a dog-collar, Toon's consternation was absolute. His first shot that night was in Saddell Bay, off the Henhouse, ordinarily a clean haul; but the net was coming up torn. As this unexpected drama was unfolding, Archie Cook was at Toon's side watching. 'Is she still open, Willie?' he enquired, concerned. 'Aye, she's still open,' Toon growled between clenched teeth. With that, the minister remarked: 'Just swear if you want to.' – 'Aye, she's still fuckin open!' Toon obliged. The crew laced the net together, however, and 'got a good fishin efter that'. [Duncan Campbell, 2000]

Sabbath observance

It is debatable whether Sabbath observance can be defined as 'superstition'. Perhaps it can now, but a century ago it was certainly accepted conduct, subscribed to from genuine belief or from a fear of being seen to flout a moral convention.

Hugh MacFarlane recollected returning to Tarbert from Girvan one Saturday. The weather was poor and darkness was coming on, so the crew decided to pass the night in Ardrossan. 'We got wir tea an got waashed up; we went tae the pictures an had a dram.' The following day – a Sunday – the wind 'wid hardly blow oot the sail'. One of the crew was eager to be away. 'Come on, let go them ropes. Up wi the sell.' Angus Livingstone, who was 'good' – i.e. religious – queried the suggestion. 'Where are ye's goin?' – 'Where, but we're gonny take the good day when it's in't,' was the answer. 'The Man that made this one will make another one,' Angus countered. 'Well, we'll take this one anyway,' was the answer to that, and away they went.

With the whole sail up and the big jib set to catch the 'wee air' on a calm sea, they arrived in Tarbert at one o' clock in the afternoon. The church bells were ringing and Hugh, carrying his kit-bag, walked home to his 'wee hoose' beside the church, passing the congregation on the way.

'Some o the good ones, they came tae doon the Bàgh mu Chomraig there (at Battle Isle), put oot the anchor tae night that the church folk winna see them. That's what they did. Och, och! Aye, many a siege wis in't at thon time.' [Hugh MacFarlane, 1975]

During the Minch spring herring-fishery of 1929, Jamie Campbell of Carradale was in Tiree with his neighbour. The crews decided to leave some time during the Sunday, and Jamie asked an islander on Scarinish quay to cast off the *Irma*. 'I'll let go your ropes,' the man said, 'but there was never any good in men going to sea on the Sabbath.' The remark bothered Jamie so much that 'he didn't stop till he got tae Crinan'. [Jim Campbell, 2002]

The Devil at the Ru

A Campbeltown skiff landed below Ru Stafnish one night when the wind had fallen and no headway could be made sailing. The crew boiled a kettle on a driftwood fire and ate their *pieces*. While seated around the fire, in the dead of the night, they were startled by the appearance of a tall stranger. Though uneasy, they greeted him in a friendly manner: 'Can we help you? Where have ye come oot o?' He enquired after a man by the name of McC—— in Southend, asking where precisely did he stay. The fishermen were able to tell him and pointed him in the direction of Southend. The stranger thanked them politely and then, to their astonishment, disappeared up the cliff-face in a ball of flame.

Terrified, the crew at once relaunched the boat and set off for Campbeltown, rowing frantically. Back in town, they reported the experience to the police, who gave them the uncanny news that the McC—— man in question had died in Southend just about the time of the mysterious encounter. It was said that, time and again, other fishermen would ply the crew with whisky in the hope of getting them to change their story, but none of them ever did. [Tom Kelly, 1996]

Nets

The 'wetting' of a new net was a general custom. It was given the 'first dram', but, as Robert Ross remarked, 'It winna be a very big yin wi some o them!' [2001] Campbeltown fishermen, however, would never haul a new net aboard on a Friday or when the tide was ebbing.

A restless soul

There was a certain skiff, bought into Tarbert from Carradale, on which an unfortunate fisherman – 'Archie' in this account, to conceal his identity – committed suicide by cutting his throat. The tragic event apparently occurred in Carradale Bay, and when the skiff, with her Tarbert crew, used to go into the Bay to lie with north-west wind during the Brown Head fishing, one of that crew would become 'hellish nervous'. If a pot, perhaps, would tumble in the hold with the motion on the sea, this individual would immediately declare, 'That hoor Erchie's on the prowl agane', and beg his skipper to lift the anchor and clear out. [Robert Ross, 2001]

Perka's sou'wester

The following anecdote probably qualifies as an example of superstition, albeit at an extremity of spontaneous irrationality.

Sandy Galbraith – a grandfather of the informant – was a keen fisherman but inclined to become 'very agitated if he cou'na get things tae go his own way'. He and his neighbour were off Skipness and every other pair of skiffs was shot but his own. 'Och,' he was complaining, 'are we no gonny get a shot at all?' Then he spied his brother Archie – invariably called 'Perka' – wearing a sou-wester with the rim down over his ears. 'Is it any bloody wonder we canna get a ring? If ye'd go an put off that bloody sou-wester!' – 'Well,' replied the good-natured brother, 'A'll put it off, Sandy, but it'll no make wan damn bit o difference.' And neither it did, of course. [Archibald Paterson, 2000]

Pranks
· · · · · · · · · ·

Fishermen formerly had more leisure, particularly during the summer herring-fishing, when darkness was brief and fishing time correspondingly brief; not only that, herring-fishermen could indulge in a species of optimism – absent now from the weekly grind of 'prawn'-trawling and clam-dredging – which was supported by the knowledge that no matter how slack the fishing became, one catch alone could provide the necessary 'touch' and restore prosperity overnight. The fishermen's outlook on life was therefore cheerier and lent itself to practical jokes and mischief-making. Such devilment – which was generally taken in good part – no longer thrives in the grim struggle for economic survival which is modern fishing.

Andy and the frying-pan

A Dalintober skiff was out at the back of Davaar Island, her crew fishing with hand-lines for a *rasher*. Andy McKinlay went below to light his pipe and while he was gone somebody hauled in his line. There was a rusty frying-pan hanging in the boat's hold, and the pan was hooked on to the end of the line and lowered over the side. When Andy came back on deck and caught the line to loosen it – he had it tied – he didn't say a word, but hauled up the weight. When he saw the pan, he remarked: 'Bloody pan!' Then he mentioned the name of a boy who had lost it two years previously: 'Jeest on this very spot!' Andy always had an answer. It was the practice, after the boy had fried herring, that he would dip the pan over the side while it was still hot, and the sudden immersion in cold water would 'clean everythin off it', and this fictional boy of Andy's 'near went ower the side an let the pan go'. [Henry Martin, 1974]

Andy's share

Andy McKinlay was near-blind. During the 'Harvest Slack', around October, when herring became scarce, Andy would go to otter-trawling with a small net. After the catch of white fish had been landed, the small unmarketable fish would be divided equally into chip-baskets and allocated to each crew member by an elaborate system of back-turnings and finger-pointings and the repeated question: 'Whose acht?' (Whose is it?) Willie 'The Bolt' McLellan, however, had surreptitiously loaded the bottom of Andy's basket with ballast stones. 'That's yours, Andy,' he said. 'Oh, is this …?' Andy began, surprised by the great weight he was feeling. 'That's yours there, Andy,' the Bolt repeated. Andy lifted it. 'Aw, is this aa for me?' – 'Aye, that's yours, Andy,' said the Bolt and away went Andy, home to Kinloch Place. When he got in, he just emptied the basket into the sink and smashed it. [George Newlands, 1975]

The 'Bolt's' Lights

'The Bolt' was a 'wile man for playin tricks'. He and his crew were looking for herring in the *burning* out off Machrie one night, growing dispirited and seeing no lights anywhere. One torch going up signified a net being shot; two torches signified a fishing secured. It was a lovely dark, starry night with not a ripple on the water. 'Ach,' the Bolt said to George Newlands, 'stop the engine.' They lay and listened a while for herring, but there was nothing to listen for, no herring. So the Bolt left the tiller and went below to the forecastle and got a bit of wood and two condensed milk tins. He nailed the tins to the plank, stuffed a bit of paraffin-soaked tow into each can, put a match to them and dropped the plank over the quarter. 'Start her up, George,' he said. George started the engine. 'Full bit,' he ordered. 'Gie her full bit.' Away they went for Davaar. Boats were known to be up about Iorsa and from that across to Carradale Point, and they began to converge on the lights from all 'erts an perts'. The first pair to arrive was the 'Grey Boats', Dan Conley's *Frigate Bird* and the *Sweet Home*. They came up and up on the lights and finally got 'waarped up' – fouled their propellers – in a 'bing o wreck an stuff'. 'Oh, hoot the hell's that?' And there were the two burning milk-tins, floating on the water. 'The Bolt wis off!' [George Newlands, 1975]

Uncle Angus

The following anecdotes concern Angus Paterson, an old uncle of Archie Paterson's. Archie was shipmates with him, when a boy on the Rolling Wave *of Carradale during the Second World War.*

On one occasion, Archie tied a string to the end of old Angus's bedcovers and passed it over the top rung of the iron ladder that led from the scuttle down into the forecastle. Concealing himself in a corner on the opposite side of the forecastle from Angus's bunk, Archie proceeded to pull on the string. The covers, of course, left the bunk and mysteriously floated towards the scuttle. The old man gazed in terror at this phenomenon and then dived at the covers and hauled them back. Archie would wait a while and then repeat the action until the old man was 'demented'.

There was a wireless aboard the boat and Archie would switch it on in the forecastle when the Nazi collaborator, William Joyce – 'Lord Haw Haw' – was broadcasting. This would make old Angus 'mad in his bunk' and he would always conclude his denunciations with: 'Shut up, ya bugger – ye're full o asthma!'

Angus sometimes took too much drink and would lie in his bunk speaking to himself all night. One night he kept requesting, 'Fill ma pipe,' so Archie filled it for him, but he packed in with the tobacco the broken off head of every match he could find and when the old man eventually lit the pipe there was an explosion! [Archie Paterson, 2000]

A couple of ton of coal

There was one Ayrshire 'character' whose mischief was legendary. On one occasion, when boats were moored at Port Bannatyne, Bute, a coalman came along and asked the fishermen if they wanted any coal. 'Aye,' said the joker, 'a couple o ton.' The coalman said that he would have to come back because he didn't have that quantity in the cart, so the man duly returned to his yard and loaded up with two ton of coal and carted it back to the pier, where the joker told him that he didn't want a couple of ton, only a hundredweight. 'He got away wi this kinna thing,' Matt Sloan remarked. 'Now, how did he manage it? Did he manage tae bluff his wey oot it?' [Matt Sloan, 1976]

Anchorless

There was a fleet of Ayrshire boats working in the Kilbrannan Sound one night. 'Kruger' – James McCreath – came back from market in the *May* and dropped his anchor at Skipness. He and his crew then turned in, and while they were asleep Tommy 'Tarry' McCrindle lifted his own anchor and edged close to the *May*. Without actually going alongside, Tarry picked up Kruger's anchor-rope, lifted the anchor, unshackled it and shackled on an ordinary bucket, then dropped the lot away again. There was a westerly breeze and the bucket, of course, failed to hold the *May*. It wasn't until she had drifted half-way between Skipness and the mouth of the Kyles that the increasing motion began to disturb the slumbers of the Girvan crew. They got up, wondering what was wrong. They couldn't understand why the anchor should drag, and 'when they lift it up they discover there's nae anchor in it an there's a bucket on'. [Matt Sloan, 1976]

Hallowe'en in the Track

It was Hallowe'en of 1953 and the ring-net fleet was fishing in the Track. The neighbours *Irma* and *Florentine* of Carradale came together for 'a wee yarn' – there was no radio-transmitter on either boat at the time – and had been lying for some 10 minutes when another boat was seen approaching slowly. She came alongside the *Irma* and the first thing Jim Campbell – a boy of 15 – noticed was a man leaning out the wheelhouse window with a false-face on and smoking a pipe. 'Where'll we go now, boys?' he enquired. Then Jim realised that the entire crew was wearing grotesque masks – of old men, witches and clowns – and not only that, but they were plainly inebriated to a man. This was a Tarbert crew that had lost its neighbour and mistaken the *Irma* for the missing boat. Another Tarbert boat that had radio later reported that the missing boat was 'last seen goin up by the Skate makin for Tarbert'. [Jim Campbell, 2001]

Dunky Donal's brush

One night in the Kilbrannan Sound, Duncan MacDonald's echo-meter in the *Golden Hind* wasn't functioning. He had 'fiddled about with it' and discovered that it needed a new brush. So, Dunky came on the air and began 'shouting about', asking: 'Any o ye's got a brush for an MS-24?' There was no favourable response until Matt Sloan called him up on the radio: 'Duncan, A hear ye enquirin everywhere for a brush.' – 'That's right,' Duncan replied. 'If ye come over alongside us, A'll gie ye a brush,' Matt said. 'Whereabouts are ye?' Duncan queried. 'We're in the middle o Machrie.' – 'Och,' said Duncan, 'A'm at the Isle o Ross,' which was on the other side of the Sound. 'Well, if ye're wantin a brush, Duncan, jeest come tae us,' Matt repeated. Half-an-hour later, one of Matt's crew announced: 'Here's Duncan comin.' Matt switched on the *Watchful's* deck lights and primed his crew for the encounter. Duncan brought the *Golden Hind* alongside. 'Haev ye got a brush for us, Matt?' he called. 'Aye.' With that, one of the boys on the *Watchful* yanked a deck-broom off the side of the wheelhouse and threw it aboard the Campbeltown boat. 'Oh,' Matt recalled, 'ye should've heard Duncan – he didnae half go aff his nut that mornin!' [Matt Sloan, 1976]

Making a Bender

John 'Jonah' Edgar's *Hercules* of Dunure was in the Kilbrannan Sound with her neighbour, *Britannia* BA 130, one night in the early 1960s. There was a bright moon, which is detrimental to herring-fishing, besides which the herring were swimming at 12 and 15 fathoms … too deep to catch, unless at slack water. So the fleet was steaming aimlessly about the moonlit Sound, when Jonah noticed that the *Golden Hind's* deck was lit. Some time later, puzzled, he shouted Duncan MacDonald on the radio: 'Ye're steamin aboot a long while wi yer lights on, Dunky. Are ye mendin or what?' – 'Naw, naw,' Dunky replied, 'the boys are makin a bender, John.' – 'Whit's that?' queried the Dunureman, more puzzled than ever. 'It's a machine for throwin shite at the moon!' was Dunky's reply. [Hugh Edgar, 2000]

Fern-Cakes

In the summer of 1967, the *Amy Harris* of Carradale had a higher than normal number of youths in her crew and devilment was consequently rife. Half-a-dozen fern-cakes – so-named from the iced decoration – were brought aboard each evening from the village bakery. In theory, each crew-member should have had a cake, but in practice the boys ate all the cakes. 'Bungalow', one of the two men aboard, resented this greed and decided, one evening, to secure his cake early on. This he did, remarking triumphantly, as he secreted the paper-bag in his bunk: 'Ye're naw gettin it this time.'

Once he'd gone on deck to look for herring in the water, however,

John 'Vandal' Paterson located the cake, sliced the top off it with a heated knife, scooped out the filling, replaced it with a mixture of mustard and pepper and then carefully replaced the top. When Bungalow reappeared later for a cup of tea, he produced his cake and began laughing at the success of his strategy. His was an infectious laugh and soon the boys too were all laughing.

'We wir laughin at what wis tae come, but he wis just thinkin we wir laughin because he wis laughin. An while all the laughin wis goin on, he bit into the cake and his expression – A can see it tae this day – changed fae mirth tae absolute horror as he swallowed a big chunk. Of course, his throat went on fire.'

He spat out the chunk and, enraged, made a grab for the nearest boy, clearing the table of cups and cutlery and all else in his haste to exact retribution. In the meantime, the Vandal, who was the real culprit, had 'shot up the scuttle' and made his escape. As a punishment, Bungalow confiscated the bottle of orange-juice and pretended he'd flung it over the side; actually, he had 'plunked it behind the brailer'. [John Galbraith, 2001]

'A glorious gag'

The *Watchful* and *Wistaria* were leaving Kilbrannan Sound one Friday morning. They'd been working among Campbeltown and Carradale ringers on the north and west side of the Rock, but the bulk of the Ayrshire fleet was 'scouting about looking for wee herring' mid-channel on the other side of Arran. The *Wistaria* was going round the north end of Arran for Ayr, and the *Watchful* was taking a southerly course to go home to Maidens. Before the brothers Sloan parted on the fishing grounds, Matt in the *Watchful* told Billy that when he got round the north end of Arran and was going down through any boats and their skippers called him on the radio: 'Under no circumstances have ye tae speak tae them. Ye've tae keep quiet. Ye've jeest no tae speak. And supposin they see ye an call ye up, ye've no tae answer them.'

As Matt steered his course around the south end of Arran, he was hearing Ayrshire skippers talking on the radio, reporting 'wee puckles o poor herrin'. Craig McCrindle in the *Silver Lining* came on the air and remarked: 'A huvnae heard the *Watchful* an the *Wistaria* the night.' – 'Och,' somebody replied, 'they wir up in the Soon or somewhere lik that.' – 'Aye, there wisnae much daein amongst the boats in the Soon,' Craig said. 'A don't think they'll be there noo.' By this time Matt was three or four miles off Turnberry. He picked up the microphone, pressed it and said: '*Wistaria, Wistaria* – dae ye see us here?' The other skippers heard this and silence ensued. Matt repeated his appeal, this time in more urgent tones: '*Wistaria*, dae ye see us here? Dae ye no see wir en goin away there?' Then Billy came on the air: 'Aye, A see ye – we're nae distance fae ye.'

Then everybody began calling them. 'Whereabouts ir ye?' Matt kept silent, but Cameron Weir on the *Wistaria* replied and simply said: 'Pladda. Turnberry.' Not another word was heard from either of the Sloan boats. 'A widnae answer them,' Matt recalled, 'but I had created the impression in these fellas up at the Lady Isle, ye see, that we wir ringin … Well, Cameron let the secret oot, supposedly, that we wir between Pladda an Turnberry, so there's a mad rush takes place then.' For the next hour, there were boats steaming into the south-west from between Lamlash and the Lady Isle, trying to locate the Sloans and the mythical spot of herring. Of course, they never found the boats where they had expected them to be and were shouting on the radio and getting no reply.

By that time, the *Wistaria* was in Ayr and the *Watchful* was in Maidens. Before Matt and his crew had got 'squared up' and turned in, the *Silver Lining* entered Maidens harbour. Next thing, Craig called up the rest of the boats to announce: 'The *Watchful*'s in here on his own. This is only a glorious gag. We've a' been diddled!' [Matt Sloan, 1976]

GLOSSARY

A – I

a', aa, aal, aw – all
aafu – awful
aback – behind
abaird – aboard
aboord – aboard
aboot – about
acquant – acquaint
aff – off
afore – before
agane – again
aheid – ahead
ain – own
alane – alone
amang – among
an – and
as – than
atween – between
auld – old
aw – all
awa – away
aweh – away
awfy – awful
aye – always

bairnie – child
bate – beat, beaten
bate – bet
beeried – buried
belang – belong
bey – bay
bi – by
bing – a heap
birled – spun round
bonny – fine, lovely
bow – buoy
brash – a sudden burst of activity
braw – fine
breckin – breaking
breid – bread
breist – breast

bridle – the rope, on each end of a
    ring-net, to which the sweepline
    was knotted for towing the net
brock – broke
broon – brown
bucket – a large quantity of drink
bunnet – cap

canna, cannae – cannot
cannle – candle
canny – cautious
cerry – carry
chap – knock
chip-basket – a flat wicker basket
    used in discharging herring
chow – chew
chug – tug, pull
coulda – could've
cou'na, couldna – couldn't
crabbit – cross
croon – crown

dacent – decent
dae – do
dae't – do it
daik – deck
deh – day
deid – dead
deifen – deafen
den – forecastle
didnae – didn't
dinna – didn't, don't
doesna, doesnae – doesn't
doin – a doing, or telling-off
doo – dove, pigeon
dook – duck, plummet
doon – down
dorr – door
dose – a large quantity
drap – drop
dreg – drag

177

dry – of herring, when a ring-net has been hauled in as far as it can be and the catch is floundering almost literally in a dry state
dug – dog
durt – dirt

efter – after
en – end
erm – arm
err – air
erts an perts – airts (quarters of the compass) and parts
ett – ate
everhoot – whatever

fadom – fathom
fae – from
faither – father
farrid – forward
feel – to sense herring by smell
feenish – finish
fella – fellow
fether – father
flambeau – paraffin torch
flott – float
flow – the wing and shoulder netting of a ring-net, particularly in the act of hauling; the billow of a net
foo – full
footer – potter about, fiddle about
forby – besides, as well as
forrid – forward
furst – first
fuul – full

gan – going
gell – gale
gie – give
gied – gave
gless – glass
gloaming – evening
goat – got
gonny – going to
grip – a seabed obstruction liable to catch a net

haal – haul

hadna, hadnae – hadn't
hae, haev – have
haena, haevna – haven't
haes – has
hame – home
han – hand
han' lin' – hand line
hanna – hadn't
heid – head
heppenin – happening
herm – harm
himsel – himself
hing – hang
hit – it
hivna – haven't
hoor – whore
hoot – what
hunner – hundred
hut – hit
huv – have
huvnae – haven't

in't – in it
intae – into
ithir – other

jabble – choppy sea
jaloosed – figured out
jeest – just
jist – just
jeenk – jink, dodge

ken – know
killt – killed
kinna – kind of
kist – chest

laik – like
lang – long
lea – leave
leid-line – lead-line
lice – tiny shrimp-like creatures
licht – light
lik – like
lipper – ripple
loast – lost
loat – lot
lug – gable or end of net

ma – my
machrel – mackerel
mair – more
maist – most
male – meal
masel – myself
mash; mashin – mesh; meshing,
    when fish have been caught by
    their gills in the meshes
me – my
meenit – a minute
merr – more
mightna – mightn't
moarnin – morning; also, a glass of
    spirits habitually taken before
    mid-day
mooth – mouth
mush – a confused mass
muxed – mixed

Nabby – a round-sterned, lug-sailed
    boat which evolved on the eastern
    side of the Firth of Clyde in the
    18th century
nae – no
naethin – nothing
nane – none
naw – not
nawthing, nawthin – nothing
neebor – neighbour, partner
needna – needn't
nesty – nasty
noo – now
norrid – northward

o – of
oan – on
on't – on it
on tae, got – criticised
oor – our, hour
oorsels – ourselves
oot – out
o't – of it
otherwheres – elsewhere
ould – old
ower – over

park (of herring) – a mass of herring,
field-like in the greenish phospho-
    rescence
pickle, puckle – quantity of
piece – sandwich
pit – put
play – a loud rush of fish on the
    surface of the sea
poacket – pocket
poun – pound
putt – put

rasher – a meal, specifically of fish
redd – clear, tidy up
reenged – searched thoroughly
rether – rather
richt – right
rid – red
ring – a set, or 'shot', of the ring-net;
    to encircle a shoal of fish
rinkle – a muddle or mess
rivin – pulling vigorously
riz – rose
roon, roond – round
rowl – roll
ryse – rise

san – sand
sar – a light breeze
scad – faint appearance of light
scatter – a few
scoored – scoured
scran – a perquisite
scuttle – the covering built over the
    hatchway to the forecastle
seck – sake
seeck – sick
seh – say
sell – sail
Seterday – Saturday
shoart – short
shot – shoot
shottin – shooting
showlin – shoaling
sile – herring-fry
skiddoag – a boat-hook designed
    specifically for catching the end of
    a ring-net and lifting it inboard
skift – skiff

sling – bag, or centre, of ring-net
sma – small
soarted – sorted
sooked; sookin – sucked; sucking
sooth – south
sorta – sort of
sowl – soul
spale – spell
spannie – spawning, close to
    spawning
spot – a shoal of fish
squared – (of a pair of ring-netters)
    brought together for discharging
    herring from net
steyed – stayed
stokered – sold 'on the side' and the
    proceeds shared among the crew
stoot – stout
stracht – straight
stroke – a big, solid flash of herring
    showing in the phosphorescence
sweem – swim

tae – to, until
teirin – tearing
thegither – together
themorra – tomorrow
themsels – themselves
thir – their, that
thon – those
thonder – yonder
tim – time
tooslin – a tousling, a roughing-up
touch – a lucrative catch
trevellin – travelling
turnt – turned

unner – under
unnerstan – understand

waalk – walk
waasna, wasnae – wasn't
wae – with
wan – one
wance – once
wanna – wouldn't
watter – water
wey – way
whaur – where
wheen – a quantity
wherr – where
whit – what
whoot – what
wi – with
wid – would
widna, widnae, widn't, winna –
    wouldn't
wile, wild – wild, terrible
win – wind
winky – lit end-buoy of ring-net,
    from its blinking
winna, winnae – wouldn't
wir – were, our
wirna, wirnae – weren't
wis – was
wou'na, wouldna, wouldnae –
    wouldn't
wrang – wrong
wreck – wrack, or seaweed
wrocht – wrought, worked
wunner – wonder

ye – you
yer – your
yersel – yourself
yin – one
yit – yet
yon – those

INDEXES

Boats

Code:

CS   Canoe/cruiser-stern
F   Fifie
LFS   Loch Fyne Skiff
N   Nabby

A blank has been left whenever a boat's type is doubtful or confused; likewise when a registration number is doubtful or has not been determined.

Virginia (BA 66, BA 202) *CS*, 28, 29, 122

Vision (OB 390) 96

Volunteer (CN 670) *LFS*, 75

Watchful (BA 124) *CS*, 27, 83–5, 86, 123, 148, 162–3, 166, 173, 174–5

Waterbird (CN 113) *LFS*, 52, 133, 161

Wistaria (BA 64, BA 208) *CS*, 27, 83–4, 123, 148, 162–3, 174–5

Fishermen

Code:

Cam	Campbeltown
Car	Carradale
Dal	Dalintober
Dun	Dunure
Gir	Girvan
Mai	Maidens
Tar	Tarbert

Alexander, Andy, *Mai*, 27, 41, 149, 162

Anderson, Hugh, *Dun*, 4

Anderson, Jimmy, *Dun*, 4

Anderson, John, *Dun*, 4

Andrew, Bert, *Mai*, 163

Andrew, Davie, *Mai*, 33

Andrew, Dick, *Mai*, 103

Andrew, Jimmy, *Mai*, 121

Andrew, John, *Mai*, 33

Black, Alex 'Roarin'', *Cam*, 115, 156

Black, Archie 'Scone', *Cam*, 110

Black, Dan, *Cam*, 37, 63

Black, Dan 'Cooma', *Cam*, 120, 150

Black, Duncan, *Cam*, 109

Blair family, *Cam*, 22, 38–9, 91, 107

Blair, Archie, *Cam*, 141

Blair, Donald, *Tar*, ix, 165

Blair, Dugald, *Cam*, 91, 107, 141

Brodie family, *Cam*, 86, 104

Brodie, Jock, *Cam*, 50

Brodie, Neil 'Norman', *Cam*, 37

Brown, Alec, *Cam*, 149

Brown, Andrew, *Cam*, 120

Brown, Jamie, *Cam*, 133

Brown, Walter, *Cam*, 109

Brownie, Fred, *Car*, 83, 93, 96

Brownie, Ronnie, *Car*, 27

Bruce, Colin, *Tar*, 141

'Bungalow' Ritchie, *Car*, 173–4

Cameron, Charles, *Cam*, 49, 133

Cameron, Sandy, *Cam*, 133

Campbell, Colin 'Jazz', *Cam*, 164

Campbell, Duncan 'Kemmell', *Cam*, 116, 121, 124, 125, 150, 155–6, 165, 166

Campbell, James, *Car*, 87

Campbell, James 'Bucket', *Car*, 11–12, 39–40, 49, 94, 115, 167

Campbell, James 'Wee Jim', *Car*, 11–12, 29–30, 39, 40, 43–4, 49–50, 74–5, 83, 94, 119, 131–2, 148–9, 167, 172

Campbell, Johnny 'Colin', *Car*, 90

Campbell, John 'Nonna', *Car*, 42

Campbell, John 'Wee Jock', *Car*, 93

Carmichael, Jock 'Takins', *Dal*, 58

Conley, Dan, *Cam*, 62, 146–7, 156, 170

Conley, James, *Car*, 136

Conley, John, *Car*, 155

Conley, John, *Cam*, 57, 121, 130

Conley, Robert 'Bob', *Car*, 8, 48, 59, 69, 72, 136

Cook, Alec, *Cam*, 106

Cook, Archie, *Cam*, 75–6, 105, 163

Cook, Johnny, *Claonaig*, 77

Cook, Willie, *Cam*, 106

Coulls, *Gir*, 112

Cully, *Portavogie*, 80

Donaldson, William, 5

Dougalls, *Rothesay*, 80

Durnin, Charlie 'Duke', *Cam*, 115, 133

General